W9-BBI-150

MEXICO IN ITS NOVEL

A Nation's Search for Identity

The Texas Pan-American Series

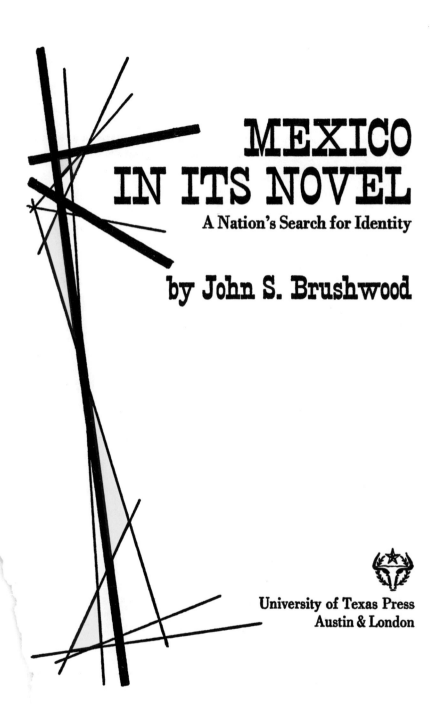

MEXICO
IN ITS NOVEL
A Nation's Search for Identity

by John S. Brushwood

University of Texas Press
Austin & London

The Texas Pan American Series is published with the assistance of a revolving fund established by the Pan American Sulphur Company and other friends of Latin America in Texas.

International Standard Book Number 0–292–73608–8
Library of Congress Catalog Card No. 65–27534
Copyright © 1966 by John S. Brushwood

Manufactured in the United States of America
Second Printing, 1970

To my friends in Mexico,
who receive my person
and my ideas
with courtesy.

PREFACE

The novel is particularly capable of expressing the reality of a nation, because of its ability to encompass both visible reality and the elements of reality that are not seen. At its best the novel explores the inner reality that is the deeper part of existing circumstance, and also the dreams that transcend the visible in a different direction. It is able to probe in both directions without mitigating its own awareness, or the reader's awareness, of visible circumstance. Obviously, not all novels are written with vision so penetrating. But novels ought always to be considered on the basis of their most complete function. Like other forms of art, the novel is a cultural organism with an ideal role, and the way in which that role is fulfilled or neglected offers one way of examining a culture's grasp of reality.

The intent of this book is to take account of the Mexican reality that is revealed through the nation's novel. In many respects, of course, this view coincides with the view of the historian, the economist, or the sociologist. But the novel reveals some aspects of reality that would not be apparent to specialists in nonartistic disciplines. We ought to know this fuller truth, because Mexico's unique experience may be enlightening in our consideration of the contemporary dilemma.

Mexico is at once a very old country and a very new one. Its roots are deep in the European tradition, and within the present-day interpretation of that tradition there are subtle manifestations of an ancient indigenous culture. Mexico does not deny its history. But, during the present century, the nation has passed through a social revolution that, from the beginning, was a mixture of proletarian and bourgeois impulses. This redefinition of Mexico gave it many characteristics of a new nation. And looking at basically individual characteristics, rather than at basically political ones, we find in Mexico a number of interesting attitudes that speak to the contemporary problem of loneliness, apartness, or lack of communication.

In spite of the fact that Northamericans live close to Mexico, and frequently travel below the border, our ignorance of the country is abysmal. Without knowing enough about it to decide whether it is important or not, we regard it as unimportant, so showing our easy inclination toward prejudice in its purest form. Least of all are we concerned with Mexico's cultural life. I recall with frankly nationalistic embarrassment the scores of times I have been faced with an ingenuous "I never realized that Mexico had novels; of course they must have them; how interesting." The fact is that even the Northamericans who visit Mexico rarely search beyond the picturesque superficialities. And I should not wish to treat them too harshly, because it is a rewarding country, even on that very elementary level. Still it seems to me that we ought to be aware of Mexico's aspirations, problems, and vitality—and especially of its long struggle toward the liberty that is self-realization. We are moving toward the estimation of nations on bases other than their military or economic prominence, past or present. It is quite possible that, in this changing world, the role of Mexico may be very important.

This book is addressed primarily to Northamericans, particularly to those who are interested in literature in general but know little of my specialization. Naturally, I hope that my fellow specialists in the United States and in Mexico will find the book interesting. While I have included some basic information that will be well known to some readers, the book is by no means a literary primer. I hope it may answer some questions, but raise even more.

I have chosen to write a history of the novel, rather than a history of the novelists. The latter can be very interesting, but the novel has a life of its own which deserves to be told without distortion for the sake of dealing with an author all in one place, or for the sake of dealing with a particular theme in one chapter. The basis for the organization of the book was a chronological list of novels written in Mexico. An abridgment of this list is printed at the end of the book so the reader may see for himself some of the unexpected sequences and juxtapositions that are hidden when the novel is discussed author by author or theme by theme. A study of the list, from the standpoint of the novel as the expression of a people, reveals some rather obvious divisions. These divisions became the chapters of the book, and the lines were maintained even if it meant that some novelists would appear in more than one chapter. In a few cases I have broken the chronological order to bring together one or more works of a single author, when that procedure served to clarify the discussion. The story begins with the present period, which is a time of realization, then goes back more than four centuries to the time of the Conquest. From that point the story of the novel is told chronologically throughout the nation's history until the last chapter meets the first.

Perhaps I should say that I have avoided any particular critical method, but have allowed each novel to dictate, by its own character, the direction of my comments. Indeed, I have thought less about method than about point of view. Trying always to remember the human character of the novel, I have written of the aspects of each work that contribute to its re-creation of reality, and have tried to search out the farthest limits of reality captured in each book.

Several technical matters call for brief explanations. First, footnotes appear only where it was hopelessly awkward to put the necessary information in the text. Second, the Bibliography is highly selective. Specialists who are interested in more bibliographical detail and in biographical data, may find both in the *Breve historia de la novela mexicana* and in *Literatura mexicana contemporánea*, which are cited in the Bibliography. Third, titles are translated or explained only when they contribute substantially to my comments. Fourth, translations of excerpts from novels are mine unless otherwise indicated. Fifth, I have used the term "Northamerican" to refer to my fellow countrymen. It is not an accurate term, but there is no accurate term that is manageable (I refuse to say "United-statesian"), and "Northamerican" is the term most commonly used in the Mexican press.

By way of confession, I should emphasize that I am a foreigner in my field. In spite of the fact that I know Mexico reasonably well, I am aware that I cannot possibly see Mexico as a Mexican sees it. I regret the errors that have inevitably come from my foreignness, and hope they may be balanced by the advantage of a certain objectivity. I must also confess a great faith in intuition, and I have not tried to harness it in writing this book. I have given intuition greater validity by writing the book in Mexico and living each day among Mexicans, not observing them from outside, but participating in their cultural life.

One of the most rewarding aspects of my work has been the help received from so many people. I wish I could name them, but they are too many. The first investigations were made more than twenty years ago. Many years of learning followed, all of them satisfying. Recent reconsideration of what was learned earlier has been the most satisfying experience of all, and from it came the present essay. Over the years, ideas have come from teachers, colleagues, students. In the past few months, the sympathetic hearing and response given my ideas by many Mexican friends have made the subject more alive than ever before. All these people contributed to what is here, but the version is mine, and mine too is the blame for the errors.

John S. Brushwood
University of Missouri

CONTENTS

MEXICO IN ITS NOVEL

A Nation's Search for Identity

A NOTE ON MEXICAN HISTORY

The terminology used by a people to describe its history may be confusing to the people of another nation because similar terms are sometimes used for very different events. For instance, the "Revolution" in the United States means the war of independence, while in Mexico the "Revolution" refers to a twentieth-century social upheaval. Since it is necessary, in this book, to make frequent references to the history of the country, a few words about the main currents may be helpful. The most convenient procedure is to consider four major events: The Conquest, The Independence, The Reform, and The Revolution.

THE CONQUEST

Hernán Cortés landed at Veracruz in 1519, invaded the territory of the Aztec emperor, Moctezuma, reached the capital city, Tenochtitlán (Mexico City), and conquered the Aztecs in 1521. This event amounted to a clash between Spain, then at the height of her power, and an advanced Indian civilization. The Conquest brought Spanish domination, but the Indian was not eliminated. The Colonial Period lasted three hundred years.

THE INDEPENDENCE

The War of Independence began with the revolt led by Father Miguel Hidalgo, who called his followers to arms on September 16, 1810 (Mexican Independence Day). Some other leaders of the movement in subsequent years were Javier de Mina, Father José María Morelos, and Agustín Iturbide. Independence was finally achieved under the leadership of Iturbide when he entered the capital on September 27, 1821.

The ideology behind the Hidalgo revolt was the liberal thought of the period that led to the establishment of many representative governments. However, the political situation in Spain was so uncertain that some conservatives joined the liberals in the fight for Mexican independence. Their victory was the result of a compromise that soon turned into political chaos. The struggle between the liberals and conservatives fed the opportunism of Santa Anna, and was one of the causes of the secession of Texas. Then the nation suffered the Northamerican Invasion (1845–1847), by which the United States took approximately half of Mexico's national territory.

THE REFORM

Under the leadership of Benito Juárez, a group of dedicated liberals, determined to bring order out of chaos, created the Constitution of 1857. Their political ideology was capitalist-democratic, and their goal was to make Mexico a progressive nation. The conservatives reacted violently for three principal reasons: the Reform attacked the power of the Church, it threatened some personal interests, and it proposed a governmental structure which the conservatives considered too weak.

The War of the Reform lasted from 1857 to 1860, and the liberals were victorious. However, Napoleon III saw an opportunity to establish an empire in the New World, and he conspired with Mexican conservatives to place Archduke Maximilian of Austria on the throne of Mexico. The French Intervention began in 1862 when the troops of Napoleon III entered the country. In 1864, Maximilian and his wife, Carlotta, arrived. Threatened by external pressures, Napoleon III withdrew his troops and the liberals were again victorious. Maximilian was captured and shot in 1867.

The next several years showed that the noble intent of the Reformists was too advanced for the state of the country. In 1876, Porfirio Díaz, a Reformist general, assumed the Presidency. He served a four-year term, allowed a political associate to serve the next four years, then returned to the office which he held until 1910.

Díaz paid lip service to the principles of the Reform, and quietly allowed the Church to regain power and the bourgeoisie to fatten their purses. The age of Díaz was one of relative stability, foreign investment, overt prosperity, and exploitation of the poor.

THE REVOLUTION

By 1910, there was a great deal of dissatisfaction with the Díaz dictatorship. Some of the thinking was entirely political, but there were also some questions about social justice. The Revolution started late in 1910 under the leadership of Francisco Madero, idealist and martyr. Other names rapidly became prominent: Villa, Orozco, Zapata, Carranza, Obregón. The Revolution was a chaotic struggle that had no apparent unity. Ideologies differed, power struggles created strange alliances. For some, the Revolution was always political, for others it was a social crusade.

In 1917 a Revolutionary constitution was promulgated. Based on the Constitution of 1857, its radical provisions were more specific. Then the administrative phase of the Revolution began. From the beginning, the Revolution had been a middle-class movement and a proletarian movement at the same time. Its administrative interpretation has varied, depending on the political position of the leaders during each presidential term.

1. The Novel
of Time and Being
(1947–1963)

Town of women in mourning clothes. Here, there, at night, in the dawn approaching, in the blessed river of morning, under the fiery brilliance of midday, in the afternoon light—strong, clear, gaunt, in extremis— old women, mature women, young maidens, little girls; in the entrances to churches, in the street silence, inside shops and some of the houses— so few—furtively opened. Cloistered town. Shamefaced saloons . . . Town with no pool parlors, or phonographs, or pianos. Town of women in mourning clothes . . . Desire, desires pretend not to breathe. You have to be still a moment to hear their breathing, to know that it exists behind the barred doors, in the trail left by women in mourning clothes, by grave men, by healthy young bucks, by pale little boys. You have to hear it in the ecclesiastical prayers and chants where it takes refuge. Deep breathing, feverish breathing held back . . . Life goes by among the women in mourning clothes. Death comes. Or love. Love, which is the strangest, most extreme form of dying; the most dangerous and frightening way of living one's death.[1]

The "Acto Preparatorio" of *Al filo del agua* (*On the Edge of the Storm*)[2] is Agustín Yáñez's setting for a novel that discovers the relationship between the outer and inner lives of the people in a small

---

[1] Agustín Yáñez, *Al filo del agua*, 2nd ed. (Mexico City: Porrúa, 1955), pp. 3, 5, 14.

[2] Yáñez explains that the title of his novel is a rural expression which refers to the moment just before the rain begins. It can also mean to be on the brink of any event.

Mexican town. It is more than a mood setting, because Yáñez prepares the reader to know and to see the town and the individuals who live in it. It is an introduction which looks forward and backward, up and down, as does the book. The characters emerge from the preparatory act, identify themselves with their severely circumscribed world, then transcend the limits of visible reality and move into the reality of all men, enlarging at the same time their own objective experience.

Al filo del agua was published in 1947, three decades after the promulgation of the Revolutionary constitution. It is an historical novel in the best sense, because it re-creates the reality of Mexico on the edge of the Revolution, during the fading moments of the "peace and order" of the age of Porfirio Díaz. Yet it is not an historical novel that moves the reader back into a past that he wishes to get to know or to relive. In this novel, the past is the present, for two reasons. One is that the Revolution did not completely change the circumstances that are apparent in the novel. The condition of being on the edge of the storm is not entirely different from being in the midst of the storm, or even after the storm. The second reason is that, in the case of the Revolution, awareness followed reality. The significance of the Revolution was not easily understood at first. What must have appeared to be a series of rebellions gradually acquired an element of unity. And later, men were so impressed by the *movement* of the Revolution— movement that was physical, social, spiritual, and to a lesser extent intellectual—that they responded only with *movement* in one form or another. In the case of prose fiction, the *movement* was generally expressed in a lineal account of the action of the Revolution. Sometimes the line formed a pattern, but more often it kept moving on the same plane, as if the author were seeking to take account of what had happened.

It would be unfair to say that *Al filo del agua* changed the direction of the novel. But it does mark a turning point, embodies the characteristics of a new direction. It incorporates and surpasses the anecdote, the *costumbrismo*,[3] the social protest, the studied artistry that are present in earlier novels, though hardly ever in combination. And

---

[3] This is a term used in Hispanic literature to refer to the novel of customs and similar prose.

it accomplishes a degree of interiorization seen only rarely in earlier Mexican prose. The book itself is indeed "*al filo del agua*" literarily. And it is in a similar position as an expression of the Mexican nation because it transposes the reality of the moment of its setting, historically past, to the reality of the present, the moment of awareness. It also transposes another reality—a literary one— from past to present, for it is the blossoming of the intent of the *Contemporáneos* group in the late 1920's and early 1930's, an intent that had to wait until awareness became a fact.

It is typical of Yáñez's way of expressing himself that the titles of his novel and of his introduction involve the reader in speculation beyond the minimal understanding of what the author says. In all his works, Yáñez uses his mastery of prose, names of characters, sequence of events, proverbs, place names, and association of ideas to propel his reader into creative participation. A fair appraisal of Yáñez calls for the use of the word "propel," for it is important to understand that Yáñez does not drag a hand-clutching reader behind him. Sometimes it appears that he is making an allegory; and in a sense, that is what he is doing, but the allegory is not carried to completion or resolution. His intimations are to allegory as thought is to systematic philosophy.

Yáñez's use of the language contributes greatly to the feeling of a hermetic situation which is about to change. His prose has an inner rhythm that suggests the regular movement of day-to-day existence; and this rhythm flows into a larger one which is produced by the writer's movement from simple narrative statement to a poetic quality that is based on his understanding the exterior and appreciating the interior at the same time. The town is closed, but only temporarily. The future is open.

It would be reasonable to say that the town's hermeticism is ecclesiastical, for its rhythm and its apparent reason for being are controlled by the Church. But *Al filo del agua* is not a complaint against the Church, because the Church itself is as circumscribed as any inhabitant of the town. The Church has become either its own victim or the victim of some force that is greater than the life of the Church or the life of the town. The members of the clergy do not move in a common direction, have only glimpses of the quality of being. Neither ritualism, nor organizationalism, nor even ordinary human understanding, can break the spell of restraint, fear, death, cast by the circumstance which past attitudes and actions have created. The town, afraid to die, is living its death. In this respect, Yáñez's town is not very different from other towns, and not just in Mexico, where restraints placed upon the natural inclination to live have made life die. This fact alone would give *Al filo del agua* universal appeal.

Yáñez narrates from the point of view of the reader, assisted by the author's omniscience. The reader learns of events in the town as if he lived there, and later finds out how and why they happened. But it is the author whose interiorization completes the reason, and the reader whose projection considers the significance. Many characters move within the setting. None becomes a single central figure, but all who are affected directly or indirectly by the possibility of change from the outside contribute to the anticipation that is the focus of the novel.

The fact of the coming Revolution identifies the novel with Mexican history. But the town is as clearly the cause of the Revolution as the Revolution is the cause of change in the town. And if the Revolution had not taken its historical form, the town's hermeticism would have been broken in some other way, because it was *"al filo del agua."* The change brings hope to some, despair to others. Frustration and fulfillment are equal possibilities; life is given a chance against death. Potential self-realization stands before everyone. Damián Limón, who has worked in the north, knows that a more attractive material life is possible. But his anxiety cannot wait for the expected moment. His death comes less from the tragedy he precipitated than from his trying to live. The priest, after the Revolution has swept through the town, says Mass because it is the only thing he can think of to do. Gabriel, whose bells have marked the progress of the days, of the years, of life, has before him the possibility of artistic creativity, the opposite of Damián's material ambitions. Victoria, from the outside, knows that the change will bring life to some, but only to some. María, whose dreams would have broken the shell from within, is swept along with the Revolution into the World, which is a substitute for dreams. The town remains, changed but not remade, its hermeticism broken by the Revolution, a Mexican fact, its future to be determined by its awareness of its own identity, a human concern.

Al filo del agua is the best Mexican novel to date, whether judged purely on the basis of its artistic worth, or on that basis combined with its merit as the expression of the nation. It brought the author national and international prominence. Some may consider this book a first novel because Yáñez's earlier narrative prose is autobiographical to a considerable extent, and its form is not clearly novelistic. But the earlier works are a preparation for the masterpiece, and they all show an important characteristic of the author which is extremely significant in present-day Mexico: the ability to move outward from the particular, the intimate, the commonplace, toward a general identification with the human condition. He is like Ramón López Velarde and, in a somewhat different way, Alfonso Reyes. All three have been particularly successful in being Mexican and universal at the same time.

Yáñez's preparation began with his work on a literary review in Guadalajara, *Bandera de Provincias*, which was published during the lifetime of *Contemporáneos*[4] and which professed to be a provincial organ sharing the goals and interests of the review published in Mexico City. During the years between this beginning and the publication of *Al filo del agua*, Mexican fiction was concerned mainly with objective social discovery: narrative accounts of the military phase of the Revolution, analysis of the social results of the Revolution, awareness and description of the Indian problem. Some good fiction was produced during these years; but as a general rule, art was considered subordinate to message, and sometimes was disregarded entirely.

It is easy to let the importance of a work like *Al filo del agua* distort the facts of literary history. It is wrong to let the impression stand that this novel, because it is indicative in many ways of the direction taken by the best fiction in later years, brought about an immediate

---

[4] From 1928 to 1931 the review *Contemporáneos* was published by some of the most eminent literati of the present century: Torres Bodet, Novo, Cuesta, Ortiz de Montellano, Villaurrutia, Owen, *etc.* The group was frequently accused of being un-Mexican because they were profoundly interested in foreign literatures. Their fundamental Mexicanism was not recognized by extreme nationalists and propagandists. The nature of this nativist-universalist argument is extremely complicated, and, in addition to comments at various places in this book, I have tried to provide some clarification in an article, "*Contemporáneos* and the Limits of Art," *Romance Notes*, V, 2 (Spring, 1964).

change in the characteristics of the Mexican novel in general. Yáñez's novel is only one of many published in 1947, and right at that moment was hardly more indicative than any one of several others.

The other novels of 1947 that received more than just passing attention hardly indicate the beginning of a new phase, though a few promise a deeper understanding and broader interpretation of the Mexican circumstance. As far as subject matter is concerned, these novels look rather traditional: the tale of the Revolution, personalistic leadership (*caciquismo*), rural social protest, and the like. María Luisa Ocampo published her first novel, *Bajo el fuego*, which is another lineal account of experiences of the Revolution similar to many that were published in the thirties and forties. It demonstrates the same need to recount the recent past in an attempt to become aware of what had happened, by sharing experiences with others. Rogelio Barriga Rivas' *Guelaguetza*, another first novel, deals with the *caciquismo* theme, but it is really nothing more than a piece of competently written *costumbrismo*. The critical reception accorded José María Dávila's *El médico y el santero* is especially revealing in that it shows an interest in the possibility of expressing the Mexican character in fiction combined with a willingness to accept an extremely superficial interpretation.[5] Dávila was an accurate observer and reporter. The humor and cynicism of his novel have a kind of picaresque appeal that is reminiscent of José Rubén Romero. Its frankness gives the impression of an uncommonly realistic view of Mexico. Actually it is no more realistic than many others, and the book contains nothing that will take the reader beyond the objective account.

Some other authors show new and varied tendencies toward an idea of the novel that is very different from what had become more or less traditional in Mexico. One of these novels has to be regarded as a special case: Jesús Goytortúa Santos' *Lluvia roja*. In this novel, as in his earlier one, *Pensativa*, the author makes a successful combination of fact and imagination, which is a good deal closer to what a novel ought to be than is the lineal tale of the Revolution. Goytortúa is not a great novelist, because he lacks the ability to accomplish a refined

[5] A discussion with suitable quotations of this critical reaction may be found in Manuel Pedro González, *Trayectoria de la novela mexicana*, pp. 388–390.

shading of characters, and tends to overstate emotional response. In the earlier novel, he dealt with the *cristero* rebellions, and in *Lluvia roja* he deals with the end of the Obregón administration. Both novels are written with the obvious intent of involving the reader in the action; and if the author gives us little or nothing more, it is to his credit that he knows how to attract readers who are not already involved in his own interests.

In the rather vague category of the novel of social protest, Magdalena Mondragón published a kind of rural version of *Yo como pobre.* Her earlier novel describes the life of the very lowest social elements in Mexico City. Mondragón's technique is direct description, and the effectiveness of her protest depends largely on the compassion with which she presents the problem. *Más allá existe la tierra* shows a similar concern for the rural problem. In both cases, she succeeds in arousing her reader; but the later book is better because a deeper psychological penetration of the characters directs the reader's sympathy toward the plight of individuals rather than toward the generalized problem. For the most part, during the 1930's and early 1940's, the novel tended to be so concerned about the social condition that the authors were led into a kind of abstraction of the problem that left individuals bereft of significance.

The same year saw the publication of an inferior novel, *Lola Casanova,* by a very important writer, Francisco Rojas González. This novel is the reconstruction of an old legend, and its only possible importance in the history of the genre is that the author's psychological insight is considerable. He had earlier shown the same ability in a better novel, *La negra Angustias,* which is a novel of the Revolution. We may sometimes question the validity of the author's psychological insight, but there is no doubt that his novel moves forward from the lineal account. Rojas González wrote no more novels, but his interpretive ability is amply apparent in his short stories which probably contribute more to the contemporary novel than his longer works do.[6] He can write about various sectors of society without implying that one or the other is the *real* Mexico. And although his subject matter is un-

[6] Joseph Sommers, "La génesis literaria en Francisco Rojas González," *Revista Iberoamericana,* XX, 56 (julio–diciembre, 1963), 299–309.

questionably Mexican, he bases his fiction on human characteristics that are common among men rather than peculiar to Mexico. Still, his reader does not feel that he is struggling to be universal. His base may be resignation or abnegation or any other universally understood condition, and his identification with Mexico rests on that universality.

Undoubtedly the most important book of the year, next to *Al filo del agua,* is Miguel Lira's *Donde crecen los tepozanes (Where the tepozanes grow),* a *novela indigenista.*[7] The book is the first novel of an established poet and playwright. It is radically different from the usual idea of what an *indigenista* novel is, because it does not protest the Indian problem nor undertake proposals for the integration of two cultures. Rather, Lira's attitude seems to be that this culture is partly integrated, but different, and that the proper starting point is recognition of its nature.

Lira wrote a kind of learned folkloric poetry in which his poetic sensitivity changes the commonplace into the legendary. A similar transition takes place in *Donde crecen los tepozanes.* The chronological setting of the novel could be at any point after a few Christian-European customs and beliefs had infiltrated the native ones. Lira presents this partial conjunction of cultures as if it were quite natural, and he purposely suspends time, which indeed reflects the actual situation since the development of the native culture was halted by the European intrusion. It is not possible to tell where one culture ends and another starts, where reality ends and imagination begins, where fact becomes superstition.

It is possible that some might criticize this novel because it does not present easily recognizable characters in a *costumbrista* setting. The fact is that it does not have the quaint, touristic charm that is often expected of Indianist novels, but presents the disturbing fact of a world different from ours. The people live in a cultural Nirvana where life, death, and time are entirely different from what they are to us. And the contrast with our own attitudes provokes astonishment and speculation.

[7] This is a term used to identify novels that deal with the life and problems of the Indian population, and to distinguish them from the nineteenth-century novels that idealized the Indian.

Lira wrote four novels in all, and each one is worthy of special attention as representative of an era. One year after *Donde crecen los tepozanes*, he published *La escondida*, the first of two novels of the Revolution. He selected some folkloric, revolutionary figures and set them against the background of the last days of the Díaz regime. These characters tend toward the heroic, but they are not dehumanized. They are similar to the characters in the author's folk-type poetry, and so achieve something of the realist-legendary value of the heroes found in old Spanish romances. They are more authentic than the people that belong to refined society, and Lira used them to set up a confrontation of their world and the other side of Mexican life of that period. If the reader ignores this confrontation, the novel will seem to have two poorly integrated plots: one that deals primarily with Revolutionary action, and one that is the love story of one of the revolutionaries and a woman of the favored social class. If the Revolution was to have any meaning, certainly it would call for some sort of integration of the society. So Lira moves his characters beyond the act of fighting into the problems of a personal relationship where he contrasts the basic with the superficial aspects of Mexican society. If we define a message in this novel, it is that the reality of the folk-type characters must prevail, but not without the influence of more cultivated people. However, it is unfair to imply that Lira actually states a message. He only describes a possible situation.

Lira's second novel of the Revolution was written ten years later, and is one man's retrospective view of the Revolution. *Mientras la muerte llega* is, like Fuentes' *La muerte de Artemio Cruz* and Almanza's *Detrás del espejo*, an attempt to bring the reality of the Revolution into focus, not by personal reminiscence, but by the recall of a fictional character. By using this technique the author enhances the possibility for analysis rather than mere observation.

Una mujer en soledad, which Lira published in 1956, is quite removed from Revolution or from social problems in the ordinary sense of the term. That is, it does not have to do with the plight of any group. It is an epistolary novel, miraculously saved by the author's ability to breathe life into his characters, which has to do with a personal relationship in contemporary life. To be more specific, it is the story of a woman who is made to become what she really is not, by the pressures of modern society. It is also the story of a man who is irresistibly attracted to her, but cannot save her from destruction. At first glance, this story appears to be the naturalist's account of the woman's fall. But it is not a fall, it is the enforced negation of self.

Sometimes novelists appear to deny the importance of social protest and to ignore the great social problems. On the other hand, there are still some writers who examine the problem from the outside, not caring to study the relationship of the problem to the state of being Mexican, of being man. María Elvira Bermúdez, in her review of Concha Villareal's *El desierto mágico* (1961), says: "What is important above all things [in this novel] is to denounce and redeem. That is why this is a *social novel*, a type that is abundant in Mexico. And it will keep on being abundant as long as there are oppressed to redeem and oppressors to denounce."[8] The point is not whether a book does or does not present a social problem, but whether it does anything else. I do not mean that the author is obliged to present a solution to any problem he may describe, but that he needs to relate the problem to the basic human qualities and allow the coincidence to be seen in individuals. Herein lies the art of the novelist, whether or not he wishes to emphasize a problem. There is little point in a novelist's being a poor sociologist.

It is not possible to understand recent Mexican fiction without knowing that the country passed through a social revolution that did not create utopia. Some believe that the Revolution has been betrayed, others that a predictable human compromise has been made between what was hoped for and what was possible. The fact is that, although a very large number of Mexicans enjoy a higher standard of living than before the Revolution, the distribution of wealth and the national product are still far from satisfactory. And it is also necessary to point out that certain elements of society, like those in Magdalena Mondragón's *Yo como pobre,* and some rural groups, do not live within the national economy at all, but subsist on the margin of it. We may hope that in a world where, in spite of the many self-incurred dangers, men appear to be more concerned than they used to be for the material welfare of other men, a combination of individ-

[8] *Letras.* XXXI, 165 (julio, 1962), p. 2.

ual human concern and the principles of the Revolution will assure the continuation of the progress that has changed Mexico into a modern nation in the last fifty years.

A great deal of Mexican fiction since the Revolution shows dissatisfaction with the social interpretation of the change. Not much of this fiction is revolutionary in the sense that it advocates another revolution. But it does show plainly that such an upheaval is within the realm of possibility unless attention is paid to the needs of the nation as a whole and confidence expressed in its future. In general, the attitude of the novelists is hopeful. But the clearest hope is apparent where the author goes beyond the presentation of a social problem and attempts to find the reality that is deeper than the problem.

The fiction that is chronologically closer to the Revolution than the books that we have just been dealing with shows that Mexico, after the Revolution, went through a process of introversion and of extroversion at the same time. The country felt a need to understand its own nature and its problems; but at the same time it needed to understand its relationship with the rest of the world. But what was the nation? To a considerable extent, it was new. Mexico has an important history, and present-day Mexico is rooted in that history; but the *modus operandi* from the time of the Revolution has been quite different from what it was before. The most important single reason is that a larger part of the population is incorporated into the life of the country.

During the years when Mexico was first going through the simultaneous and conflicting processes of introversion and extroversion, the attempts to understand the nature of the country were often inhibited by the lack of awareness of the fact of the Revolution.[9] This question of awareness can best be understood in terms of the individual. If a person is affected by a favorable change of circumstances, he may profit from the change before he is quite aware of what has happened to him. He may recall an event that precipitated the change, but its significance in relation to his changed circumstances half eludes him. He does not really *know* what has happened. And only

[9] It should be understood that such a generalization must necessarily have notable exceptions. Perhaps the outstanding example is Samuel Ramos.

time will enable him to appreciate fully the nature of the present and, indeed, the fact that he is a different person. So it was in the case of the Mexican change; and by the year 1947, I believe enough progress had been made toward the state of necessary awareness so that at least the mainstream of fiction goes beyond the description of the problem to study the nature of Mexico and of man. And it is important to observe that the relationship of one nation to another has changed in such a way that Mexican reality cannot be apprehended except in terms of universal man. So it is perfectly understandable that if a particular kind of anxiety focuses the attention of a writer on a social problem, the obverse of that anxiety might cause another writer to ignore the problem and address himself to man's universal condition. And it is possible for a novelist to combine the two procedures effectively.

Not long after the publication of *Al filo del agua*, Agustín Yáñez entered politics and became governor of the state of Jalisco, an act thoroughly in accord with his idea of what a novelist should be and do. Both jobs require the same vision, the same projection beyond objective fact. His political activities broke the thread of his novelistic production temporarily, and a number of important books were published by other authors before his next novel appeared.

The first novel of really major importance after *Al filo del agua* was Juan Rulfo's *Pedro Páramo* (1955). During the years between these great novels, almost all the important novelists who had published before 1947, ended their careers. The most important of them was Mariano Azuela, whose *Sendas perdidas* was published in 1949, followed by two posthumous novels, *La maldición* and *Esa sangre*, in 1955 and late 1956 respectively. *Sendas perdidas* is a somewhat better novel than the quarrelsome books that Azuela had been writing toward the end of his career. Instead of being petulantly disgusted with the loss of ordinary moral values in the new Mexican society, he seems to be probing for deeper causes. The book suggests that the author senses the need for common concern among men, and that he is willing to consider this need rather than insist blindly on the perverseness of the modern world. *La maldición* is more like the novels published immediately before *Sendas perdidas*, and adds neither to the stature of the writer nor to his interpretation of Mexico.

The most important of the three books is *Esa sangre*, a novel which rounds out Azuela's production because it is about the return of Julián Andrade, the male protagonist of *Mala yerba*, one of the author's earliest novels, in which he clearly draws the contrast between the landed aristocracy and the rural poor. Azuela does not defend the morality of either class in these novels, but concerns himself with where the power lies. In *Mala yerba*, whatever we may think of Andrade's conduct, power is on his side. When he returns, in *Esa sangre*, he is essentially the same person, unwilling to assume that power has deserted him. But he is obviously wrong, and his intransigence leads to his death. This book is the final comment of a great novelist whose works give us his view of the whole spectrum of the Revolution: the society from which it burst, the military phase, the chaos, and the organized social result. However much he may question some of the values of the new society, Azuela recognizes the fact of its existence.

The addition of *Esa sangre* to Azuela's works gives his view of modern Mexico a depth of perspective that it could not have without the dovetailing of time and circumstance that is effected by the return of Julián Andrade. Mauricio Magdaleno achieved a similar perspective in *Tierra Grande* (1949), a long and complicated novel that looks backward to the time of the Revolution and examines its effect on a large and important landholding family. The novel has a structural protagonist in the person of Gustavo Suárez Medrano, but the spiritual protagonist is the family as a whole. Following his usual custom, Magdaleno went back several generations to set the stage for the members of the family who are contemporary with the principal action of the novel. Gustavo is the most ruthless of the young generation, and perhaps the most devoted to the land.

For the Suárez Medrano family, the land is essence. Even though they are removed from the direct act of extracting life from the land, they still feel the relationship so deeply that defense of the land is almost equivalent to defense of life. Indeed, there have been moments in the family's past when land was more important than life. Magdaleno makes no attempt to justify the cruelty that has grown out of the family's passion, but he does show that their ownership is important to them for reasons that are much deeper than the purely economic. The land is belonging, and it is identification. Relationships may be broken within the family, but the integrity of the land remains.

The Revolution comes to destroy this relationship between the family and its property. Gustavo, courageous and ruthless, admirable and hateful, holds on as well as he can to the meaning of his existence. But as the Revolution progresses, he gradually degenerates, and hope is found only in a new generation.

Magdaleno's central theme in this novel, the feeling for the land, functions exactly as it should and serves as the focal point for the study of a multitude of characters. Many of the people are seen with admirable clarity, but the dominating characterization is of the family. The social role of this family, as a unit, is destroyed, but there is no doubt that the strength of character that has grown from their well-founded sense of belonging will cast them in new roles. At the same time, the land takes on new significance for some to whom it has been denied, and their roles too will change.

Magdaleno, who had neglected the novel for many years, published two in 1949, and then lapsed into another long silence. His second novel of that year, *Cabello de elote,* is an ambitious failure, but a significant one. It is a panoramic view of a small Mexican town during the Second World War. The picture of the town in the process of change is superb. Magdaleno shows the communication and lack of communication among the different social classes, the conflict between political conservatism and progressivism, the influence of immigrants from Europe, the effect of the changing agricultural economy. The novel's great fault, and it is major, is that the central theme is not strong enough to justify the enormous, panoramic backdrop. Indeed the panorama becomes so important the theme is sometimes forgotten.

The title of the novel, *Cabello de elote,* refers to the blonde hair of the protagonist, who is the daughter of an Indian woman and a foreigner. Although she is rescued from a poor economic environment, her social position in the town remains nebulous and she is alternately accepted and rejected. Her goal is to find a new environment where she can be an integrated person. The theme is a perfectly good one, and the author is sensitive enough to its implications. The trouble is that there are too many things going on around the theme.

Magdaleno's town was at one time almost entirely dependent on a nearby hacienda. It is not hard to imagine a place similar to the town in *Al filo del agua*. But the economy of the town had to change when the land was redistributed, and it is anything but hermetic when Magdaleno describes it. It is open to all kinds of influences, and change and confusion are apparent everywhere. A new middle class has appeared, and it has some of the characteristics of Azuela's *"nueva burguesía,"* but Magdaleno does not have Azuela's bitterness. European immigrants have brought an awareness of the size of the world. A movie theater is the symbol of a new sophistication. The old aristocracy clings to its conservative point of view, but cannot remain separated from the new middle class. Neither the one nor the other knows exactly what the relationship is, and neither the town nor its individual constituents can be sure of an exact identity. The personality of the protagonist is, to an extent, a reflection of the town's confusion. The Indian is apart from the rest of the town; and although Magdaleno does not exclude the possibility of integration, the hope belongs to a future that is farther away than tomorrow.

Magdaleno's position here, among the "older" novelists, is strange. His earlier works do indeed belong to the preceding period because of their concern with the social problem; but even these early novels are concerned with the condition of man in a way that is not characteristic of the novel of protest. Rather, they are to a considerable extent forerunners of *Al filo del agua* and Magdaleno's own later works. His neglect of the novel is based on his decision to turn his efforts in another direction, not on his having rounded out his novelistic circle or having reached a conclusion. His work stands with an open end pointing toward the future, and he really should be publishing currently.

José Mancisidor, on the other hand, obviously finished his work when he published his last two novels in 1953, *Frontera junto al mar* and *El alba en las cimas*. The first is about the invasion of Veracruz by Northamerican marines in 1914, the second about the expropriation of oil. Both novels are intensely nationalistic, and they will certainly make a conscientious Northamerican aware of why his country is not universally loved. *El alba en las cimas*, like all of Mancisidor's novels except *Frontera junto al mar*, promises more than it produces. On beginning a Mancisidor novel, the reader is likely to expect a penetrating study based on a social position. It is unfortunate that the author's ideological anxiety overshadows his interest in authentic creation; and while the novels are never quite devoid of art, they do not come up to the reader's expectation or the author's ability. *Frontera junto al mar* fares better, perhaps because it is the account of an event in which the author participated. In this book, the author's position is so closely identified with his action that one would hardly overshadow the other.

Entresuelo, published by Gregorio López y Fuentes in 1948, has to be mentioned only because of the author's reputation. It is a middle-class novel of the city, subject matter in which the author had shown no earlier interest, which is written in the realist tradition and might more properly belong to the nineteenth century than to the twentieth. It has nothing of the legendlike value that is the outstanding characteristic of the earlier novels that used folkloric or indigenist themes. And without that quality, not much is left, for López y Fuentes was never a great literary artist. *Entresuelo* tells us that there is a middle class, but it does not take us beyond the fact.[10]

Among the younger writers, several followed the lead of Magdalena Mondragón in *Yo como pobre.* This theme of indignation concerning the plight of the urban poor is a compelling one, but apparently not a rich one. It is the theme of the only novels of Benigno Corona Rojas (*La barriada,* 1948) and of Felipe García Arroyo (*El sol sale para*

---

[10] It should be noted here that this discussion cannot hope to include all the novelists whose names are respected. Some were writing in this period whose work, in my opinion, does not need to be considered at this point. Rodolfo Benavides, an uncultivated writer, wrote with considerable native force. His protest is strong, but his view is entirely personal, and his work neither benefits from nor contributes to what other novelists were doing. Fernando Robles published *Cuando el águila perdió sus alas,* an account of the Northamerican invasion, in 1951. It it a good historical novel, but not different from his earlier works. Luis Rivero del Val published his only novel, *Entre las patas de los caballos,* in 1953. This lineal account of personal experiences in the *cristero* rebellions really belongs to an earlier period. Artemio de Valle Arizpe, raconteur, author of colonialist and quasi-picaresque novels, continued writing in the same vein until his death in 1962. A charming anachronism even in his youth, he was doubly so in his later years.

todos, 1948); and even in cases of more productive writers, only one novel by each author is on this theme. *Yo como pobre* is the only one by Mondragón, *Candelaria de los patos* (1952) is Héctor Raúl Almanza's treatment of the theme, and Barriga Rivas published *Río humano* (1949) between a novel on the theme of the *cacique* (*Guelaguetza*, 1947) and an *indigenista* novel (*La mayordomía*, 1952).

These novels of misery, of the dregs of urban society, have relatively little artistic value. They are mainly descriptive of a deplorable social condition. The blame is not clearly fixed, though Corona Rojas tends to place it on corrupt officials. In general, the assumption is that the social condition is the fault of society as a whole, and that it is society's duty to change the condition. Usually there is some impulse in one or another of the characters to improve himself—the strongest is in *Candelaria de los patos*—but the general picture is one of hopelessness.

There are a few people who like to say that these novels portray the real Mexico, and they like to make a contrast with cafe society, ignoring the tremendous upward impulse of the majority of the Mexican people. The fact is that both social extremes are false, both groups are actually less alive than the middle. While the social propagandists make active use of the novels of misery, there is no reason to think that the writers consider these criminals, prostitutes, and thieves as representative of the real Mexico. If they did, surely they would write more about them. They do consider this subhuman element to be a part of visible reality in Mexico, and they know that its existence cannot be ignored.

The different novelists' approaches to the subject matter vary widely. None of them has actually experienced the life he describes. Magdalena Mondragón tries hard for identification, but the best she can do is be compassionate, so her novel is not entirely convincing. García Arroyo tries to be a Luis Buñuel, and it is possible that more experience as a writer might have enabled him to succeed. His novel has two major faults: a lack of precision in character delineation, and a tiresome use of nouns for descriptive purposes. He insists on describing the revolting scene to the point that the reader reacts against the novelist. Corona Rojas' novel has a different focus: the exploitation of the poor by dishonest officials. His protest is so violent that he breaks the action in an editorial fashion. Almanza's novel is the most positive of the group, because his emphasis is on hope. Barriga Rivas is the most objective. *Río humano* is a series of snapshots of the people who pass through a police station on a given evening. The structure is weak, and the author is in no way involved with his socially condemned characters. But it is probably the most convincing of all these novels because the author does not make a futile attempt to identify with characters whom he could know only from the outside.

Barriga Rivas is a *costumbrista* novelist, and that quality is the dominant characteristic of *Río humano* as well as of his other novels. Among the works of Mondragón and Almanza, on the other hand, the novels of urban misery amount to one aspect of a wide range of social protest. Almanza's began with *Huelga blanca* in 1950. And after *Candelaria de los patos*, came *Brecha en la roca* in 1955, and two more novels after that date. He has dealt with wetbacks, the exploitation of oil workers by foreign companies, the fishing industry, and the meaning of the Revolution. In many ways, Almanza is an old-fashioned writer. He has no stylistic tricks, no significance beyond what is readily apparent. The truth is that his novels are sometimes a welcome relief from those that intend to involve the reader beyond what the writer actually says. In his earlier novels, his characterizations are carelessly done, or else they are purposely stereotyped. He obviously holds Northamericans in very low regard, and his evaluation of their moral standards is unjust to the point of being ludicrous. But Anglo-Americans should be aware that Almanza is not alone in this evaluation, and that some Northamerican evaluations of Mexicans are just as absurd. In his later novels, Almanza shows some improvement in characterization, and starts to move beyond the descriptive.

The *indigenista* theme constitutes a particular kind of social protest because it involves not only an economic issue, but a cultural one as well. Indeed, this kind of novel is less a novel of protest than of cultural analysis. While it is obviously important to incorporate the Indian population into the national economy, it is even more important to understand the significance of the Indian influence in the national culture. The discussion of nativism has been long and sometimes bitter, and only recently has there been much calm clarification of it.

Since there are still almost as many positions as there are people, any statement is likely to bring upon its maker the wrath or indignation of a substantial number of critics. My opinion is that indigenous culture in Mexico is alive but static, as it has been since the time of the Conquest. Large segments of the Indian population had reached a high degree of civilization at that time. In some ways the Indians were more civilized than the Spaniards. But the egocentric anxiety of the Spaniards, their desire to make the world over in their own image, was so overwhelming that the impact of the confrontation of two cultures brought the development of the indigenous to a standstill. Yet the indigenous culture was not destroyed. Miguel Lira says something to this effect in *Donde crecen los tepozanes*. Since that time, a fusion of the two cultures has been in process, though not always in the most desirable way. If we think of the indigenous culture as an identifiable and independent reality, it exists only among small and isolated groups of Indians. If, however, we think of how indigenous culture has modified the European culture which throttled its development, we find that the influence is considerable. Movements to revive indigenous culture are futile and reactionary. Attempts to understand indigenous culture, on the other hand, are absolutely necessary, because the result of the fusion can never be understood in any other way.

From the time of the Revolution the Indian was given more serious attention in the novel as well as elsewhere. The new treatment certainly differentiated him from the romanticized Indian of the last century. But it tended to generalize him and to recognize his dignity without searching for a deep-rooted cause of that dignity. Miguel Angel Menéndez moved toward improvement in *Nayar* (1941), in which he sends his protagonist into the world of a special group, the *coras*. A different, but even more mature, approach was used by Lira. In 1948, a great push in the same direction was given by two books dealing with the *tzotziles*: *Juan Pérez Jolote* by Ricardo Pozas A., and Ramón Rubín's *El callado dolor de los tzotziles*.

The more influential of the two has been *Juan Pérez Jolote*, which is not a novel but the account by a social anthropologist of the life of a *tzotzil*. Its accuracy is generally accepted, and it is read with the intense interest that a fine work of this type deserves. Actually, the book is something between scientific description and novel. Pozas limits the amount of detail and in his language captures the simplicity of his subject. By doing so he brings his reader within the situation, and the effect is something like that of a good historical novel, where the author re-creates the feeling of a time past and moves his reader into it.

If Pozas' documentary tends to be novelistic, Rubín's novel tends to be documentary, and they come out nearly even. Of the two books, Pozas' is the more compelling because his choice of detail attracts the reader while Rubín loses his reader by his insistence on too much detail. However, Rubín's interests are more varied, and he has written of other Indian groups and also of mestizos.[11] It is a pity that he does not see the value of more careful character development and plot construction. If he would take this care, the re-creation of an unfamiliar culture would be more complete, and he would make a greater contribution to the understanding of the fusion of cultures and to the understanding of man. One of the principal values of the ethnological tendency in the *indigenista* novel is the representation of man in a culture sufficiently different from our own to make us aware of facts that we normally ignore. At its best this kind of novel goes far beyond the representation of an isolated group.

However insistent the social problem theme may be in the recent Mexican novel, this kind of writing has tended gradually to do more than just describe the problem. Sometimes the desire to transcend the immediate leaves the author in an unresolved mess which he cannot clarify adequately. José Revueltas, one of the most strongly committed and most artistically capable of Mexican writers, has failed even after several attempts to write the novel that many consider him capable of. Revueltas maintains a strong leftist position politically; and although this position is apparent in his novels, the author wishes to base it on the condition of man rather than on the volume of his

[11] *El canto de la grilla* (1952) concerns the *coras* and *La bruma lo vuelve azul* (1954) concerns the *huicholes*. The author calls *La canoa perdida* (1951) a "*novela mestiza*." It is not really a *novela indigenista*, but the author's insistence on a kind of documentary use of folklore makes this book interesting in a consideration of the fusion of cultures.

protest. The impression left by a Revueltas novel is that somehow the author gets lost and is never able to do what he sets out to do.

Revueltas' first novel, *Los muros de agua* (1941), deals with political prisoners and is notable mainly because the author is fundamentally concerned with them as people. The second novel, *El luto humano*, was published in 1943, and it indicated to many critics the author's tremendous potential. It also suggested that a politically committed novelist could write a novel without forsaking either his commitment or his art. The people are rural, destitute, facing death; but the meaning of death is controlled by the meaning of life—if it can be called that—which has had no significance except on the most basic level. They are lost, utterly lost; and although they have participated in the Revolution, in strikes, in whatever they were asked to do, these actions have had no meaning, the participants have never known the why. Their land is nothing, their religion is nothing, their actions are nothing, their life is nothing. They only die.

Revueltas has the elements of a very powerful novel, yet somewhere he misses. Three faults are identifiable. One is that the reader is thrown off by inconsistent characterization. Revueltas knows how to make characters, but some are seen in the clarity of daylight, others in the mist of poetry. A second fault is lack of narrative organization. Revueltas does not use a line straight or even in a pattern, but breaks it up and puts the pieces in a bowl that is his novel. The third fault is that the author seems not to be able to express his ideology adequately through his creating of characters, and the reader feels the strain and confusion that are the author's. Yet, in spite of these faults, Revueltas is a compelling novelist because he makes his reader anticipate greater things. The same criticism could be made of *Los días terrenales* (1949), which the Communist Party caused him to renounce, and *Los motivos de Caín* (1957) which is an indictment of the brutality of Northamerican soldiers in the Second World War. Nowhere is the feeling of human isolation stronger than in this last novel, but the strength of the book is mitigated by the author's forcing it to say what his political position demanded.

In novels of social protest, the author's most effective tool is the ability to construct a narrative. Neither perceptive observation nor

strong commitment can be as effective as a story that will involve
the reader in the world of the fictional characters. In this respect,
Revueltas has repeatedly failed. Luis Spota, with considerably less artistic sensitivity than Revueltas, has had amazing success. His characterizations are often superficial and he is inclined to be sensationalist, but his ability to tell a story is one that other novelists cannot
afford to overlook. From 1948 to the present, Spota has published
novels that give the inside stories of the bullfight, migrant workers,
cafe society, and other subjects in which the author finds injustice
and hypocrisy. The novels are to a considerable extent a refinement
and enlargement of what the author does in his newspaper column.
Murieron a mitad del río (1948) set the tone of Spota's fiction and
it hasn't changed much since. His most widely read work is *Casi el
paraíso* (1956) which is a condemnation of cafe society in Mexico
City. In this book, as in many others, Spota expresses himself so
strongly he becomes silly. It has been widely read because it is easy,
it is scandalous, and it belabors a group toward which few feel any
particular generosity.

Spota really doesn't pretend to be enough of an artist to be included
in the tradition of the deeply searching novel that was established by
Yáñez in 1947. The contribution of Spota to the new novel is his
cosmopolitanism combined with his honest concern for the welfare
of Mexico. His work would naturally help the novel of social protest
move from its position of isolation.

During the years when an older generation was disappearing and
a younger one establishing itself, the short story acquired an unusual
importance in Mexican fiction. Three specific volumes probably did
more to enhance the artistic awareness of the novel than did any three
novels of the same period: Juan José Arreola's *Confabulario* (1952),
Juan Rulfo's *El llano en llamas* (1953), and Carlos Fuentes' *Los días
enmascarados* (1954). All three writers later turned to the novel,
though Arreola not until late 1963, and then with a kind of anti-
novel. Fuentes is the only one who can be called prolific.

It is not easy now to think of these collections outside the framework of their subsequent influence and the later work of their authors. Trying to place myself in 1952, when *Confabulario* was published, I think that if it were not for Rubén Salazar Mallén's *Ejercicios,*

Arreola's stories might appear to be lost in a sea of concern for immediate problems and past memories. *Confabulario* is a work of the imagination, though I don't mean to say that Arreola is unaware of the world around him. Quite to the contrary, he is probably more deeply aware of it than most of his contemporaries. But the world that comes out of Arreola is one that has passed under the spell of his particular way of looking at things.

Salazar Mallén's *Ejercicios* contains a story, "Soledad," which, according to its author, is "the only novel that has been written in Mexico from within and toward within and with interest in immortality rather than in the present moment."[12] This statement would have been an exaggeration in 1952, and it was nonsense in 1958. But if we assume that its author, writing in 1958 about his own work, recaptured the feeling he had when he wrote the story in 1952, we may understand that he felt some uneasiness about the lasting value of Mexican fiction. "Soledad" is a sound and penetrating view into the life of an isolated and insignificant individual. What the author did not take account of in 1952, but should have known by 1958, is that the attitude he describes had been present for many years and was becoming characteristic of the mainstream of Mexican fiction. The evidence is apparent in many works, Arreola's *Varia invencion*, among them.

As for Arreola's stories, *Varia invencion* and *Confabulario* are of one piece, and indeed they do later constitute a single volume. It is necessary to say something about Arreola's way of looking at things. Arreola is perhaps a bit of a pixie, and the unexpected is likely to happen. In spite of Arreola's easy expression and amazing flow of ideas, I suspect he is really an introvert, because the world comes out of him bearing a highly personal stamp and listing slightly to one side. A project to get a camel through a needle's eye so that rich men can go to heaven involves all the knowledge of modern science and philanthropy in such a way that if the experiment doesn't succeed, the wealthy will have become poor from supporting it and will have no problem after all ("La verdad os digo"). The national railways become part ghost, part paper empire, part reality, and part absurd-

---

[12] "Letras. Actualidad y perennidad," *Mañana*, 12 abril 1958.

ity ("El guardagujas"). No one could say seriously that Arreola is not dealing with reality. No one could say that he is not profoundly Mexican. But he speaks to all of us.

Arreola is one of those fortunate people who don't need to serve an apprenticeship; or else he's one of those wise people who don't publish until they have practiced enough. In any case, the excellence of Arreola's writing attracted attention and gave it immediate status, which was a blessing for Mexican fiction. It is not fair to consider Arreola perfect: he has his moments of failure. Sometimes his humorous slant leads him overboard and at other times it leaves him standing with no place to go. And it must be observed that some of his pieces are not stories, but little bits of poorly developed inspiration. Still there is no doubt that he had a liberating effect on fiction.

Juan Rulfo's stories are entirely different from Arreola's; and although it may not be just to select between such different works, I believe Rulfo's have more value as a body of literature because their quality is more consistent and because they represent a clearer involvement of the author, his immediate environment, and the larger world of all men. *El llano en llamas* (*The Plain Aflame*) is a collection of rural stories, though sometimes the rural values are made apparent by the injection of an "outsider" contrast. Common to all the stories is a certain parched quality, a feeling of dust in the throat, of dogged living in spite of what happens, of resistance to change, of belonging to something that is hostile or at best senseless and at the same time indispensable. Sometimes an attitude or a custom will be based on primitive logic that will not work in a complicated society; but Rulfo's stories are in no way *costumbrista*, because the author's reason for writing is not to show quaint customs, but to examine the actions of men. A valuable comparison can be made with the writing of William Faulkner, whose aim is certainly not to show the quaint customs of Mississippi, but to use them for other purposes.[13] Rulfo's

[13] Some people have seen further similarities between Faulkner and Rulfo, as well as other Spanish-American novelists. See, for example, James E. Irby, *La influencia de William Faulkner en cuatro narradores hispanoamericanos* (Mexico City: n.p., 1956). I doubt that this influence is very profound. It is quite possible that Faulkner demonstrated for these writers the validity of

style is entirely different from Faulkner's. His language is strong, simple, even coarse. It has characteristics of rural speech; but it is not rural speech because objectively we know that the characters would not speak that way, nor would Rulfo. The closest I can come to describing this style is to say that he captures and uses the essence of rural speech so that we accept his language as authentic, but allow it to remove us from a folkloric plane to a mythic plane where we observe not customs but symbols of customs.

The stories of *Los días enmascarados* are more in the nature of exercises than are the stories of Arreola and Rulfo. Fuentes is primarily a novelist, and his stories are preliminary to the main event. They show two extremely important characteristics: the author's interest in the role of indigenous culture in contemporary Mexico, and his willingness to enter a world of fantasy which, at its best, becomes superreality.

Juan Rulfo was the first of these three writers to publish a novel. *Pedro Páramo* (1955) is, on the first reading, one of the most difficult novels ever published; but on subsequent readings we are more and more amazed by its unique clarity. I suppose we might make interesting speculations about different influences; and since Rulfo has read other novelists, the speculations would perhaps have some justification. But I think it would be impossible to say that *Pedro Páramo* is like any other novel. Precisely for this reason, the initial reading is difficult, because the book cannot be read as other novels are read. Nor can it be described as other novels are described.

It is possible and desirable to make some objective statements about what *Pedro Páramo* is, but it should be remembered that such statements alone cannot describe the novel. Pedro Páramo is a *cacique*, and the novel is the story of his hate and the people who are tyrannized by it, including himself. Hate is both the cause and result of his power and his obsessive love for one woman. He is the epitome of egocentricity. There is no time. It is wrong to say that Rulfo suspends time; he doesn't suspend it, because it doesn't exist. Charac-

---

moving from the regional to the universal. Faulkner's influence was that of a teacher, not a model.

ters pass back and forth between the two states we call life and death
with no regard for what we consider possible. The style is fundamentally the same as in the author's short stories. The narrative viewpoint
is varied and changes as is required by Rulfo's reconstruction of reality. It is possible that the author is subject to criticism on this last
point. It may be that the frequent changes make the novel unneces-
sarily difficult, but I am inclined, after several readings, to believe
that the author is right.

The story opens with the arrival in Comala of Juan Preciado, one
of the many sons of Pedro Páramo, sent by his dying mother to claim
from his father what was his due. The town is dead, and so is Doña
Eduviges, who receives Juan Preciado into her house. Or perhaps this
death is life. Eduviges talks with Juan about his mother who was her
friend. "Poor Dolores. She must have felt abandoned. We promised
each other we'd die together. . . . So she's ahead of me? But you can
be sure I'll catch up with her. I know how far away heaven is, but I
know how to find the shortcuts. It's a question of dying, God willing,
when you want to and not when He wants you to. Or if you'd rather,
you make Him want it ahead of time."[14]

Beyond the first few pages of this book, any reference by the reader
to either life or death is utterly useless. There are states of being in
the novel, but an exterior comment on them is impossible. The book
must be read with the subconscious. The reader cannot stay outside
the novel. And he must do even more than just enter the book. He
must unite with it, entering into the book and allowing the book to
enter him. Once the subconscious is open, the reader's problem is
solved. Since time does not exist in the subconscious, the major obstacle is removed, and what at first seemed unreal now appears to be
quite the reverse.

Páramo's obsession becomes a lyric and is perfectly placed wher-
ever it interrupts the throat-parching narration.

"The wind made us laugh. Our eyes met as the kite string ran between
our fingers after the wind, until it broke with a gentle snap as if it had
been cut by a bird's wing. And up above, the paper bird fell somer-

[14] Juan Rulfo, *Pedro Páramo*, 4th ed. (Mexico City: Fondo de Cultura Económica, 1963), p. 16.

saulting, dragging its rag tail, disappearing in the green of the earth. "Your lips were moist as if the dew had kissed them."[15]

Pedro Páramo's love-obsession, his hate, and his power are one. The church bells ring in Comala, they ring until they deafen the people, who learn that they are tolling the death of Susana. People come, vendors come, musicians come, a travelling circus comes. The festive air grows, and even when the bells stop, the fiesta goes on. Around Páramo all is quiet. He looks at Comala: " 'I will fold my arms and Comala will die of hunger.' And that is what he did."[16]

The fate of Comala, of Susana, and of Páramo are one. However you comprehend the change, it is the natural fruition of existence, and the change in Páramo is interior as well as exterior. He is a ripe fruit dropping. "He leaned on the arms of Damiana Cisneros and tried to walk. After a few steps he fell, pleading within, but not saying a word. He made a dry thud against the ground and crumbled as if he were a pile of rocks."[17] We can only ask if this is the death of life or the death of death.

Nowhere in Mexican literature has the *caciquismo* theme been treated as well as in *Pedro Páramo*. There is not the slightest doubt that Rulfo knows what he is talking about, that he understands his theme, and that he is able to show the reality of it as it had never been shown before. Quite naturally, some readers object to the difficult access to the novel, and some prefer to reject it rather than work for what it says. I can sympathize with the reluctance to participate so actively, but it seems to me that the result is worth the effort. Even more disturbing to me is the occasional assumption that a simple, descriptive novel of protest is a more patriotic undertaking than an artistically important novel. Such an attitude seems to me to be equal to saying that an observation is worth more than a reason. Certainly observation has its uses, but I think it does not speak directly to the present need in Mexico. The continuation of the movement of the Revolution in Mexico seems to me to depend on the development of a deep understanding of Mexican reality. Rulfo has contributed not-

[15] *Ibid.*, p. 18.
[16] *Ibid.*, p. 143.
[17] *Ibid.*, p. 152.

ably to this end. And unless I read the contemporary novel poorly, such is the general orientation of the writers. Just as Rulfo's work is based on a social circumstance that can be defined as a problem, so the other writers begin with the problem and transcend its visible reality. And even if, in some cases, the visible reality is not a typically Mexican social problem, the universal human reality discovered by the author also contributes to the Mexican act of self discovery.

It is perhaps unnecessary to say that treatment of the novel becomes more difficult as we approach the present day. Current criticism is not very helpful, because it is not really independent. Personal friendships or enmities, the pressure of literary cliques, and political and professional associations inhibit objective, professional criticism. And since the number of novels published is increasing steadily, it is difficult to separate wheat from chaff, and even harder to say which of the wheat is best. My notes reveal the names of something more than eighty novelists who might be given a place in this chapter. The exigencies of time, space, and sound judgment demand a considerable reduction in that number, and we must proceed bravely, knowing that some injustice will be done.

It is not easy for a novelist to achieve the wide and deep reality of *Pedro Páramo*. Two other good novels of the same year show how the novelist's view rarely acquires the dimensions of Rulfo's: José Alvarado's *El personaje* and Almanza's *Brecha en la roca*. Alvarado, a keenly perceptive observer of human nature, had already published *Memoria de un espejo* in 1953. Both works are short novels that make fine contributions to the tendency to look beyond the immediately apparent. It is unfortunate that Alvarado has not written more. Almanza, on the other hand, is the hard-hitting, indignant corrector of injustice—honorable, but not very enlightening. Considering these and other novels of the year, we find that quantitatively, the novelists still take a view that is turned inward upon Mexico, but not toward the basic nature of man.

The following year shows less nationalistic concern. Among its books are Azuela's *Esa sangre*, Lira's *Una mujer en soledad*, a minor Revueltas work (*En algún valle de lágrimas*), and *La veleta oxidada* by newcomer Emilio Carballido. Although he is well known and properly respected as a playwright, Carballido's stories and novels are

often overlooked. *La veleta oxidada* and *El norte* (1958) are short
pieces, but they are novels and good ones. Both are concise examina-
tions of human relationships. Like many contemporary novels, they
show the loneliness of the individual, whose relationships are either
nullified or perverted by the failure of contemporary society to be
significant. The two novels are similar in many ways, but *El norte* is
the stronger of the two. It concerns the misery-ridden love affair of
a middle-aged woman and a young boy. The egocentricity of one or
the other member of this unnatural union forbids the realization of
every decent tendency on the part of either the woman or the boy.
The reality of the situation is made apparent by the author's movement between past and present. He writes a neat but sketchy prose
that invites the reader to fill in what the author does not say.

Carballido is utterly pessimistic, and some people believe that this
kind of pessimism, which is found in many contemporary novels, is
characteristic of the writer who does not base his work on an intimately known situation, regional or personal.[18] It is true that novels
like those of Yáñez, Rulfo, Fuentes, Castellanos, and others, leave a
somewhat more positive impression. It is difficult to say whether they
actually are less pessimistic. Their affirmation may be only in the
implication of possible action. And that action may be nullified by
the same living of death that is at the root of more abstract pessimism.
The novelist's aim would be the same in both cases: to discover life.

Whatever its shortcomings, the most spectacular novel of 1956 was
Spota's *Casi el paraíso*, because of the direction of its attack and because of its sensationalism. In addition to the fact that the people
who are the object of the attack are an unlovely bunch, these same
people represent the greatest threat to the progress of the nation, less
on account of their accumulation of wealth than on account of their
lack of human concern. They are, of course, just as disoriented as
the characters of Carballido or anyone else. The novel is important
because it reached a very large number of readers. Its place in history, however, will be slight, because Carlos Fuentes did the job much
better two years later.

The appearance in 1957 of a lineal account of the Revolution, José

[18] Rosario Castellanos, "La novela mexicana contemporánea," *México en la
Cultura*, no. 597 (21 agosto 1960), pp. 1 ff.

Pérez Moreno's *El tercer canto del gallo*, indicates the persistence of
that kind of novel; but it looks completely out of place beside Revueltas' *Los motivos de Caín* and Rosario Castellanos' *Balúm Canán*, both
of the same year, and sandwiched between the extraordinarily imaginative works of 1956 and 1958.

In *Balúm Canán*, Castellanos goes back to her childhood as a means
of discovering reality that is hidden from an adult, and deals with
a dispute between the Argüelles family and an Indian group. Her approach to the problem is not sociological but personal. The situation
she describes is really a frontier situation where the two cultures come
into contact. Castellanos has all the necessary ethnological information, which combined with her desire for human understanding, makes
a very different and welcome approach to the *indigenista* theme. In
1962, she published a more mature novel, *Oficio de tinieblas*, which
probes similar material even more deeply. The Indian is not at all
generalized. Although the reader is aware of the customs that lie behind the behavior of the characters, each one is seen individually.
Once in a while the author falls into the "many-moons-will-pass" pre-
tentiousness that has bedevilled so much Indianist literature, but the
total effect of the novel is far removed from such foolishness.

Castellanos' thought is contained within the action of the novel, a
story of the confrontation of two cultures. These cultures have been
mutually influential; but there has been no real marriage of them,
and human relationships fall into the abyss that exists between the
two. *Oficio de tinieblas* is an eloquent demonstration of how this happens. The author's optimism consists of the suggestion that new and
more radical approaches to the problem are needed, but it is not clear
what these approaches should be.

The richness of 1958 is overwhelming, both with regard to the
number of good novels published and with regard to the breadth and
depth of the authors' view. The outstanding novel of the year is Carlos Fuentes' *La región más transparente* (*Where the Air Is Clear*),[19]
the first novel of one of Mexico's best writers, and probably the most
widely discussed book written in Mexico. The reaction to it reflects
both its merits and faults, but no one opinion of the novel has given

[19] The reference, well known in Mexican literature, is to Mexico City.

adequate importance to both the good and the bad. Interestingly enough, the best review of *La región más transparente* was written by Anthony West[20] after the translation appeared in the United States. It is a tribute to the author that Anthony West, who so far as I know has no particular knowledge of Fuentes' material, comprehends so well what this vigorous author is saying.

Putting aside the temptation to argue with opinions already expressed, I shall give one view of the novel. It is the story of life in Mexico City, all social classes, all kinds of people. Fuentes has a wonderful ability to re-create the feeling of a city—he has done it in other places—and this feeling is one of the basic values of the novel. The reader feels adequately placed. The central character in the narrative is Fernando Robles, an old Revolutionary, now a financial tycoon whose affairs have become so complicated that even making money has no point to it except to make more money. Robles cannot extricate himself from this meaningless web of obligations except by throwing over the whole business and returning to the most primitive way of life open to him. Through this story move businessmen, poets, philosophers, actresses, servants, prostitutes, laborers, film directors, mistresses, opportunists, aristocrats, *nouveaux riches*, the whole gamut of society.

The story deals with the events leading to Robles' ruin. Anthony West describes the narrative technique as "a rapid, cinematic movement that cuts nervously from one character to another every time a new life intersects a strand in the cable of Robles' affairs. The focus of attention moves from within one character to give an exterior view of the point of intersection in a brilliantly written narrative passage, and then moves inside the mind of the new character." While Robles is the central figure of this action, he is not really the center of the author's attention. The character of Robles is seen through the effect he has on others, and Fuentes intends to direct the reader's attention to the others as well as to Robles.

The world in which Fernando Robles moves is a representation of the Revolution betrayed. It may be interpreted as a condemnation of capitalism in Mexico. But it seems to me to be even more susceptible

[20] *The New Yorker*, 4 March 1961, pp. 123–125.

to another interpretation: that power runs contrary to human concern. Far worse than Robles himself are the inadequates and opportunists who attach themselves to his power. Robles had at least been a man at one time. Some of his satellites have never known the adventure of being human. As pathetic as these revolting people are, they are hardly more so than the humble people who, on a different level, are equally lost in modern society. For both groups, the values held are not those required for authentic living. Objectively, we can observe that Fuentes describes people who do indeed live in Mexico. Their vulgar senselessness, their inhumanity are brilliantly apparent. But it is also true that people like these are present in any large urban situation. And if the Revolution is what gave them to Mexico, it means only that the Revolution made Mexico resemble a large part of the rest of the world. To have done anything else, the Revolution would have had to change men, not institutions.[21]

Moving in and out through the action of the novel is Fuentes' major mistake, a shadowy character named Ixca Cienfuegos. It is a good thing that Fuentes was bold enough to write a novel of such heroic proportions, otherwise Ixca Cienfuegos would have destroyed it. As well as I can determine, the enigmatic Ixca is intended to be the conjunction of cultures or the indigenous spirit, or something similar. The trouble is that he is neither man nor myth, and his presence refuses to make sense because he persists in being one when he would more reasonably be the other. Perhaps Fuentes meant him to be this way. I have wondered if Ixca's meddling in the affairs of the characters of the novel could be the author's way of showing the indigenist influence in Mexican culture. But it all could have worked out the same way without him. It appears that Fuentes would like to give Ixca an importance that is not justified in the novel.

A combination of memory and present circumstance is the basis of Fuentes' portrayal of Mexican reality. The proportions vary according to the specific situation. In spite of the youthful impetuosity apparent in some parts of this novel, it is carefully worked out. Readers of the English translation should be warned that the second-rate,

[21] An observation to this effect was made by Mariano Azuela in connection with his disenchantment concerning the Revolution. *Cien años de novela mexicana*, p. 222.

neo-Naturalist prose of the English version belongs to the translator, not to Fuentes.

Perhaps the most general criticism of *La región más transparente* is that the author attempted to do too much. His second novel, *Las buenas conciencias* (1960), indicates that he gave consideration to the criticism, because it is a much less ambitious book. Fuentes studies the provincial background of one of the characters mentioned rather casually in the first novel. The setting is less hermetic than the town in *Al filo del agua*, but it has some of the same qualities. The author has to examine the customs, many of them religious or semi-religious, which control the pattern of life. This culture has been subjected to only a small amount of the antitraditional tendencies that constitute pressures in cosmopolitan Mexico City. Fuentes writes about it with less assurance than in the earlier novel, and I think *Las buenas consciencias* has to be regarded as a minor work.

In 1962 Fuentes published two other novels, one major and one minor. The lesser of the two, *Aura*, is a short novel in which the author allows himself to enjoy his taste for fantasy. A young man answers an advertisement for someone who knows French, and finds himself in a ghostly old house whose owner is an elegant lady of years long past. This withered belle also appears as a beautiful young woman with whom the protagonist falls in love. Fuentes doesn't tell his reader the secret of the dual woman; but he doesn't fool anybody because the whole atmosphere of the story informs the reader from the beginning that he has already heard or read it in several different versions. Fuentes tells the story well, narrating in the second person singular, a technique he probably learned from his French contemporary Michel Butor. The viewpoint is effective for a while, but I find myself taking the "you" personally rather than impersonally, and consequently rebelling.

Salvador Reyes Nevares recently observed that the atmosphere of *Aura*—the persistence of a worn out past: musty old houses, antique furniture, and elderly people that are semi-ghosts—is a recurrent preoccupation in the works of Fuentes. Reyes Nevares understands this atmosphere as a representation of the reactionary element in society—an element which is repulsive because it insists on surviving although it is really dead. The idea is interesting, and may well be valid. The social criticism that Reyes Nevares sees in *Aura* gives the novel a reasonable place in the trajectory of Fuentes' work.[22] There is certainly no doubt that Fuentes reproduces the same atmosphere many times. I have assumed—perhaps too innocently—that it is no more than a neo-Romantic obsession. Whatever the interpretation, Fuentes has already used it too much.

La muerte de Artemio Cruz is an altogether different proposition. In my opinion, it is Fuentes' best novel to date, though it has not been praised as highly as *La región más transparente*. Artemio Cruz is another Fernando Robles, but here the spotlight is on him rather than on the people about him. The reader is introduced to him when he is on his death bed, and through changing narrative viewpoints which use all three persons, is told what Cruz's thoughts are at the moment, what his external situation is, and what his life has been. The last is revealed through a pattern of flashbacks that recede in time until the heart of the matter is finally revealed. He spent his early years in a situation that frustrated almost every act that would have given meaning to life. The opportunism of his later life was originally self-preservation, and he has cast aside every possibility that might have made his death significant in terms of what had gone before. Now, at the point of death, isolated from those who should be related to him, he is in no way prepared to accept death which has no more meaning than life.

A great deal of Mexico is seen as Artemio Cruz moves through it. The scene is not as panoramic as in *La región más transparente*, but the novel gains through its tightness. Comparing the two novels is something like comparing a sonnet and a long lyric poem. The changing narrative viewpoint is extremely effective, providing a clarity that could not have been accomplished any other way. I doubt that there is anywhere in fiction a character whose wholeness is more apparent than in the case of Artemio Cruz.

The ideology of the novel is somewhat disturbing. It is much the same as in *La región más transparente*, but without the apparent insistence on the indigenist influence. I assume that the life and char-

---

[22] Salvador Reyes Nevares, "Una obra maestra," *La Cultura en México*, no. 127, supplement to *Siempre* (22 julio 1964), 19.

acter of Artemio Cruz are the author's representation of Mexican reality. It is not that Fuentes has created a gigantic symbol, for Cruz is every inch an authentic, flesh-and-blood character; but it does seem that the life of Cruz can be understood as one way of looking at the attitudes of the nation and why they are as they are. If my assumption is correct, Fuentes sees Mexico as having deceived herself by accepting values that will not allow her to realize her potential. Foremost among the false values of Cruz is the accumulation of wealth and power. And here again is the possible condemnation of capitalism that is also apparent in *La región más transparente*. It is not surprising that Fuentes should express such a position in his novels, since his leftist position is amply apparent in his political essays. However, his novels do not make clear whether the accumulation of wealth and power is an economic disadvantage or a cultural error. Much of his displeasure is directed against the influence and imitation of the United States. His belief is that Mexico should take account of herself and maintain her independence. Fuentes' novels indicate that many Mexicans of all social classes will have to develop more faith in their country's present and future if this independence is to become reality.

Fuentes' two great novels show the Revolution's inherent dynamism and also its loss or acquisition of various characteristics through the years that followed the military phase. Even if we disagree with his understanding of the Revolution, we can hardly doubt that the broad conception of these works is one of their greatest values. In 1958, the year when *La región más transparente* was published, Miguel N. Lira published *Mientras la muerte llega*, another retrospective view of the Revolution. Lira's is a good novel, but its relatively limited view is unsatisfactory when it is compared with Fuentes' panorama.

Carballido's *El norte* is an example of a strong tendency to examine the human dilemma without particular attention to the Mexican scene, though the writers who take this road certainly are not avoiding Mexico. It is simply a question of whether the Mexican problem or the human problem constitutes the basis of the author's search. One is as authentically Mexican and as authentically human as the other. The novels refer to a contemporary human condition that is often called "solitude" or "isolation." I should prefer to think of it as a problem of self-realization. It is difficult for the individual to untangle the complications of society so he can see what he really is, what his relationships with others ought to be, and what he can become. The path to this self-realization is blocked by numerous tyrannies that man imposes upon himself. His need to overcome them, for the sake of the individual and for the sake of the nation, was made apparent in *Al filo del agua,* and this same need has become increasingly a preoccupation of the novel.

The attempt to understand, to see more clearly, has led to different methods of isolating a segment of human experience so its nature may be accurately observed. In *El norte,* Carballido used only three characters. In *1956* (this is the title of the novel published in 1958), Carmen Rosenzweig examines the year of the slow death of the narrator's father. In *El solitario Atlántico,* Jorge López Páez goes back to childhood, as Rosario Castellanos had done in *Balúm Canán,* to establish a beachhead on reality. Josefina Vicens makes *El libro vacío* a study of the reactions of a man whose potential is never realized. Her novel, though focused on one individual, is an eloquent example of how man is subjected by his self-made tyrannies. Her protagonist is bored by the repetition of one day following another. Living in a state we call security, he knows what each day will bring, he knows every detail of his life. Vicens' use of excruciatingly small and meaningless detail overwhelms the reader with the uselessness of living. And yet, the protagonist cannot break down the walls that enclose him, in spite of the fact that he knows that by nature he has the capacity for the heroic act. He cannot realize himself, he cannot change death into life.

Sergio Galindo, in *Polvos de arroz* and in two subsequent novels, uses family relationships as the basis of his study. He is one of the best of current Mexican novelists because of his keen understanding of human reaction, his fluent narration, and his ability to build characters through careful choice of detail that resembles the choice of the exact word in poetry. Galindo is an unobtrusive novelist. He uses none of the spectacular tricks that advise the reader to expect a novel of great significance. His novels expect the participation of the reader, but he does not use unexplained symbol or elliptical development to inform the reader that his participation is expected. The reader could happily finish a Galindo novel without exerting himself at all, but the opportunity for active participation is present if the reader chooses to recognize it.

Polvos de arroz (Rice Powder), a short novel, is the author's first venture into longer fiction. It is a tragedy, as are all his novels. A woman reaches middle age in her family home, having devoted her life to what has appeared to be her duty. She starts a lonely-hearts correspondence with a young man in the city. Her vicarious self-realization becomes an obsession; and when her niece's family provides the opportunity for her to visit the city, she accepts with the hope of changing dreams to reality. Like the protagonist of Vicens' *El libro vacío*, circumstances build a fence between her and the person she might be. The circumstances are not quite the same, but the result is.

The only fault one could find with *Polvos de arroz* is that it might have been developed more slowly and more fully. Galindo's second novel, *Justicia de enero*[23] (1959), shows greater maturity in organization and development. The thread of action is the search by officers of the Immigration Service for a poor devil who is supposed to be deported. However, Galindo changes the focus of the story from one investigator to another, showing the relationship between each one's personal life and his job. "Justice exists only in the minds of people who have had nothing to do with it," says one of the characters.[24] This startlingly cynical comment seems less and less strange as the author shows how trivial things in the lives of the officers may affect the destiny of a man they seek. And the reverse is also true: the exigencies of the job have their influence on the private lives of the officers. What is really startling is not the cynical view of justice, but the awful responsibility that rests upon each person with regard to every action. Galindo is so skillful in his portrayal of human interactions that almost every act seems to be performed as some sort of compensation for a preceding one.

In *Justicia de enero*, Galindo shows a middle-class world in which

[23] The title (*January Justice*) is a saying that refers to inconsistency on the part of those who judge. January is regarded as the month when the weather is most likely to change abruptly.

[24] *Justicia de enero* (Mexico City: Fondo de Cultura Económica, 1959), p. 89.

people barely manage to live decently, where there are dreams but not much hope. The officers try to squeeze some degree of satisfaction from their work, and it often takes the form of injustice toward another person. In *Polvos de arroz*, Galindo used a rural setting and a more secure economic situation. His third novel, *El bordo* (1960), is also rural. In both of these rural novels, the study of relationships is less intricate than in *Justicia de enero* because financial security eliminates some of the complicating questions of individual integrity that are present in his urban novel.

In *El bordo*, which is his best novel, Galindo manages a remarkably full and interesting development of the relationships within a single family, while maintaining admirable unity of action, time, and locale. By restricting himself to such a tight situation, he makes the problem of human relationships stand out with compelling boldness. Since so many rural novels deal with the economic problem, it should be repeated that *El bordo* has nothing at all to do with the landless peasant. The ownership and working of the land are important factors in the characterizations, but they are elements of security rather than the reverse. The novel focuses on Joaquina, the aunt and dominant personality in the family. The wall between her and self-realization is a secondary one that grew after she had had a chance for fulfillment and had lost it. The tyranny under which she suffers is her attempt to compensate for what she has seen clearly and has missed. Tragedy is inevitable from the beginning, though its form is not immediately apparent. Galindo gradually intensifies the sense of impending tragedy and suggests its probable form without giving away the moment or the fact until the situation is perfectly ripe. Meanwhile, he has drawn his reader into the family circle, mainly by a nearly miraculous choice of detail, to such a degree that concern for the several characters is inevitable.

In addition to the publication of *Justicia de enero*, the year 1959 saw two other events of particular significance in the novel: one was the publication of another good *indigenista* novel of the ethnological kind, the second and more important event was the literary return of Agustín Yáñez. Carlo Antonio Castro's *Los hombres verdaderos* is an ethnological study similar to *Juan Pérez Jolote*. *Juan Pérez Jolote* has enjoyed greater popularity, probably because of its small-boy charm, but *Los hombres verdaderos* makes an even clearer presentation of the confrontation of two cultures. The title indicates the Indians' assumption that they are the real people and that outsiders are not authentic; and the book shows the impermeability of the culture. As in *Juan Pérez Jolote*, the author bases his story on representation rather than on imagination.

La creación, Yáñez's first novel after *Al filo del agua*, is the story of Gabriel in the realm of artistic creativity after the Revolution. The novel is generally regarded as a failure; but I think it deserves more than summary dismissal, if for no other reason than that Yáñez always writes with a serious and well-founded purpose. And it is also true that a book of equal value might well be praised if it were written by a lesser novelist. Trying to discover why this novel went awry, I find one major failure, which is in the author's description of the creative process. Gabriel is a musician and a composer. Yáñez, who has interesting ideas about the process of artistic creation, has to describe the process of musical composition without the benefit of music. He cannot do it. Although his excellent control of the language takes him as close as anyone could get, both author and reader stay outside the artist and talk about the process rather than experience it. I think Yáñez might have avoided this failure if his protagonist had been a poet.

Gabriel's artistic career is tied to his relationship with Victoria and María, both from *Al filo del agua*. The relationship with Victoria is more imagined than real. She represents for Gabriel a combination of mother-figure, love-object, redemption, and inspiration. Because of his dependence on this imagined relationship, Gabriel cannot easily see worldly reality. María, on the other hand, is the representation of worldly reality which Gabriel cannot accept. She is now in a position of power and able to help the young composer, but he is reluctant to compromise his independence. Because of the author's inability to capture the authentic quality of the creative act, the specific problem of Gabriel is less interesting than the background against which his story is told.

I have said elsewhere that after the Revolution Mexico had many of the characteristics of a new nation. There was a tremendous impulse to re-create everything: the government, the society, and, of course, the arts. These were the years of Diego Rivera, Carlos Chávez, Alfonso Reyes. They were also the years of influence of Ramón López Velarde's special kind of Mexicanism, the youthful years of the men who were to become the *Contemporáneos* group, and the time of the "discovery" of *Los de abajo*. It is possible that Yáñez's insight into these years is one reason *La creación* has been so generally disliked, because the arguments that arose then are still not forgotten or resolved, and opinions are many and strong. Mexico was faced with the necessity of understanding itself. And the contradiction of simultaneous introversion and extroversion made understanding difficult. If Yáñez had been successful in capturing the essence of the creative process, the possibilities of seeing beyond visible reality in this novel would have been stupendous. The creative act would have had meaningful reference not just to Gabriel, but to every individual and to the nation anthropomorphized. But even if the novel is not successful to that extent, it is still a fascinating picture of artistic activity in a nation that is remaking itself.

Although the subject matter of Yáñez's novels varies a great deal, they all concern the discovery of reality that is below the surface, and we must put them all together to have the picture as it should be preserved. *Ojerosa y pintada* (1960) is another case of a novel generally regarded as poor but which deserves a second look. The title is taken from López Velarde's *Suave patria*, where the words refer to Mexico City and imply the worldliness of the city as contrasted with the starched purity of the province. Yáñez intends to capture the rhythm of the city's life, and the novel fails probably because it is too ambitious. The action covers a period of twenty-four hours, and is tied together for narrative purposes by a taxi driver who works those hours consecutively. The story begins with a birth and ends with a death, and it has a kind of interlude when a homespun philosopher talks with the taxi driver about the life around them. Between birth and death, we see a variety of individuals, social conditions, ambitions, and attitudes. Presumably all these factors should combine into one impression, but they don't. Still the novel is written with love, and anyone who has ever looked out over a great city and felt the miracle of its existence will find that feeling recalled in *Ojerosa y pintada*.[25]

Almost simultaneously with *Ojerosa y pintada*, Yáñez published *La tierra pródiga*, whose reception has been most favorable. With regard to Yáñez's success or failure in fiction, it seems to me that the result is a question of luck. He is a courageous novelist, both in technique and in conception of the work. He probes deeply, because his purpose is one of discovery, for his reader and for himself. At his best, the discovery is brilliantly communicated. *La tierra pródiga* is a novel of the land, the same land that was discovered by the Spaniards. The story is a kind of twentieth-century re-enactment of the Conquest. The land is a woman, fertile and redemptive. It is there to be dominated, subjugated, exploited, seduced, or raped. The active role is masculine, and the treatment of the land depends upon the interpretation of the masculine role.

Yáñez uses a combination of exterior and interior narration. With one he shows the surface relationships that exist among the several men who would exert different forms of domination upon the land. The shift to the interior reveals the real driving force behind each one. The significance of the novel is greatly enhanced by the quasi-allegorical techniques that Yáñez uses so well. Machines come and the land will be developed, but this kind of victory will call for some self-evaluation on the part of each man who has felt a relationship with the conquered.

Las tierras flacas (1962) is a kind of counterpoint to *La tierra pródiga*. There is no really adequate translation for *"tierras flacas."* The word *"flacas"* means that the land is reluctantly productive. The feeling of the novel as a whole is similarly contrastive. *Las tierras flacas* is drier, sharper, stingier, than *La tierra pródiga*. Men are related to the land, but it is a dogged relationship. The region is dominated by a *cacique*, Don Epifanio, who considers himself a modern patriarch and begets children throughout the region. In his patriarchal fashion, he cares for them and has favorites among them. The one woman whom he wants and cannot obtain dies but leaves an extraor-

---

[25] The most favorable and most carefully analytical study of this novel is one made by Emmanuel Carballo in *Nivel*, 25 enero 1963, p. 3.

dinary legacy—a sewing machine which becomes a kind of me-
chanical saint. For Epifanio, it symbolizes the woman he wanted;
for the rest of the people it represents a kind of freedom from Don
Epifanio's imposition of himself.

This too is a novel of the land and of the coming of progress. The
relationship of the people to the area is expressed through hundreds
of proverbs which Yáñez uses as a means of interiorization. There is
some question about the effectiveness of this technique. Certainly the
proverbs give keen insight into the ethos of the area, and Yáñez uses
them very cleverly to indicate what is inside a character and how he
is fundamentally related to the region. But proverbs have the quality
of quaintness, and strings of them used for purposes of characterization tend to lose their initial effect and to end up seeming precious.
If the reader does not react in this adverse fashion, the proverbs assist
in moving from one generation to another, which sometimes happens
in the timeless realm of the interior.

Much of the subliminal reality of *Las tierras flacas* is suggested by
Biblical names and the events attached to the people and places who
bear them. The religious aspect of the regional culture is similar to
the dogged relationship with the land. The strange role of the sewing
machine is not intended to indicate the religion of the people, but to
comment on their means of assuring their identity. Folk practices
have joined with Christianity, but Yáñez is not portraying a primi-
tively superstitious people. Miguel Arcángel, one of the many sons
of Don Epifanio, rebels against his father and brings progress to the
region. The reaction to him is confused, as it reasonably would be
in a place where the recent Revolution was something the people had
heard of but really didn't comprehend.

The novels published in 1960 show a marked interest in discovery
of the inner and deeper reality: *Ojerosa y pintada, La tierra pródiga,*
Fuentes' *Las buenas conciencias,* Galindo's *El bordo.* Some others of
importance, like Almanza's *Pesca brava* and Rubín's *Cuando el Táguaro agoniza,* probe less deeply, and their significance is correspondingly limited. The tale of the Revolution appeared again, Spota published another of his many novels (*El tiempo de la ira*), and several
novels were published by writers who probably will never become a
real part of the literary world. It is hard to say whether these writers

have only one or two books to write or whether they are discouraged by the difficulties facing a beginning writer.

It is entirely possible that one of the most highly publicized books of the next year, Ema Godoy's *Erase un hombre pentafácico*, may be another case of an isolated work. Godoy has written poetry, and a volume of philosophical dialogues that are a preliminary exercise to *Erase un hombre pentafácico*. This novel-essay, undoubtedly the product of an intellectual pilgrimage, has attracted more attention in the United States, where it won the William Faulkner prize, than it has received in Mexico. The book suffers from a certain negativism on the part of the author. She calls it "soliloquies or perhaps a novel." Then in a preliminary note she supposes that the book will not please anyone, saying why it will displease various groups. Her reasons are amusing and perceptive, but the fact remains that her attitude is negative.

The book deals with one man: his Existence and five aspects of his Essence. Existence is identified with Free Will; the five aspects of Essence are Religion, Reason, Worldliness, Sentiment, and Sex. The protagonist cannot make a decision because the five aspects of Essence struggle with each other in an effort to dominate him. In general, the allegory is interesting, but the book is not one to be read at a single sitting. The most disturbing thing about it is that its conclusion could be reached by a simple act of faith which would make the intellectual exercise unnecessary. Perhaps it is the fate of an intellectually oriented person to live with the tyranny of his commitment. I suspect that *Erase un hombre pentafácico* represents a problem worked out by the author for her own enlightenment. She is right in thinking that her book is not quite a novel in the generally accepted sense, and the reader has no way of guessing whether this book is a terminal intellectual journey, or a first step.

First novels were published in 1961 by two writers who were already known in literary circles for their shorter works: Vicente Leñero and Ana Mairena. Leñero's *La voz adolorida* is the monologue of a man who is mentally ill. The reader learns his background and his present circumstances, following his "reason" through his disoriented periods as well as through his lucid ones. Then, with a "double-take" reaction, the reader realizes that he has been accepting irrationality as completely rational. Those who were aware of Leñero's deep sensitivity were not surprised that a new novel, *Los albañiles* (still unpublished at this writing) won the international "Biblioteca Breve" prize late in 1963.

Ana Mairena is something of a mystery. No one seems to know who she is or exactly what she has written. Works known to be hers include some poetry. So far as I know, *Los extraordinarios* is her only novel.

Mexico City receives a constant stream of uprooted provincials who, driven by the hope of a better material life, add to their other troubles the problem of adjusting to a life totally different from the one they have known. Some make a successful adjustment, others sink immediately into anonymity, still others have anonymity forced upon them in spite of their efforts. The protagonist of *Los extraordinarios* belongs to the third group. Even a murder, which we know from the beginning he will commit, will not identify him, and he disappears into the city.

Mairena uses an effective time device for her narration. All the action takes place as the murderer is waiting for his victim. The flashbacks are related to actual time in such a way that time's passage, while he is waiting, indicates the importance of each episode in the life of the protagonist. The boy's Indian background and provincial upbringing are what he can comprehend. But they make no sense in terms of the world in which he is lost. His repeated attempts to find himself add up to nothing. The depth of his dilemma adds a new dimension to our understanding of life in the rapidly growing city. Some earlier novels, particularly Azuela's *Nueva burguesía* (1941), recognized the external manifestations of this lack of direction. From the external viewpoint, the transplanted provincial is pathetic and ridiculous at the same time. Given the dimension added by Mairena, his problem demands a more radical solution than Azuela's suggestion that traditional provincial values be recovered.

The year 1962 was unusually rich, both in quality and in quantity. Its long list of novels is dominated by Fuentes' *Aura* and *La muerte de Artemio Cruz*, Yáñez's *Las tierras flacas*, Castellanos' *Oficio de tinieblas*, and Almanza's *Detrás del espejo*. A general view of the lesser novels shows that social protest from the external point of view still persists, but that the more searching novels are exercising a healthy influence in enlarging the novelists' understanding of their world.

After years of silence, Arreola published a longer work in 1963. I have just read *La feria,* and the only thing of which I am certain is that the book raises many questions that probably only time will answer. It is not a collection of short stories. If it is a novel, we must change our understanding of what a novel is. Still it is unquestionably a form of fiction. Arreola has put together many pieces of prose of varying length, from a single line to several pages. These pieces are memories, regional legends, history, impressions, narrative accounts, individual reactions of some of the characters. They all concern a town in Jalisco. There is no single story line, no traditional character development. But the town and its people do come alive, and the reader finds himself incorporated within the life of the town.

The author's well known virtuosity is amply apparent throughout *La feria,* and the reader's early reaction may well be that Arreola would do well to forsake his virtuoso role and work harder at being a novelist. The unity of the book is not apparent at first. Indeed, its unity is never really *apparent,* but enters the reader's awareness unexpectedly. I think Arreola has put into words his subconscious knowledge of the town. This procedure would explain the patchwork quality of the book. And this approach would, of course, involve its own internal unity which would have nothing to do with unity as we usually think of it. It would also explain the difference in the lengths of the passages, and the fact that there is no attempt to make chapters.

La feria is a kind of interiorization; but it is not the interior of the town that Arreola shows, it is the interior of Arreola. And here we find that *La feria* is quite similar to the short stories, though I think the author never opened his subconscious as completely in any of the stories as he has done in *La feria.* Many people will be happy that he has chosen a visibly Mexican basis for this book, but it seems to me that what he has done is valuable to Mexican culture not because of the locale he has chosen, but because what the reader sees is what Arreola sees, with those penetrating eyes that are at once very personal, very Mexican, and very universal.

Two other short story writers enlarged their form in 1963: Tomás

Mojarro in *Bramadero* and Carlos Valdés in *Los antepasados*. The latter has been treated rather kindly, probably because of the author's reputation in short fiction. It shows the characteristics of several generations of Mexicans, an approach which might say a good deal about the national character. But the book never comes alive because Valdés chose the awkward device of telling the story to an artist friend, and because he apparently grew tired of telling it long before he reached the end. *Bramadero* is more successful. It tells the story of a small town whose closed existence is changed completely by the building of a highway. This is an intelligent study of a circumstance that is fairly common in Mexico. Mojarro sometimes obscures his story line for no apparent reason, and his characterizations are trite; but he does make the desirable relationship between visible Mexican reality and universal human values.

Luisa Josefina Hernández, in *Los palacios desiertos*, studies a love relationship between two poorly adjusted persons. She deals with them carefully and in almost complete isolation, just as Carballido did in *El Norte*. Hernández, whose ability as a dramatist is generally recognized, has trouble with the novel form. *Los palacios desiertos* is her third and most successful novel, still it has serious shortcomings because it does not accomplish what the author apparently intended. She tells the story from different viewpoints, a procedure which ought to inform the reader more fully than a case history would. But it doesn't work out that way. We are aware of the author's sensitivity because her detailed study shows it. However, we do not see beyond the surface of her analysis; and the narrative technique that we expect to take us beyond, fails and simply looks awkward.

Perhaps the best novel of 1963 is Elena Garro's *Los recuerdos del porvenir* (*Memories of Days to Come*). The author has for some time enjoyed a good reputation as a minor playwright, and frequent references have been made to her unpublished works. If these references made sceptics wonder, all doubts have been removed by the publication of this novel, which is mature, profound, sensitive, and written with professional assurance that is apparent from beginning to end. *Los recuerdos del porvenir* is a novel of reality and unreality, of life and death. What the reader understands of these circumstances comes from the extended, magical communication that Garro achieves.

The town of Ixtepec looks at itself. The only really disturbing aspect of the novel is the semi-personification of the town which causes the town to speak in the first person. The town is an entity, but its speaking always strikes me as false. In any case, the town, "seated upon this apparent stone," changeless, static, looks upon itself and knows that its only life is in its memory. The story concerns life in the town during the period of terror brought on by the *cristero* revolts. If this book were nothing else, it would be the best novel written about that period. The general who occupies the town, caught between an unrequited love and a love which he does not share, is destroyed. But the overt conflict is between the general and the town, cloaked in its conservatism, in its hermetic provinciality. The attitudes of its people are remarkable. Their anti-Indian racial prejudice is frank and depressing. Class lines are clearly drawn. Ineffectiveness in the face of exploitation amounts to a custom. Their reaction to the occupation of the town is less a question of ideology than one of hating the outsider. An issue becomes important only when the church is closed. Then the battle is joined because of the interests of those to whom the church is most important and the inclination of a few who rebel against the stagnant town. But even this revolt serves only to destroy individuals, and the town sees only the mirror.

The "apparent stone" is explained at the end of the novel when we discover that it is magically a *"recuerdo del porvenir."* The question raised by this novel is, as I read it, not what will happen in a Mexican town, but whether the human condition will ever be identifiable as life rather than death. If life is the reality of self-realization, then nothing in Ixtepec is real, nor is there anything that promises reality in the future. Life is more death than life and keeps repeating itself into eternity.

I should not wish to guess the extent to which novelists are prophets. But I have no doubt that recent novelists have assumed the role of *vate*, the seer, that is traditionally assigned to poets. This role does not require them to predict events of the future by date and exact nature. It does mean that they open the road to the awareness of what is real, not what we think is real. The assumption of this role has a particular relevance in a country which, by the nature of its growth, seeks its national reality, which must be of a new sort because of the time in which we live.

Mexico is not an entirely new nation, because its history endows it with institutional problems that are familiar to all nations. There are many difficulties between these problems and their solution, difficulties that are universally understandable even if they are not universally present. Novels will describe these difficulties as long as there is a novelist who believes description will lessen the problem. But such novels must necessarily be fewer, if some see below the surface.

The change of direction in Mexico gives it characteristics of a new nation, and the discovery of the national reality will necessarily reveal its relationship with universals, because the meaning of *nation* is changing. In the process of discovering its reality, Mexico may realize itself and so be the architect of its history. A movement into the reality of life would reveal the death of the past, and only that reality would place Mexico specifically in and of the present moment. Meanwhile, the movement is related to the past, and we must examine what preceded the moment where we stand.

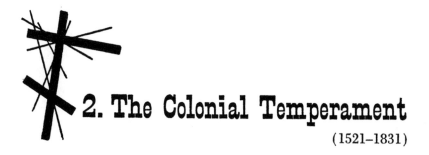

2. The Colonial Temperament

(1521–1831)

It has become almost a matter of form, when anyone discusses the novel in Mexico, to offer some theories about the absence of the novel during the Colonial Period. Although there are a few novels, or seminovels, there is nothing remotely resembling a novel tradition before the nineteenth century, after Independence. On the face of it, this fact does seem strange, since the colonial years correspond to the time of Spain's greatest creative activity. And it is even stranger when we recall that Spain's influence was extremely productive in poetry. What was true of Mexico, was also true of the other Spanish colonies, and so far as I know, of colonial cultures in general. So I suspect the reasons are to be found in the nature of the society. On the basis of this assumption, we might find some specific reasons like the availability of printing presses or official prohibition of novels.[1] But such specific reasons seem to me to be parts of a larger social attitude. And if we assume that the novel is one way a people expresses itself, its absence is an important consideration.

The fact of the Conquest is startling; the nature of it, which would be novel rather than history, would probably be overwhelming. This

[1] There actually was a prohibition of the importation of novels. Irving A. Leonard has dealt with the subject in great detail—see his *Books of the Brave* (Cambridge, Massachusetts: Harvard University Press, 1949). He shows that novels did, in fact, reach America. It seems to me that the important consideration is not how effective the prohibition was, but that it did exist, and for moral reasons.

major event has never been dealt with adequately in the novel of any language, and less so in Spanish than in some others. Considering the fact that this conquest, this confrontation of two worlds, is at the root of Mexican reality, I do not wonder that Mexicans approach the subject with reserve.

Hernán Cortés, acting without authorization, landed at Veracruz, destroyed his ships, and with his handful of men, headed into the heart of a great empire. By his side was Doña Marina, Malinche, interpreter, mistress, and guide, forever the nationalists' symbol of the Mexican who sells out to foreign influence. What thoughts he must have had when he crossed the mountains and looked out over the valley of Anáhuac! What astonishment when he became aware of Tenochtitlán, the Aztec capital, a great city full of the movement of life! And not far away were the ruins of another great civilization so old it was already a mystery to the Aztecs. All this he could give to his king, with a portion reserved for himself, of course. This civilization, this land, could be a gift because none of it was real, it was "other."

The pristine prejudice of Cortés could not admit the reality of a world different from his own. His Spain was all: defender of the faith, bulwark of culture, epitome of progress, discoverer, explorer, mistress of the world. Why should he disabuse Moctezuma, who thought he was divinely sent? Cortés agreed with him, or at least a part of him did. The shock had to come with Moctezuma's disbelief and the ensuing struggle which showed that the "other" had a soul. So the gift to be given had to be won, and it was. The Conquest was to clear the path for Spain to impose herself. But beneath this fact moved the soul of "other"—still not quite real because it was different. Surely, Moctezuma was not alone in wondering.

It was not a time for novels, for no novel could have competed with the accounts that took their place. There are many accounts of this time, and perhaps others that we do not even know about, but the main ones are Cortés' own *Cartas de relación* (*Letters of Report*) and the account of one of his soldiers, Bernal Díaz del Castillo's *Verdadera historia de la conquista de la Nueva España* (*True History of the Conquest of New Spain*). The *Cartas de relación*, since they amount to Cortés' official report and justification of his action, were soon published. Bernal Díaz's history had a different fate. Late in his life, the old soldier wrote his account to tell the story from his point of view, and especially to correct accounts that seemed to him to give Cortés more than his share of credit. First the manuscript was lost. Then later, its publisher took the liberty of changing it so it would be in accord with what the author had wished to correct. Bernal Díaz's view was hidden for many years. His history and Cortés' *Cartas* complement each other in several ways. Although the human quality of Cortés sometimes cuts through the formality of his report, it is Bernal Díaz who really makes the Conquest belong to living men. His style is more narrative, and there are lapses in the thread of narration which the author goes back to cover. They give the story an oral quality. Díaz is less anxious to justify himself than is Cortés. He is also more inclined to be aware of the soul in this astonishing "other," though he never indicates that he thinks it deserves any particular respect from him. Together, the two accounts paint a brilliant and startling picture of what happened.

Gazing on such wonderful sights, we did not know what to say, or whether what appeared before us was real, for on one side, on the land, there were great cities, and in the lake ever so many more, and the lake itself was crowded with canoes, and in the Causeway were many bridges at intervals, and in front of us stood the great city of Mexico, and we— we did not even number four hundred soldiers! . . . Let the curious readers consider whether there is not much to ponder over in this that I am writing . . . But let us get on, and march along the Causeway . . . When Cortés saw that the Great Montezuma was approaching, and he saw him coming, he dismounted from his horse, and when he was near Montezuma, they simultaneously paid great reverence to one another . . . And it seems to me that Cortés, through Doña Marina, offered him his right hand, and Montezuma did not wish to take it, but he did give his hand to Cortés and then Cortés brought out a necklace which he had ready at hand . . . and he placed it round the neck of the Great Montezuma and when he had so placed it he was going to embrace him, and those great princes who accompanied Montezuma held back Cortés by the arm so that he should not embrace him, for they considered it an indignity.[2]

---

[2] Bernal Díaz del Castillo, *The Discovery and Conquest of Mexico*, trans. A. P. Maudslay (New York: Farrar, Straus and Cudahy, Inc., 1956), pp. 192, 193.

There is a kind of beauty in the simplicity of the Spaniards' prejudice, which was not cluttered by the need of choosing between two
circumstances. When Moctezuma took Cortés to see his gods, the
Spaniard's immediate suggestion was that Moctezuma take them
down and put up a statue of the Holy Virgin. Cortés even offered a
lecture on Christian doctrine, and took pride in informing his king of
his missionary work. Moctezuma was not greatly impressed, and suggested that each of them retain his own gods. But Moctezuma's gods
were no more real for Cortés than was the rest of the civilization; and
later he did take it upon himself to destroy the images. I suspect that
still later, the missionaries, in spite of their concern for the Indians as
living beings, were equally unaware of the reality of these gods. When
Christianity was superimposed upon native religion, the latter's persistence was probably only superficially disturbing, because it wasn't
real anyway.

Bernal Díaz and Cortés wrote unwittingly of their own blindness.
Their accounts not only reveal that the strange civilization was unreal
for them; they also reveal its reality, but without being aware of what
they are doing. Unreal or not, the new world was spectacular, and
they wanted to describe it to the folks back home. Cortés, of course,
was eager to make it as grand as possible. As he does so, the life and
spirit of the people come through in places, and these incidents, when
the account goes beyond the chronicler, give the works their novelistic value.

Some four hundred years later, Alfonso Reyes came closer than
anyone else has ever come to capturing the moment of the Conquest
when he wrote *Visión de Anáhuac*. This essay begins in the realm of
imagination, and imagination elevates us to the moment of excite-
ment, of suspense, when the Spaniards are cast by their own daring
upon a vibrant world, colorful, active, complicated, as victimized by
its own tyrannies as the Spaniards were by theirs. Reyes takes us into
the activity of this world and we see its brilliance as the Spaniards saw
it. Then he takes us into its soul and writes of its poetry, and especially
of the role of flowers. In his final lines, Reyes declares the need of
preserving this beauty, whatever the relationship of the two worlds
may be.

Whatever the historical faith to which one subscribes (and I am not one of those who dream of an absurd perpetuation of the native tradition, nor do I even put too much faith in the survival of the Spanish), we are linked to the race of yesterday, without entering into the question of blood, by a common effort to master our wild, hostile natural setting, an effort that lies at the very root of history. We are also linked by the far deeper community of the daily emotions aroused by the same natural objects. The impact of the same world on the sensibility engenders a common soul. But even if one refused to accept as valid either the one or the other, either the fruits of a common effort or the results of a common outlook, it must be allowed that the historic emotion forms a part of our modern life, and that without its glow our valleys and our mountains would be like an unlighted theatre. The poet sees, as the moonlight shimmers on the snow of the volcanoes, the shade of Doña Marina outlined against the sky, pursued by the shadow of the Archer of Stars; or dreams of the copper ax on whose sharp edge the heavens rest; or thinks to hear, in the lonely desert, the tragic weeping of the twins the white-robed goddess bears upon her back. We must not ignore the evocation or turn our backs upon the legend. Even if this tradition were not ours, it is, at any rate, in our hands, and we are its sole repository. We must never renounce, O Keats, a thing of beauty, the creator of eternal joys.[3]

The missionaries, who formed the second wave of conquerors, left their own accounts of what they did and what they could learn of the history of the Indian civilizations. These documents are priceless for historical reasons, and they show the.friars' humble concern for the Indians. But not one of these accounts goes beyond the intent of the author. And it is amply evident that, whatever the intentions of the missionaries, the Indians constituted a second estate. And this position was soon even further separated from the Spaniards' by the interposition of the *criollos*, people of Spanish descent who were born in America.

Criollista anxiety is apparent in Mexico from the earliest possible time. It is found in satirical poetry, in trenchant praise of Mexico, and in eagerness to be worthy of the Spanish heritage. The colonials' principal literary expression was poetry, which followed exactly the same

[3] Alfonso Reyes, "Vision of Anahuac," in *Position of America and Other Essays*, trans. Harriet de Onís, (New York: Alfred A. Knopf, Inc., 1950).

tendencies that were apparent in Spanish poetry of the time. The Italian-style poetry of the Renaissance flourished in the sixteenth century and then gave way to the baroque. The amount of poetry written gives ample proof that there was plenty of time for literary pursuits. The fact that the outlet was poetry rather than novel is perhaps an indication of *criollista* desire to be worthy. Poetry was an art; the novel was not. At that time, the novel was a semilegitimate form of expression at best. It was considered frivolous and sometimes immoral. From the point of view of the Spaniard, *criollista* society was simply another manifestation of "other," and was not a real, considerable fact. The *criollos*, therefore, were moved to show their excellence.

The first *criollo* to write a work of fiction was Bernardo de Balbuena. One of his poems, *La grandeza mexicana*, has an important place in Mexican literature because of its praise of all things Mexican. The casual reader might be impressed only by the laudatory adjectives, but Balbuena really does a better job than that, because his choice of words and ideas captures qualities that are distinctively not Spanish. His novel, *El siglo de oro en las selvas de Erífile* (1607) is a far more conventional piece. Indeed, it is so conventional its description need not say more than that it is a pastoral novel. It is nature cloaked in drawing-room artificiality. The plot is weak and, therefore, typical of the genre. The work as a whole is designed to satisfy the preciousness of the time. It is pointless to criticize this novel, as some have done, for being what it was intended to be. Considered within the framework of characteristics of the pastoral novel, it turns out to be the only real novel written in Mexico during the Colonial Period.[4]

A few years later, in 1620, Francisco Bramón published a pastoral novel, *Los sirgueros de la Virgen*, for a didactic purpose. He used the form that he knew to be in vogue as a means of explaining the doctrine of the Immaculate Conception. The combination of didacticism and heavy-handed narration makes reference to this book as a novel, an act of charity. It obviously was not intended to instruct the Indians, as were so many religious works of that time, but to explain the doctrine to a more sophisticated audience. There is a certain ingenuous-

---

[4] José Rojas Garciadueñas first made this point in his "La novela en la Nueva Espana," *Anales del Instituto de Investigaciones Estéticas*, VIII, 31 (1962), pp. 57–78.

ness about the presentation that has a degree of charm. Read seriously, it is a huge bore; but read as a curiosity, a small amount of it is pleasant. The idea of classical shepherds and shepherdesses wandering over hill and dale discussing the Immaculate Conception is amusing. Where we expect to find talk of love, we find doctrine. And at the end of one dialogue, which appears to be more conventional, the shepherd informs the shepherdess that he wants it to be quite clear the love he speaks of is not for her, but for the Holy Virgin.

Bramón injects a small amount of action by having the characters arrange a fiesta in honor of the doctrine. Each character is charged with a particular aspect of the arrangements. One of them writes an *auto* which is presented during the fiesta. It is a lively little allegory quite different from the stodgy book. The protagonist is Sin, who is presented as a highwayman. He subdues several biblical characters, but is finally conquered by the Holy Virgin. The play calls for a *"danza indígena"* at the end, which indicates that the *auto* was meant for the instruction of the Indians, a purpose which must surely have been different from the purpose of the novel—unless we assume that the Spanish mind would insist on believing that what was acceptable to Spaniards must also be acceptable to everyone else.

The literary style of the seventeenth century changed to baroque. Much poetry was written, some bad and some very good. Apparently almost every literate person considered it his duty to write poetry, just as it was a duty to learn everything. One of the great savants of the time was Carlos de Sigüenza y Góngora, an almost exact contemporary of Sor Juana Inés de la Cruz, the finest poet of the Colonial Period. Don Carlos wrote poetry too, but we had best forget it. His sense of dedication was stronger than his inspiration and his best efforts were in other directions. He was historian, bibliophile, geographer, astronomer, and mathematician. His name belongs in a history of the novel because of a narrative work he published in 1690, *Los infortunios de Alonso Ramírez*.

Alonso Ramírez, probably a real person, came to Mexico from Puerto Rico to seek a better living. After suffering several misadventures in different jobs, and a marriage which ended in the early death of his wife, he decided to go to the Philippines. He was captured by English pirates, and eventually finished a trip around the world. At last the pirates freed him and several companions in a small ship which was wrecked on the coast of Yucatán, whence he made his way to Mexico City. The story is told in the picaresque manner, which was well known to the author because of its popularity in Spanish literature. The first-person account reels off the series of misadventures with a tone of self-pity that is authentic enough. There is, however, relatively little of the humor which we expect from the *picaro's* devilishness. What there is does not suffice to make Alonso come alive, and the reader's identification with him depends largely on sympathy aroused by his suffering.

On first acquaintance, it seems strange that such a learned gentleman as Don Carlos should spend his time writing a picaresque tale. Closer examination suggests that he was primarily interested in publishing information he had about geography and navigation, plus some additional information he learned from Alonso Ramírez. José Rojas Garciadueñas theorizes that Alonso Ramírez made his way to the court of the viceroy in Mexico City, and that the viceroy or some other authority sent for Don Carlos because they knew he would be interested in Ramírez' story and would set it down. The nature of the story lends itself to picaresque treatment, and the cruelty of the English pirates, appropriately exaggerated, offers dramatic possibilities. A novelist might indeed have made a real novel of it. Sigüenza y Góngora does not exert his imagination. Some chapters of the book are hardly narrative at all, and careful reading even suggests what the author knew and what was told him by Alonso.

It is by no means an exaggeration to say that the eighteenth century was not very productive literarily in Mexico, and there was nothing about the century that would increase the production of prose fiction. As time passed, there were definite signs of tendencies toward independence. Although Spanish administration of the colony improved in some ways, the influence of the mother country was not a vigorous one, and the Spanish still considered the colony a chattel. The lines between *criollo* and Spaniard were ever clearer, and resentment on the part of the *criollos* grew stronger. The Indian occupied a third estate if he occupied any estate at all. Except in rare circumstances, he was hardly considered a part of society. The French and English social thinkers became known along with the facts of the revolutions in France and Anglo-America. The ideas suggested by these intellectual activities were not translated into revolutionary action until 1810, but the shift from beauty to intellect was started earlier.

In 1792, Joaquín Bolaños published a didactic work, *La vida portentosa de la muerte*, which has nothing whatsoever to do with revolution or independence, but which is certainly the product of an intellectual era. In an allegorical fashion, the book deals with man's knowledge of death. We are told that Death is the offspring of the sin of Adam and the fault of Eve; we see several Biblical personages described as ambassadors of Death; there are descriptions of the relationship of Death to different kinds of people. There is an amusing chapter in which Death, an empress, is concerned about the population of the empire. Two of her ministers, Appetite and the Devil, promise to supply the desired inhabitants by inducing gluttony and malice in men. There is another chapter in which Death mourns the passing of a physician who had been one of her strongest allies.

A description of *La portentosa vida de la muerte* can be disturbingly deceptive, because it tends to point out the possibilities of the book rather than what it actually is. The table of contents promises many amusing incidents, and there are a few, but most are disappointing. One of the reasons is, as Agustín Yáñez has pointed out,[5] the startling inconsistency in the role of Death. An empress in one chapter, she is a picaresque character in another. At other times, she is little more than a name. If the reader is delighted at one point by a humorous presentation, he should not be deceived, because the going is likely to get dull very shortly. In spite of its faults, the book is indicative of its time, both in its doggedly intellectual base and in its occasional picaresque humor.

The War of Independence, which began with Father Hidalgo's revolt on September 16, 1810, and ended with Iturbide's triumphal entry into Mexico City on September 27, 1821, was one of the manifestations of the new consideration of man which is found in the intellectualism of the eighteenth century. The "literary society" that

---

[5] *La portentosa vida de la muerte*, prol. y sel. de Agustín Yáñez (Mexico City: Biblioteca del Estudiante Universitario, 1944).

Father Hidalgo and other liberals belonged to was an association in which discussion of Rousseau, Diderot, Voltaire, and Condorcet gradually became a plan of action. And this particular association is indicative of the general trend of the time. Man's mind was reaching out to discover his meaning and destiny; and even if the mind imposed its own tyranny in the process, the resulting restlessness demanded change. Reform was the objective which was reinforced by the right of self-determination.

The vision of Father Hidalgo was noble and comprehensive. The rights of men could be demanded, and they belonged to all men. It is probably fair to say that, for Hidalgo, the circumstance of political independence was secondary. And so it generally was, I believe, for the men who were reformers rather than opportunists. But the secondary possibility of independence was to become a prerequisite to reform. The War of Independence in Mexico was fought against a background of political confusion in Spain. Similar intellectual forces had been at work there, and the Spanish authority was alternately liberal and conservative. The result was to transfer the confusion to Mexico in such a way that both liberals and conservatives participated in the independence movement. It was a coalition of political interests that finally achieved independence, and the right of self-determination had lost most of its significance because the victors lacked the homogeneity that would have been furnished by a clearly dominant political ideal. The vision of Father Hidalgo had been obscured by the need to compromise; and the reformist impulse, which under Hidalgo and Morelos had incorporated all segments of Mexican society, now became a middle-class dispute, and the Indian was retired to his customary social position from which he could move only by exercising tremendous personal initiative.

The attitude of urgency which was expressed by the Hidalgo revolt brought with it a new kind of writing. The activity of rebellion was added to ideas, and the result was a great deal of political writing in the form of pamphlets and periodicals. Some of the periodicals had very short lives, ended by the whim of the editor or by the disappearance of freedom of the press when the Spanish authority changed. The best known of the pamphleteers was José Joaquín Fernández de Lizardi, the perfect human representation of the movement from ideas to action. He had faith in the new ideas and defended them bravely; he also had faith in the common people, understood them, and considered it his mission to communicate to the masses the ideas that he cherished. His great sensitivity to the popular enabled him to capture the speech of the ordinary people, and he used it, to the disgust of many, for the propagation of liberalism. Whenever he wrote in the popular vein, he was a successful writer; when he deserted it, he failed. Like Hidalgo, his vision incorporated the whole society.

The best known of the several periodicals that Lizardi published was *El Pensador Mexicano* (*The Mexican Thinker*) which lasted from 1812 to 1814. Its name was Lizardi's pseudonym, and appropriately so, because it is typical of the writer at his best. His ideas are firmly rooted in the academic security of the eighteenth century, but his manner of expression belongs to the people. Without regard for correctness, he captured the flavor of their speech with their own informalities and imagery. His range of subject matter is wide, and it varied according to what the particular time demanded or allowed. With the same aplomb, he wrote of the natural rights of man, or the nuisance of dogs wandering in the streets of the city. He was critical of the power of the Church, he found the education of the time totally inadequate, he deplored poor sanitation. His topics are sometimes humble, sometimes elevated, but they are always dealt with honorably and sharply.

Lizardi wrote in all genres, but it is only in the political essay and in the novel that he cultivated his popular touch. *El Periquillo Sarniento* (1816)[6] is generally considered to be the first novel published in the New World. Censorship made the 1816 edition incomplete—it is surprising what the censors didn't see—and the first complete edition was published in 1830–1831. In all there have been more than fifteen editions.

El Periquillo Sarniento is a picaresque novel, a development of the characteristics already apparent in *El Pensador Mexicano*. It is

---

[6] The title is a play on words which is typical of the author. "Periquillo" is a double diminutive of Pedro (Pedro, Perico, Periquillo) and also means parrot. The name refers to the boy's green and yellow clothing. "Sarniento" is a play on the family name, *Sarmiento*, and Lizardi's version means "itching" or "mangy."

also full of moralizing digressions that all but destroy it. But we have to remember that the author was first of all a reformer. The character of Periquillo is fairly typical of the Spanish *picaro* with the important difference that Periquillo mends his ways and hopes that his life will serve as an example of what not to do. Throughout his many adventures, he is properly opportunistic and cynical, regularly punished and just as regularly deserving of punishment. Some of the types with whom he comes in contact are standard, like the well-known but still amusing Dr. Purgante (Dr. Purgative) who is professionally inadequate and personally ridiculous. Other types are more characteristic of the time, and all of them together present a fascinating picture of Mexico City at the beginning of the last century.

Over and above the plethora of opinion and advice offered throughout the novel, Lizardi does have an overall judgment which is apparent to the reader. It is that society is hypocritical in that men are dishonest with themselves and with other men. This conviction is apparent without taking into account the author's moralization, and we are inclined to say that Lizardi would have done well to have left out his digressions. Indeed, it is possible to edit the novel so that the digressions are cut to a minimum and we are left with an excellent picaresque story. Given an edition of this kind, the reader's reaction will depend on his acceptance of picaresque humor. If we cringe at the cruelty of every trick of the *picaro*, we will surely be miserable. If, on the other hand, we suspend our reluctance to view cruelty and enter into the cynicism of the *picaro*, the story is uproariously funny. But to read only the story of the *picaro* is not to read Lizardi, because his teaching, his desire to improve the world, his wish to make men reasonable, constitute an essential part of his effort.

Lizardi's second novel, *La Quixotita y su prima* (1818), loses the sprightliness of the *Periquillo* and becomes overbearingly didactic. Probably inspired by *Emile*, and certainly encouraged by his own dim view of education, Lizardi undertook to show the horrible consequences of the frivolous education of women, and to demonstrate how they ought to be taught. Since the presentation of the argument involves the treatment of two families who are related to each other, the structure of the novel is somewhat more complicated than the picaresque. Pomposita, the victim of an education that has taught her to write social notes, dance, and eat bonbons, is the epitome of frivolity. And so are her parents. She marries imprudently and is deserted by the man who was not what he pretended to be. The death of Pomposita's improvident father leaves mother and daughter with no recourse short of prostitution. Cousin Prudenciana, on the other hand, is given a sound education, knows how to run the house, and even learns watch-making, a trade which can provide a living in the absence of her husband. But Prudenciana and her good parents take no chances on the husband either—they have as many recourses as we have fringe benefits—and select a serious, older man whose lack of glamor is his greatest attraction. Prudenciana's life is secure, if boring. The trouble with Lizardi's moral lesson is that the reader finds Pomposita and her devil-may-care father a lot more attractive than their opposite numbers. And there are times when we may ask whether the author's advice concerns the nature of education, or the proper standards for choosing a husband.

The truth of the matter is that *La Quixotita y su prima* will not stand by itself. It is an interesting part of Lizardi's work, but interest in it depends upon interest in the author's total production. No one would read the book for pleasure in our time, a fact that makes it entirely different from *El Periquillo Sarniento*. Happily, Lizardi returned to the kind of novel that was most suited to his talents in *Don Catrín de la Fachenda*, which was published posthumously in 1832.

The second picaresque novel is traditionally considered inferior to the *Periquillo*, probably with good cause, but it does not deserve the relative oblivion into which it has been cast. Don Catrín is not the same kind of *pícaro* as Periquillo. He lacks his forerunner's conscience, and his antisocial attitudes are less justifiable. His model is the "dandy" of the period who thinks the world owes him a living and who is willing to do anything to avoid legitimate work. This character does not attract the sympathy that Periquillo attracts, but enjoyment of the novel depends only on the reader's ability to take one further step into the world of *pícaro*. If our judgment is controlled by the attractive qualities of the character, the book will not provide a pleasant experience; if we accept Don Catrín as an instrument of satire, the novel is funny.

Whatever the reader's personal reaction to Lizardi's novels, there is no doubt that they show a great deal of the world in which he lived. Lizardi died in 1827, after independence had been achieved, Iturbide had declared himself emperor, and the republican forces had brought about his abdication. The arguments for reasonable, just behavior that were so important to *El Pensador Mexicano* were lost in the struggle between federalists and centralists, republicans and monarchists. In the midst of great confusion, Mexico began the arduous task of establishing itself as a nation. Noise and violence dulled the effect of Father Hidalgo's "Cry of Dolores," and only the strongest voices—supported by the strongest wills—could be heard against the tumult.

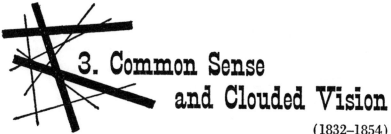

3. Common Sense and Clouded Vision

(1832–1854)

In the middle of the 1820's—the years of transition and confusion that witnessed the crossing paths of colonialism and nationalism, of conservatism and liberalism, of Neo-Classicism and the Romantic revolt—a novel called *Jicoténcal* (1826) was published in Philadelphia, anonymously and in Spanish. Its place in Mexican literature has always been uncertain, since no one has ever been able to prove that the author was Mexican. Although there is indeed no proof positive, and there probably never will be, *Jicoténcal* is precisely what should have happened in the Mexican novel at that time.[1]

The novel is based on the noble savage theme, and from the theme spring an insipid love story and an exposition of the liberal ideals of the time. In many later novels of Romanticism, the contrived poignancy of the love theme becomes all important; but for the author of *Jicoténcal*, it served as a coating for his ideology. He has boundless respect for the goodness of man in his natural state, and he questions the value of social institutions that deny the common origin and equality of men. Jicoténcal, the protagonist, contends that he must have been created by the same God that created Christians, and that if his moral values are the same, it makes little difference how he

---

[1] Luis Leal, in "Jicoténcal, primera novela histórica en castellano," *Revista Iberoamericana*, XXV, 49 (enero–julio, 1960), deals with the problem clearly and thoroughly. He agrees with the majority of scholars that the novel was written by a Spanish American, rather than by a Spaniard, but he doubts that the author was Mexican.

chooses to worship that God. The author takes a "common sense" position in his liberalism, which is not based on ethnology but on the respect of man for man.

The Spaniards, symbolized in Cortés, respect institutions rather than men, and are portrayed as essentially inhuman. Only one Spaniard is shown sympathetically in the entire novel, and he is an obvious exception. As the anonymous author proceeds with his condemnation of human blindness, it becomes apparent that there will be no life in the novel. Its characters are moved around to suit the needs of ideological proposition, and there is no feeling of the past re-created. The author judges the Conquest strictly on his own terms. Society is the victim of the divisiveness that it has created, and he advises his countrymen to unite if they love liberty, recognizing the natural unity of men. He could hardly have said anything that would have been more pertinent to the Mexican dilemma of that time, when the vision that belonged to the early movement toward Independence had been clouded by irrelevancies.

As Mexico moved into a period of independence achieved, the novel was as rudderless as the government. There were no teachers. Even if the relationship with the Spanish novel had not been broken early in the Colonial Period, it would have offered little in the last hundred years. Mexican writers were adrift, poorly oriented, but aware of the country's need for them to participate in the national life. They looked for their masters particularly in France but also in England and occasionally in Germany, and started the long road toward authentic expression of their world. One major Hispanic influence remained, the picaresque inclination. And it was strengthened by the Spanish *costumbrista* writers of the nineteenth century.

The novelists looked for their way in the midst of the Romantic revolt, which had two faces. One was the liberalism that came primarily from Rousseau through Lizardi and others. The second face was violence and exaggerated emotional response. I doubt that any of the early novelists recognized the relationship of the two faces, though both are apparent in the works of some writers. A question of art was involved, and sometimes a novelist would remove himself from his surroundings in an attempt to discover truth, only to end up in a mire of improbable sentimentality. Others wrote under the *costumbrista* influence, whose interest in particularity makes it a special kind of Romantic expression; but always the action is colored by Romantic sensitivity that too frequently degenerates into the opposite of reality.

It is not at all surprising that early fiction after Independence should interest itself in Mexico's past. No particular point in the past becomes the focus of attention, because Mexico had no Middle Ages to which the novelists might return as the Europeans did. The most interesting themes are the Inquisition, the idealized Indian set against the Conquest, and defense of the *criollo*. The brevity of many of the novels probably indicates that the writers lacked experience. Certainly brevity cannot be called a characteristic of Romanticism, and some Mexican novelists became magnificent examples of the opposite tendency. It is possible that the undeveloped novels may be related to the anarchic conditions of the time which were obviously not conducive to concentration on literature. But it is more likely that they were written by authors who had not yet had time to learn the art of making a novel.

As early as 1832, José María Lafragua published *Netzula*, the tragic love story of a young Indian couple. The author managed to strip the story of all significance and builds only an ironic twist of fate, of the kind that so delighted the Romantics. He is obviously more interested in breaking the hearts of sensitive readers than in breathing life into his characters. A far better story is J. R. Pacheco's *El criollo* (1836) which uses the discriminatory society of the Colonial Period as the cause of the love tragedy. Simply because he saw life in the tragedy, rather than sensationalism, he is more a novelist than Lafragua. But Pacheco's insight is the exception rather than the rule. In the same year, Mariano Meléndez y Muñoz set *El misterioso* in the Spain of Phillip II, and failed miserably because he lacked the ability to re-create the time of his setting. It is entirely reasonable to suppose that the author had read some historical novels and decided to furnish one to Mexican culture, without understanding at all how he should go about it. Even Ignacio Rodríguez Galván, who felt the influence of literary currents more than most of his contemporaries, failed to produce an authentic atmosphere in *La hija del oidor* (1836). Interest in the story depends entirely too much on its outcome, and the author's attempt to fix the setting by reference to historical personages is exterior to the movement of the novel.

In three successive years, Rodríguez Galván published three novels whose general characteristics are the same: *La hija del oidor, Manolito Pisaverde* (1837) and *La procesión* (1838). The plots turn on hidden or mistaken identity, and the author does little else to attract the reader. Surprisingly, and in spite of knowing approximately what the author has in mind, the reader is caught up in the movement of the plot and wants to know how it is resolved. The melodramatic quality of Rodríguez Galván's fiction elicits the accusation that he misunderstood the nature of Romanticism and was attracted only by its most superficial aspects. I should not wish to defend his comprehension of all aspects of Romanticism, but the fact is that in these three novels, he reflects one of its aspects—action—which was often forgotten by other novelists. Rodríguez Galván's famous patriotic poem, *Profecía de Guatimoc*, has the same quality. The poem moves in a confusion of Romantic mystery, dreams, and overstatement, but it does move. So it is with the three novels. They suffer from many of the quirks that some Romanticists thought were essential, but they do have the movement of the period. And in still another short novel, Rodríguez Galván showed that he could descend from the heights of imagination to see the ridiculousness of the human estate. He called the story *Tras un mal nos vienen ciento*, a title that suggests an unfortunate situation where there is no apparent relief from a series of unhappy events. The date of its publication is uncertain, but it was probably written at the same time as the others. The difference is in the author's mood. It is a kind of *costumbrista* sketch in which an invitation to dinner with friends leads a man into a series of awkward situations, but never to dinner. The author takes the opportunity to change the perspective in which he sees a number of commonly accepted human foibles. It is interesting that in this story, where he is dealing with matters close to his experience, Rodríguez Galván confined himself to a very simple story and developed it fully, while his other novels have enough action in a kind of outline form to supply some novelists with material for two or three volumes.

The length of a novel is not always indicative of the adequacy of its development. Cultivation of the serialized novel produced a number of monstrous narratives that hang action onto action for as long as the author wished, with absolutely no concern for structure. Some are as devoid of development as Rodríguez Galván's novels, which he could have strung together with the same effect if he had chosen to do so. Manuel Payno's famous *El fistol del diablo* would be among them if it were not saved by the author's attack on the lack of common sense in the society of his time. *El fistol del diablo* was published serially in 1845 and 1846, and it is fairly apparent that Payno wrote the installments separately and without much concern for what had gone before or what was to come later. As he originally thought of the novel, it did have a connecting device, but even this weak attempt at unity was forgotten long before the end. There is no point in reading *El fistol del diablo* as an example of the art of writing a novel. Even in the few attempts that Payno made to give form and style to his work, he failed. Its value lies in what the author did unconsciously, in the society re-created, which is authentic because of Payno's intense interest in social improvement. Even so, he is often boring; but there are many parts of the novel that place the reader, not the characters, genuinely within the period.

The world of Payno was chaotic, to say the least. Society was disorganized, the people did not have common goals and aspirations that were specific enough to allow the country to function. Political thinking was split in several different ways. The economic situation was deplorable. Class divisions were firmly established. All these factors were conducive to individual self-preservation rather than to concern for the common good. The conditions of the time make the reader feel that he is witnessing a great pretense, that the nation existed only in form and that, within this form, frantic activity led the country backward rather than forward.[2] Only a time like this would have permitted the opportunism and folly of Santa Anna. Only a lack of national awareness could have permitted the country to drift as it did, even to the point of losing more than half the national territory in a war which, however unjustified the action of the aggressor, might

---

[2] One of the best treatments of the early years of Mexico's history is a novel by Leopoldo Zamora Plowes, *Quince Uñas y Casanova* (Mexico City: Talleres Gráficos, 1945). It re-creates the years from 1844 to 1853, the heyday of Santa Anna.

not have happened if the Mexican nation had been better organized. Nationalism was the product of desperation rather than of deep understanding.

Manuel Payno saw what was wrong with the country, and his understanding kept him in a moderate political position, without the burden of commitment to either liberals or conservatives. From his point of view, the nation was behaving illogically, and the need was to restore common sense. His criticism covers the whole social spectrum, but it is always essentially the same. Life in Mexico was, as he saw it, a series of conspiracies made with someone's personal advantage as the goal. He is equally critical of the generals who made up their armies for their own personal power, and of the sheep who followed them with no apparent hope of contributing to the national good. But the general is hardly different from the society matron whose associations with others are destructive rather than mutually helpful. Payno believed that personalistic conspiracies were the result of social stratification, and that class lines were supported by economic problems.

El fistol del diablo does not contain much economic or political theory. Payno's argument rests on what he considers a reasonable attitude among men. Since he accepted the liberal principles of his time, it was apparent to him that general acceptance of these principles would naturally solve the problems he saw. He describes the problems always with the intention of showing how foolish men are. Usually his descriptions have a picaresque attractiveness with less sermonizing than Lizardi's. The one case in which he overworks the problem is his discussion of imprisonment and rehabilitation. This was a special interest of his and he had spent a great deal of time studying its effect on the nation. Since he was careless of structure anyway, the length of his presentation was governed by his interest. It is apparent that the incorporation of the reader was enough for Payno; and because he allowed his characters to remain outside, he wrote a series of *costumbrista* sketches rather than a real novel.

The weaknesses of *El fistol del diablo* exist partly because it was published in serial form. But Justo Sierra O'Reilly shows in *La hija del judío* (1848–1850) that the serialized novel can overcome many of the difficulties imposed by the manner of publication. Sierra's novel is historical and deals with the injustice of the Inquisition. It is far better than other Romantic novels on the same subject, mainly because Sierra caught the novelist's magic that escaped Payno and many others: his characters live under the effect of the world that surrounds them.

Sierra was a political and religious liberal, a position that is clear enough in his novel; but he makes it clear within the novel, not by intruding for purposes of explanation. It is true that he judges a past time from the standpoint of his present position, but this fallacy affects reality on a different level—the re-creation of the past. He makes up for it to a considerable extent by detailed description of place that rivals Sir Walter Scott. Within this detailed setting, Sierra places two lovers, an appropriately worthy young man and a girl whose rightful inheritance is demanded by the Inquisition for reasons that are explained in a romantically complicated manner. In spite of some exaggeration, the author evokes the reader's identification with the young couple, and together they live under the Inquisition's shadow. The principal character, however, is a Jesuit who befriends the girl and determines to save her inheritance, reserving part of it for his order. The Jesuit may well be the best characterization in Mexico during the years of Romanticism. He is one of the few who are not either all good or all bad. In his case, the reader's sympathy rises and falls. Although the Jesuit sincerely wants to help the girl, this inclination has its terminal point because he also considers the welfare of his order, which Sierra understands as a kind of selfishness. The plot interest depends on the Jesuit's skillful maneuvering to gain his end. However, this action is well related to the love story, and Sierra's novel is the most complex and best constructed in Mexico before Juan Díaz Covarrubias. The second, and perhaps more important, contribution of Sierra is that he was the first to see an aspect of Mexican reality in the perspective of time. His successful re-creation of the past gives reality to information that might be nothing but words; and Mexicans looking at it could see, in addition to the mirror image, a part of the basis of what they were.

The common sense advocated by Payno, Lizardi, and in a somewhat different way by Sierra, filled Romantic novels with concern for a kind of moral behavior that is rarely related to any profound

consideration of the social circumstance, but plays on the sympathy
of the reader by tearful description of the tragedy of one person who
has been victimized by another. These tragedies may be described
as the social norm in the novels of Romanticism. Perhaps the most
distinctive writer of such novels was Florencio M. del Castillo, who
made an extraordinary effort to find psychological reasons behind
the human difficulties of his characters. Let it be understood from
the beginning that Del Castillo was not a good novelist. His psychology, though interesting for his time, is often awry and sometimes
puerile. He is pedantic. His narration is poor, because impatience
with development of the story makes him forsake the narrative and
tell the reader directly what happened. He piles tragedy upon tragedy
to the point of being ridiculously unbelievable. His shadowy characters do little but suffer. He wrings every tear from misfortune, sub-
stituting maudlin sentimentality where stoic and entirely human no-
bility would be more inspiring. He insists on intruding to explain to
his reader what he has already made clear. This last fault is common
enough among Romantic novelists, but Del Castillo may well hold
the international championship. In one of his novels the poetic protagonist looks from his window upon a late afternoon scene that
would depress the staunchest optimist. But Del Castillo was not satisfied with his effective description, and felt compelled to explain to
the reader that this scene was just the sort of thing that would depress
the protagonist.

Some of Del Castillo's faults are common to Romantic novelists,
others are peculiarly his own. On account of both his faults and his
virtues, it is not enough to call him a Romantic novelist and assume
that he is therefore adequately described.

In 1850 Del Castillo published a volume of short novels, *Horas de
tristeza*, some or all of which had been published a year or two earlier. The date of another novel, *Culpa*, is not clear, but it probably
belongs to the same period. His last novel and most ambitious one,
Hermana de los ángeles, was published in 1854. It differs from the
others only in that it is longer. Castillo examines physical incapa-
citation through identification; the effects of sexual abstinence, of
libertinism, of unrealistic sex education; incestuous inclinations; natural desire; and holy vows. The fact that the characters writhe and

declaim in their misfortune does not alter the nature of the author's intent. The society he saw was precisely the same as that seen by Manuel Payno. And there is good reason to think that he would have been pleased by the advent of common sense that Payno yearned for. Del Castillo's obvious sympathy for the unfortunate classifies him generally as a "social" novelist, and not a few words have been written about his defense of the humble classes. The fact is that very little is seen in Del Castillo's novels of the great masses of society. His view is centered upon a distinctly middle class, though the members he chooses to describe are among the less fortunate. He saw the general social and economic ills that Payno saw, but he looked for the reason behind the lack of common sense. The misfortunes he describes are attributable to poor human relationships, and it is these relationships that he seeks to understand. It it unfortunate that his novels lack the popular appeal that Payno gained through his picaresque tone, and Sierra through his ability to incorporate the reader into the novel. There was no liberal of the nineteenth century who was more dedicated to his ideal.

A suitable contrast to Del Castillo's brevity is Fernando Orozco y Berra's *La guerra de treinta años*, which was also published in 1850. The author fills several hundred pages with an account of the protagonist's love affairs. The thirty years in the title refer to the first thirty years of his life; the war refers to his struggle to find happiness without sacrificing his ideals. Presumably the novel is autobiographical, though it is hard to believe that one man could have passed through so many different experiences. They are different, at least, in the opinion of the author; the reader is likely to find an awful sameness. *La guerra de treinta años* is a novel of sensitivity. Orozco's proposition is that a reprimand for kissing a girl when he was very young establishes inhibitions which the protagonist is never able to overcome. Every love affair is destroyed by circumstances which the protagonist cannot control, but his inhibitions are not always apparent.

The importance of this rather dull novel is not in its literary value, but in the author's reason for writing it. The motivation of Payno and of Sierra is clear enough; and if Del Castillo's motivation is not as immediately clear, a modest amount of reflection will make it so. But

La guerra de treinta años appears to ignore the world except for love. Of course, the ideal love was a favorite subject among the Romantics. The treatment of it tends to be short and idyllic, with attention focused on the long-suffering faithfulness of one or both of the lovers. But Orozco's novel is none of these things. He ignores the world, but does not remove himself from it. The action is set in time and place, but the setting does not determine what the characters do. The theme is not faithfulness, but disillusionment. *La guerra de treinta años* is the author's way of expressing dissatisfaction with the world in which he lived. I suppose he was not thinking in terms of social disorganization, but his pessimism reflects a good deal of the uneasiness that his contemporaries felt. He probably was led to express his dissatisfaction through the love relationship by his awareness of contemporary taste. Throughout the novel, Orozco takes every opportunity to state his belief that happiness must be bought by sacrificing one's principles, and what he is talking about is an ideal moral standard that coincides with the common sense advocated by Payno.

A year later Pantaleón Tovar published *Ironías de la vida* (Life's Ironies), and it is exactly what the title says, hundreds of pages of them. But the life that Tovar describes is not a slice of reality; it is a concentration of criminality, opportunism, and immorality that probably expresses the author's disgust better than any realistic picture would have done. And there is plenty of irony. Tovar works five plots simultaneously, plus a few sub-plots, and weaves them so intricately that the reader stands aghast at what is happening. He gets used to the inevitable descent of tragedy. Even when its coming is not justified by preceding events, he accepts it numbly, because he knew that something had to happen. Altamirano, the gentlest of critics, wrote that Tovar's works are marred by a bitter pessimism.[3]

Ironías de la vida is full of bitter pessimism, but I'm not sure it's fair to say that it is marred. Astounding, yes; incredible, perhaps; but the concentration of pessimism may well be the best thing about the book. And at that I doubt very much that Tovar is more pessimistic than Payno, and certainly not more than Orozco y Berra. But of

[3] Ignacio M. Altamirano, *Artículos literarios* (Mexico City: Victoriano Agüeros, 1899), p. 406.

course, his picture of a society full of scoundrels is bound to be shocking. It may be stretching interpretation too far, but it seems to me
that the cross-cutting plots and basic immorality in this book give an
adequate feeling of the deficient social organization and rejection of
responsibility that Payno described.

Ironías de la vida, in spite of its many faults, is more of a novel than
the majority of its contemporaries. Tovar knew how to interrelate the
actions of one character with the actions of other characters, an essential aspect of narration which has to be cultivated and which, when
it is absent, elicits comments like "episodic" and "poorly constructed." It is true that Tovar was carried away with his own facility and
made his novel terribly complicated; but the story incorporates the
reader much more readily than a string of episodes does. Many of
the characters, however unsatisfactory they may be from our present
viewpoint, are combinations of good and bad, and are thus distinguished from most of their fictional contemporaries, who are completely good or totally evil. Tovar's novel is so complex and so irregular that its virtues are often hidden by its faults. And it is perhaps for
this reason that the author is rarely given credit for including the
really poor class, something that very rarely happens in the nineteenth century though several novelists are commonly and wrongly
given credit for doing so. Tovar's poor are the genuine lower class,
economically nonexistent, discriminated against, outside the society.
They are not the unfortunate middle class. Tovar even gives them,
though cautiously, some of the elements of their way of speaking.

It is difficult to write off Tovar's pessimism as bitter. Rather, it is
angry, and perhaps anguished. His novel sounds very declamatory to
twentieth-century ears, but I am reluctant to close mine. Romantic
exaggeration may have been purely a product of the imagination
when it concerned the gentle sentiments; but it is not easy to imagine
anger into existence. It more likely is the result of anxiety; and ours
is not an appropriate time to take anxiety lightly. Tovar's lacks polish,
but it has strength. It is wrong to tie him in a bundle with José Rivera
y Río, who whined while Tovar screamed.

The appearance of Rivera y Río's first novel in the same year as
Tovar's is not pure coincidence, but the result of an obvious literary
influence. The title of Rivera y Río's novel, *Los misterios de San*

Cosme, would suggest the influence even if the novel did not. The influence is Eugène Sue's *Les mystères de Paris.* Rivera y Río's was the first of a long series, published over a period of many years, each novel almost exactly like its predecessors. Sue's influence is discernible in the work of the majority of Mexican Romantic novelists. His basic theme is the unfortunate individual, his narrative complex, his characters definitely categorized, his tone declamatory. The fundamental difference between Tovar and Rivera y Río is that the latter does not show the same kind of indignation. The people are the same: usurers, dishonest entrepreneurs, dandies, murderers, indeed the whole gamut of society with the accent on dishonesty. Rivera y Río's attitude is tongue-clicking disapproval that goes well with his gossipy prose style. His judgment seems to be based on his opinion of what nice people do, while Tovar's seems to be based on his idea of the kind of society intelligent people will create.

Whatever the social view of the novelists, their novels always use a love story, or a combination of love stories, as the line to which all action is attached. And very much in the Romantic manner, some novels concentrate on the theme of the faithful lover. Emilio Rey's *Amor de ángel* (1854) moves about in several European countries while the faithful woman waits for her wayward lover to come to his senses, only to learn that he was killed in a railroad accident while on his way to her. It is difficult to see in this novel anything beyond the invention of tragedy designed to wring the gentle reader's heart. It does reveal a kind of human dignity that might have some tenuous association with common sense; but Rey spends so much effort removing himself from reality, we can hardly expect him to find reality by chance.

The amount of prose fiction produced by Mexican writers in the first half of the last century is relatively slight. But the variety is important. While there are a number of obvious common denominators, practically every novelist has certain distinctive qualities. The experimentation laid the foundation for further cultivation of the novel, and gradually the foundation became recognizable. The middle of the century by no means marks the end of the Romantic novel in Mexico. Some of the influence of Realism enters early, but it is not really established until well into the 1880's.

Early in my studies of the Mexican novel, it appeared to me that the Romanticists had found some foreign models, mainly French, and had done little more than transpose these novels into more or less authentic Mexican settings. In various places the influence of Hugo, Dumas, Balzac is apparent, and perhaps to an even greater extent the influence of Sue and Alphonse Karr. The poor writing and sensationalist attitudes of the Mexican novelists didn't make my impression any more favorable. They obviously were not commendably creative. But if they had been so, they would have been remarkably different from the country as a whole. The nation was imitating, experimenting, trying to find its way, making serious mistakes, just as the novel was. Considered this way, the novel of the first half of the century is not just a good reflection of the nation, it is the nation's conscience attempting to point the way to common sense and the vision of the Independence. The Reform brought some changes in the country and in the novel, but both remained essentially Romantic.

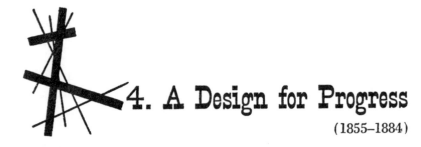

4. A Design for Progress
(1855–1884)

The Reform can be described, with a considerable degree of accuracy, as an attempt to make a nation. Out of the preceding chaos, out of the need for common sense, came a group of intellectual liberals who intended to organize the country according to their democratic, capitalistic design. Many names are important in this movement, but the most symbolic are Benito Juárez and Ignacio Manuel Altamirano: Juárez because of his gigantic leadership of the country, Altamirano because he had the vision to see that the design for reform included literature as one part of the national existence. The movement as a whole was just as Romantic as the War of Independence or any of the other great liberal movements that preceded it. Perhaps it was even more Romantic because of the persistence of its idealism, its momentary brilliance in spite of insurmountable difficulties, and its eclipse which was effected not by defeat but by impracticability. The vision of the Reform was the vision of Hidalgo, and its intention was to bring into being a land of liberty, justice, and awareness of the entire nation. The Reformists set out to limit the power of the Church, to redeem the peons economically, and to educate the masses so they might become an integral part of the nation. The conservative reaction was violent, and the country was embroiled in the War of the Reform from 1857 to 1860. Following many defeats, the liberals were at last victorious to the extent that they entered the capital. But the victory was not complete, because the people were not prepared to under-

stand the nature of the Reform, and because the conservatives plotted
to import a foreign prince who would establish their own kind of order.

The War of Reform brought Mexico's literary life to a virtual
standstill. The only novelist who published between 1855 and 1860
was Juan Díaz Covarrubias, a youth of some talent who wondered,
even while he wrote, why he was doing it. In the dedication of one
of his novels, *El diablo en México* (1858), to Luis G. Ortiz, he observed somewhat apologetically that some might think only a fool
or a child would write novels in those troubled times. Díaz Covarrubias didn't really understand those troubles. In his best novel, *Gil
Gómez el insurgente,* he comprehends the vision of the Independence.
But his novels that are not historical indicate that he did not see the
relationship between that vision and the years when he was writing.
Still, his anxiety is amply evident, and it was brought to a dramatic
end in his own death. He went with some other medical students to
the battlefield of Tacubaya to attend the wounded of both sides. He
was captured there by conservatives and ordered to be shot along
with other prisoners who were officers in the liberal army. He was
twenty-two years old.

The circumstances of Díaz Covarrubias' death cast an aura about
his work that inclines some readers to think of him as "the novelist
who might have been" and to evaluate his works more highly than
they should. He wrote one good novel, *Gil Gómez el insurgente,* and
one good short tale, *La sensitiva* (1859). The latter is one of the purest sentimental stories written in Mexico. While it is designed to
create Romantic sadness, it is gentle rather than declamatory. And
the author concentrates on the story of undying love by removing
it from time and place, thereby giving authenticity to his idyllic offer-
ing.

Gil Gómez el insurgente is an entirely different kind of novel. The
protagonist becomes one of Hidalgo's men although he had intended
to enlist on the other side. This persuasion, plus the fact that in the
end there is mutual forgiveness between people who had been committed to both sides, makes *Gil Gómez el insurgente* more a novel of
the Reform than either of the novels that deal with Díaz Covarrubias'
own period. Literarily, the novel is better than most of its antecedents.

Told in fluid if not elegant prose, the story moves well and interests the reader in both characterization and action. The historical
plot is related, though weakly, to a love story, and in both there is a
good deal of melodrama. But there is enough of value in the novel to
make the melodrama acceptable. Actually, most of the exaggeration
belongs to the love story rather than to the historical theme, where
the feeling of reality is enhanced by a certain tendency toward the
picaresque on the part of Gil Gómez.

If *Gil Gómez el insurgente* and *La sensitiva* illustrate special aspects of their period, Díaz Covarrubias' other novels are more generally characteristic of the fiction of the time. Perhaps the anxiety
that the author felt about the world around him is more evident in
La clase media (1858) and *El diablo en México*. Anxiety could be
the cause of the change in style. These "social" novels are composed in
a nervous style of repeated phrases and choppy, short paragraphs that
make the reader feel like he is reading on a pogo-stick. *La clase media,*
in spite of the fact that it is always mentioned in literary histories
that omit superior works, is one of the worst novels written in Mexico. The author's intent was honorable enough. He tried to portray
society as he saw it, and to make that society live for the reader.
What the reader finds out is not very different from what he discovers
in the novels of Tovar or Rivera y Río. Luis Leal has described the
society of Díaz Covarrubias' novels as "aristocrats, rich but perverted; the middle class, virtuous but without hope; and the people, industrious but forgotten."[1] The author's attention is centered on the
middle class who are, indeed, without hope. But he gives the impression that the salvation of Mexico depends on rescuing that middle
class, not in recognizing the needs of an even lower class. His unfortunate people are a young physician who cannot establish himself because he lacks the necessary influence, a law student who needs to
support his widowed mother while he completes his education, a retired army officer who has no pension. Díaz Covarrubias describes
many such tragic circumstances, and he makes use of enough characters so he does not have to heap too many tragedies upon any one

[1] Luis Leal, *Breve historia del cuento mexicano* (Mexico City: Studium,
1956), p. 43.

person; but once he has the large cast, he has trouble involving them in a central narrative theme. The result is highly unsatisfactory, and I prefer the bitterness of Tovar to the sweet pessimism of Díaz Covarrubias.

El diablo en México is less maudlin than *La clase media* and much less complicated. I suspect this novel has contributed something to the legend of the promising novelist, because some passages are good *costumbrista* pieces, and this kind of word painting of visible reality often creates the illusion of being more significant than it really is. The "devil" is the search for financial gain, which in this story thwarts two love matches and substitutes two marriages of convenience. Díaz Covarrubias apparently felt no particular need to develop the problem. He states it, then skips six months to the conclusion. It is interesting to note that his heroines are in good health and one of the male protagonists even recovers from a heart ailment. Such a state of health is a new departure for a Romantic novelist, and, as a matter of fact, it contributes a good deal to the credibility of the other circumstances.

The liberal victory gave an immediate if short-lived boost to the novel. Among the rather large number of novels·published in 1861 are two by Nicolás Pizarro Suárez, one of the most ardent and articulate defenders of the Reform. *El monedero* and *La coqueta* are arguments in favor of the Reform, made with the usual trappings of the Romantic novel. Altamirano knew Pizarro and had read *El monedero* before its publication, when the former was a student. He says that Pizarro revised his work, but does not say what changes were made.[2] If we consider *El monedero* as a commentary on society, we find that the author makes four suggestions. The first grows out of the fact that the protagonist, Fernando Hénkel, is an Indian who was adopted, raised and educated by a German. With the benefit of this education, he has become a successful member of society—he is an engraver—and even enjoys the privilege of being a guest at the home of Don Diego Diez de Dávila, a gentleman of extravagant social pretensions. Obviously, Pizarro is suggesting that the solution to the

[2] Altamirano, *Artículos literarios* (Mexico City: Victoriano Agüeros, 1899), pp. 411–412.

problem of the Indian is education of a practical kind. It is not surprising that the implementation of common sense should have been
carried out by a German. Many writers of the nineteenth century regarded Germans as the perfect example of industriousness, thrift, and
no-nonsense moral values. And while they were thought of as quite
different from Mexicans, they were not regarded as insensitive,
and so were usually admirable people.

The second suggestion is more complicated, and involves Fernando's encounter with Padre Luis, who established a model community
of a hundred Indian families. Incidentally, this meeting came about
when Fernando got lost and wandered into an Indian village on his
way from San Angel to Mexico City. This fact, which is similar to
many others found in novels of the time, has the charm of bringing
the past to life in an unexpected way. It is a little as if the protagonist
had gotten lost travelling from Brooklyn to Manhattan.[3] However,
what is quaint now was commonplace at the time, and Pizarro used
the event only as a means of introducing the model community. The
community must exist for the good of all, and all must contribute to
the good of the community. Everyone has a voice in the affairs of the
community, and education for everyone makes each person a responsible citizen. Its isolation protects the community from the corrupt-
ing influence of urban civilization. Padre Luis is the guiding spirit
and is concerned primarily for the earthly welfare of his people.

A particular expression of nationalism indicates the third of the
four suggestions. Don Diego Diez de Dávila affects peninsular Spanish speech, botches it, and is ridiculed by the author, not only for
his speech but for the affectation of his name as well. In another place
in the novel, Fernando sets up a business for his servant, Gregorio
Fausto Roldán, who then assumes the name Don Fausto de Roldán.
The author shows a sort of condescending charity in the latter case,
while bitterness is apparent in the first; and Pizarro's attitude in the
Gregorio incident makes one wonder just how profound was his sympathy for the lower class. The question of language was a favorite.

[3] In his *Los dramas de Nueva York* (Mexico City: Imprenta litográfica y
tipografica de J. Rivera, Hijo y Comp., 1869), Rivera y Río does give much the
same flavor to his novel by describing isolated love-nests in Harlem, *etc.*

Some years later Pizarro published a grammar of the language *as spoken in Mexico*.[4]

The fourth suggestion has to do with the clergy, of whom Padre Luis is the example. From the orthodox viewpoint, he is more social worker than priest. He does not tell his flock to bear the tribulations of this life while expecting a better life to come. His efforts are directed toward the improvement of their lot in this present world. He is seen as a good moral influence and director, but not as possessing any mystic power or inclination. This picture of Padre Luis, as well as other ideas concerning the common sense kind of life, is similar to Altamirano's attitudes in *La navidad en las montañas*.[5] Padre Luis is so far removed from the traditional concept of the priest that, at the end of the novel, he asked for and obtained release from vows so he could marry. And it is a good thing for the happy outcome of the plot that he did, because Fernando found himself in the awkward corner of a triangle, and Luis was attractive enough to distract one worthy young woman from her concentration on the protagonist.

In addition to its interest as an expresssion of Reformist sentiment, *El monedero* is not really a bad novel, given certain deficiencies that were characteristic of practically all novels of the period. Although there is a considerable amount of exaggeration and not one completely satisfactory characterization, Pizarro's interest in expressing his ideas through his characters makes them visible enough for a fair degree of identification. The book is longer than necessary, and most of what we know about the model community is told in letters from Padre Luis to Fernando. The only plot interest arising from the community itself is its destruction by the novel's villain, and its subsequent reconstruction. In this account, Pizarro is forecasting the persistence of liberal ideas. Indeed, the happy resolution of problems at the end of the novel indicates the author's faith in the triumph of liberalism. The chronological setting of the novel, at the time of the

[4] An example of Pizarro's eagerness, typical of the Reform, to straighten out the world is that he wrote the grammar in verse—or did so insofar as it was possible—since he was convinced that it would therefore be better remembered.

[5] See María del Carmen Millán, "Dos utopías," *Historia Mexicana*, VII, 2 (octubre–diciembre 1957), 187–206.

Northamerican Invasion, contributes nothing to the author's purpose so far as I can see. He relates some atrocities committed by the United States soldiers, he comments on racial discrimination in the United States, and the one Northamerican who has a role of any importance at all is a crass opportunist. Perhaps Pizarro's anti-Yankeeism is intended to warn Mexico against choosing the United States as a model.

Most people find *El monedero* more interesting than *La coqueta,* because the model community offers a clear statement of Pizarro's social ideas. *La coqueta* is a defense of the Constitution of 1857, woven into a love story, and is a much better combination of ideology and fiction than *El monedero* is. The love story itself has a special interest because Magdalena illustrates an opinion of Pizarro's on women's rights. Although she is known as a coquette, Pizarro reveals that Magdalena plays the field in her particular way because she resents the passive role of women in choosing and winning lovers. Andrés and Magdelena converse at great length on the subject of love, and these pages are not the most exciting part of the novel. But the feminist slant of these discussions makes them more interesting than the usual praise of sensitivity.

Pizarro's political ideas are expressed in *La coqueta* through conversation among the characters, a much more appropriate device than the letters of *El monedero.* Within his general defense of the Reform Constitution, the author shows two main concerns: the intransigence of the Church, and racial bias. At one point, when Andrés is thought to be near death, a priest refuses to attend him unless he will renounce the Constitution. Racial tolerance is demonstrated through the attitude of Andrés toward a Negro servant from Cuba. Andrés is democratic at least in form, but in this case as in the case of the servant in *El monedero,* the democratic attitude has an element of condescension. In an epilogue, we find Andrés running a farm on a communal basis and enjoying his family. This ending is tacked to the end of the novel, and again shows Pizarro's inability to accept anything short of victory.

Quantity if not quality supported Pizarro's work in the brief flurry of literary activity between the liberal victory and the French Intervention. José Rivera y Río published three novels in 1861. They were probably written earlier, but it is possible that they were all written in one year, because there is nothing in any of Rivera y Río's novels to indicate that he wasted any time thinking about what he was doing. The essence of his stories is that he doesn't like naughty people, and he never lets evil triumph. But evil works havoc among the virtuous until it meets poetic justice. It is difficult to see any relationship between Rivera y Río's fiction and the Reform. Available biographical information does not say whether he fought in the War of the Reform or not. Later on he fought against the French Intervention, but he could have done that for patriotic reasons that would not necessarily identify him with the principles of the Reform. Certainly he was in no way anticlerical. In one of the novels published in 1861, *Mártires y verdugos*, the most admirable character, at least from the author's point of view, becomes a priest. The amount of his publication does, of course, coincide with the general increase in literary interest, but his novels show nothing that is different from preceding years.

Even José María Ramírez showed some inclination toward the creation of a new culture in his stylistic invention. In a series of poor novels, beginning with *Celeste* in 1861, Ramírez bravely tried for effect through style. The result is silly rather than effective, and finally the reader becomes disgusted with his choppy sentences, short paragraphs, blank spaces, and tired imagery. Unable to see beyond the tragedy of love thwarted by worship of money, Ramírez attempts to be philosophical and succeeds in being trite. He is a pretentious writer who quotes others to display his literary orientation and breaks the flow of the narrative by intruding whole chapters of explanation of what has gone before. His view of society is extremely limited—he never goes farther than to show, very superficially, the need for good sense that is apparent in earlier novels—and it never changes. Even the novel which is usually cited as his best, *Una rosa y un harapo* (1868), offers little more. The historical background of the French Intervention places the book on a firmer footing than its older brothers, but Ramírez did not know how to take advantage of it.

Manuel Payno published, also in 1861, a few chapters of a novel he never finished, *El hombre de la situación*. Apparently he intended to use a Mexican just returned from Spain, where he had been studying, as a means of commenting on Mexican society. We cannot tell whether the novel would have shown a difference in Payno's opinions.

Of more importance is Hilarión Frías y Soto's *Vulcano*, the only novel of a very famous journalist. It may be wrong to call this book a novel. It is rather short, but the time span and changes of scene, as well as the personality change of the feminine protagonist, make the implied action too much for a short story. The moralistic point is that the love of money is the dominant characteristic of the time. And Frías shows how this evil is the root of other immorality, but his character representation of wealth, Vulcano, is not an evil person. The evil is done by those who sell themselves, not by the source of financial power. The strength of the woman who, in effect, sells out, is as unusual as the character of Magdalena in *La coqueta*. It is obvious that interesting things are happening in the portrayal of women. In *Vulcano*, Filomena changes from a beggar girl of primitive innocence to a calculating woman of the world, changing even her name. From one point of view, she has been corrupted by civilization; but she enjoys the pleasures of wealth too much to give them up for love. Although *Vulcano* can properly be called Romantic, there are clear signs of a Realist reaction in it: the characterization of Filomena, her attitude toward sex, the fact that Vulcano is not a villain. It is natural, of course, to expect to see Realist influences in Mexico by this time. Balzac had finished writing and Flaubert had published *Madame Bovary*. French novelists were widely read in Mexico, and imitated. But the way in which Mexico was developing kept alive the Romantic impulse; and the period of the Reform, which might be called a second generation of Romantics, was to a considerable extent an era of transition during which Realist inclinations appeared together with the persistent Romantic impulse, until Realism finally became established.

Irked by the Mexican government's policy on the payment of foreign debts, and prodded by ambition—his own and the Empress Eugénie's—Napoleon III planned the French Intervention in Mexico. He had interested England and Spain in a show of force at Veracruz, but his allies withdrew when they discovered his real intentions. Early in 1862, French forces invaded Mexico, allied with conservative elements, and the battle between liberals and conservatives was once again joined. The flurry of activity in the novel stopped as abruptly as it had started. José María Ramírez continued to write as if art and reality were his personal possessions, never realizing that he commanded neither of them. Crescencio Carrillo y Ancona composed a weak short novel, *Historia de Welinna* (1862), on the saving power of Christianity, a theme that he repeated later in *El santuario de la aldea* (1866). The only strong indictment of society to appear between 1861 and the establishment of the Empire was *El oficial mayor* (1864) by Juan Pablo de los Ríos. The basic theme of this novel is the misuse of power, whether derived from position or money. Thematically, it is not very different from many other Romantic novels. Its distinction rests on two qualities: the author's ability to write pleasant, unobtrusive prose, and the detailed description, particularly of houses. The general effect of the novel, while Romantic, is one of much more restraint than in most novels of the time. More typical of Reformist zeal is Eligio Ancona's *El filibustero* (1864), a story of the Colonial Period in which the author swings with a broadaxe at institutional religion.

The French and conservative Mexican forces advanced toward Mexico City, and in spite of the liberals' heroism at Puebla, Juárez had to leave the capital. The misguided Maximilian and Carlotta arrived in 1864 and Chapultepec Castle became the ·imperial palace. Maximilian tried to govern along fairly liberal lines, to the consternation of many of his conservative supporters, and even made peaceful overtures to some liberal leaders. While the foreign emperor and empress set up an imitation of European court life in Mexico City, Benito Juárez travelled through the north of Mexico, holding the liberals together, the government of Mexico in his old black carriage, the freedom of the Mexican people in his heart. From this austere but intensely human man, whose persistence saved a republic and guided the course of a continent's history, came the words that characterize the liberal spirit of the Reform, and will always stir men's imagination: *"El respeto al derecho ajeno es la paz"* ("Respect for the rights of the other is peace"). The statement makes a literary figure of Juárez, by its exact simplicity that says more than many volumes.

The period of the Empire is not noted for its literary productivity. Carrillo y Ancona published the second of his pro-Church novels in 1866, a remarkable contrast to Ancona's novel of two years earlier. However, the major literary event of the time of Maximilian was the publication, a year earlier, of Luis G. Inclán's *Astucia, el jefe de los hermanos de la hoja, o los charros contrabandistas de la rama*. Mexican readers have always been attracted to this novel by the author's accurate and ingenuous portrayal of rural customs. Inclán's background was rural, he even owned a ranch, and he was more than thirty years old when he moved permanently to Mexico City. He wrote, therefore, from first-hand knowledge—a fact that the reader would not be inclined to doubt even if he had no biographical information. The language of the people is present to an even greater extent than in *El Periquillo Sarniento*, and description of rural customs appears to be accurate enough, though I am inclined to believe that Inclán exaggerated reality in order to be picturesque. An added attraction is a fair amount of picaresque foxiness in the hero's personality. All these qualities evoke strong identification on the part of the Mexican reader who finds familiar things that are distinctively Mexican. I think that this perfectly understandable attitude tends to obscure some other aspects of the novel which, while it is certainly different in many ways from its contemporaries, also has much in common with them.

Like most other Mexican novelists of Romanticism, Inclán was poorly prepared for writing fiction. His advantage was that he knew perfectly a scene that was typically Mexican. Of the rural customs he describes, the most important is the rural code of honor. The protagonist, Lencho, is a spoiled brat who is finally made into a man by an old-timer who knows the way things ought to be. Faced with the choice of a career, Lencho decides to be a contrabandist—a decision which is approved by his father. The fact that Lencho lives outside the law has nothing at all to do with questions of right or wrong. These questions are decided on the basis of obligations to self and to one's friends, with no awareness of the welfare of society. The attitude is the direct opposite of the common sense that nineteenth-century intellectuals desired; and though similar attitudes are seen in some other fictional characters, I know of no other novel in which the author approves of them.

The action of the novel hinges on the struggles of the contraband gang to prevail against another less honorable gang, and against the law. Lencho, alias Astucia, is the chief of the good guys, and he feels a deep responsibility for their welfare and for the welfare of their families but not for the welfare of anybody else. In order to work in all he wants to say about rural life, Inclán interpolates the biographies and problems of the various members of the band. He integrates these stories fairly well, considering the mass of material he uses, but the novel does become tiresome because the stories are too similar to each other. Any one of the stories is interesting, but the ensemble is too much.

Although the nature of Inclán's material moves the novel toward Realism, it is a kind of natural realism rather than the studied French Realism of Flaubert. Inclán is a Romantic, and *Astucia* has many of the characteristics of that kind of novel. The men weep, many of the women are overly idealized. The structure and ethics of the gang appear to a non-Mexican to be as Dumasesque as they are rural Mexican. Both sentiment and action are exaggerated. The book is illustrated by a picture of Astucia about to commit suicide with two double-barrelled pistols, one pointed at each temple. The characters are middle-class and poor people, and they are for the most part probable characterizations. But Inclán has much of the tendency to divide his characters categorically into good and bad.

Pressure from outside France, plus apathy and some opposition within, persuaded Napoleon III to abandon his Mexican adventure, and he withdrew French troops. Maximilian's honor would not allow him to leave, and Carlotta went to Europe where she unsuccessfully sought aid for her empire. The nightmare ended when Maximilian was shot at Querétaro in June of 1867. The Republic was restored; but no sooner had the fact been accomplished than strong opposition to Juárez on the part of the more radical liberals came into the open.[6] Many of the radicals were journalists and creative writers, and they began to associate with each other in literary *veladas* (gatherings in the homes of members) for the purpose of mutual help and criticism in their attempt to revive Mexican literature. Politics probably played a role in these gatherings, but the role was a generous one, and the

[6] An excellent study of the politics of the era is Walter V. Scholes, *Politics during the Juárez regime* (Columbia: University of Missouri, 1957).

national literary effort attempted to incorporate conservatives into its plans.

The guiding spirit of the literary renaissance was Ignacio Manuel Altamirano, an able and active politician who had risen from the humblest of circumstances to a position of prominence in the life of the country. He was unquestionably the *maestro* of his literary generation. As a critic, Altamirano took the position that literature needed encouragement and could not at that time support harsh criticism. His critical opinions are interesting in the context of his total activity, but their gentleness has to be taken into account for them to have any significance. Altamirano thought of himself as a guide rather than a judge, and he tried to explain the characteristics that a national literature should have. The novelist's view should include the whole society and should enable him to re-create the people he saw and the physical setting in which he saw them. His position seems to call for Realism, but Altamirano was a Romantic. The best Romantics did indeed write about what they thought they saw, but their reality was not the objective reality of intentional Realism. In Altamirano's own work, his treatment of the countryside and the general atmosphere of small towns is rather objective. There is a gentleness about his description—we might even say it is nostalgia—that creates a rosy hue; but it is not fundamentally changed from what the author saw. What change there is belongs to the process of re-creating. The people in his novels, however, are more romanticized, because Altamirano applies to them his theories of how people should act. He believed that the novel could and should be used for purposes of instruction. What he meant was that the novel could be used to teach the nineteenth-century principles of freedom and order. Small wonder the *maestro* chose not to mention Inclán's *Astucia* in his account of Mexican novels.[7] By following these suggestions, the Mexican novel would establish its own independence from European models.

[7] Huberto Batis mentions this omission in his "Estudio Preliminar" to *Indices de "El Renacimiento"* (Mexico City: Centro de Estudios Literarios, Imprenta Universitaria, 1963), p. 128. Batis' long and carefully done essay is a masterpiece of literary history and criticism. He shows with perfect clarity the position of Altamirano's literary review in its time and in the development of Mexican literature.

Altamirano's first novel, *Julia*, was published in 1867. All of his novels are short, and *Julia* is the shortest of all. As a novelist, Altamirano was not blessed with great inspiration, but he had a keen sense of good taste, of proportion, and of reality as it was seen within the Romantic frame. *Julia* is an unpretentious Romantic love story—or appears to be so—which shows to some extent all the characteristics of the author's later novels. The story is sentimental, but it is not saccharine. It moves smoothly, and though the outcome is not an O. Henry kind of twist, it is not inevitable. The characters have more than a single quality, and they change within the story. The prose is not elegant, but neither is it tiresome. The gist of the story is that a jilted suitor's pride makes him refuse the girl when she has a change of heart. What cannot be made clear in a commentary on the book is the restraint with which Altamirano tells the story. What might have been a series of tragic scenes from the pen of one of his predecessors turns out to be a sensitive love story when written with Altamirano's good taste. The outcome of the story is more acceptable than it would be if we were left with a grief-stricken hero.

The most immediate and obvious literary response to the restoration of the Republic, however, was neither amatory nor *costumbrista*, but historical. In 1868, one or more novels were published by Juan A. Mateos, Vicente Riva Palacio, Enrique de Olavarría y Ferrari, and Manuel Martínez de Castro. They were soon joined by José Tomás de Cuéllar, whose first novel was historical, Pascual Almazán, and Ireneo Paz. José María Ramírez was also present in 1868 with *Una rosa y un harapo*, and the irrepressible Rivera y Río published *Los dramas de Nueva York* in 1869. The historical novel is much more indicative of the temperament of the time than are the other novels, which are similar to earlier works by the same authors. The historical orientation grew out of intensified national awareness which is not surprising at the moment of triumph of the Reform. The novels contain a good deal of interpretation of history by the standards of political liberalism, which was intensified by the militant position of the *puros* (radical liberals) who found themselves in opposition to the more moderate Juárez as soon as the moment of brilliance was achieved. Most of them now turned to Porfirio Díaz as their leader, and a struggle began between the Juárez faction and the Díaz faction, which finally ended in a victory for Díaz who turned out to be anything but a radical liberal.

Juan A. Mateos' first novel was *El cerro de las campanas*. Although it is generally regarded as an historical novel, the classification is hardly justified since the novel, published in 1868, deals with events of the preceding year. The author's purpose, therefore, is not to re-create the atmosphere of a time past, but to express his vehement liberal opinion of the French Intervention and the conservative collaboration. The title of the novel is the name of the site of Maximilian's execution. Mateos' liberalism was radical and absolute. He considered all conservatives scoundrels and most of them traitors. His satire, as in the references to the francophiles who supported Maximilian, is too bitter to be genuinely funny. As for the clergy, he says their support of the Intervention was entirely for selfish reasons. *El cerro de las campanas* is carelessly written and constructed, probably because the author's positive fury made him interested chiefly in laying the opponent low. His extremism affects all aspects of the novel which is woefully melodramatic. But it has been widely read and is perhaps the most popular account of the historical incident.

Mateos' other novel of 1868, *El sol de mayo*, deals with the Reform movement before the Intervention. Its general characteristics are the same as those of *El cerro de las campanas*, though it contains more historical detail. Later Mateos turned to the period of the Independence; and in *Sacerdote y caudillo* (1869) he portrayed Hidalgo as the epitome of all to which the Reformist liberals aspired. From that time until shortly after the fall of Porfirio Díaz, who resigned on May 25, 1911, Mateos continued to write novels that are more or less historical, though he tended to prefer the recent past. His last novel concerns the end of the Díaz period and is called *La majestad caída* (*The Fallen Majesty*).

The declamatory tone of Mateos' novels will disgust the reader unless he tries to understand the nature of the author's liberalism. Mateos was not being senselessly stubborn. The liberal principles that he favored appeared to him to be a clear-cut solution not only to the ills of Mexico, but to the ills of the world. So far as he was concerned, there was absolutely no reason why they should not work, if people would only follow them. They were reasonable and just, and personal gain was the only reason he could see for opposition to them. His anxiety was exaggerated, but hardly more so than Pizarro's. In most of his novels, this same insistent liberalism is apparent; whatever the period, there is a clear distinction made between the conservative forces of evil and the liberal forces of good. Only toward the end of his life was this categorical division modified at all. In some of his later works, *Memorias de un guerrillero* (1897) for example, he has come to believe that certain characteristics of the people—their traditional acceptance of religion, their lack of education—act as hindrances to the programs that would save them. So he recognizes the existence of a vicious circle, and is less inclined to denounce a particular group.

The novels of Vicente Riva Palacio and Enrique de Olavarría y Ferrari, while they are as genuinely historical as those of Mateos, are much less interesting ideologically. In all probability, all three men were attracted to the historical by their awareness of building the nation, but the latter two offer nothing that approaches the verve of Mateos' liberalist judgment. Riva Palacio was a storyteller, and a good one. His best work is a collection of stories called *Cuentos del general* which was published in 1896, though some, perhaps all, of the stories had been written earlier. Each one is interesting for its story value; and although some are old stories in a new setting, they always have a clearly Mexican flavor. The author's desire to contribute to the national literature is fulfilled in the stories rather than in the novels. What happens in the novels is that Riva Palacio's interest in telling a good story got the upper hand and dominated his writing. Removed from a familiar world and transported into a time past, he lost contact with the circumstances that surrounded the action. He does nothing to re-create the atmosphere of the period in which the action presumably takes place, and the only possible interest in the novels is the outcome of an extremely complicated plot.

Olavarría y Ferrari is inferior to Mateos for an entirely different, indeed opposite, reason. He did not know how to tell a story. His first two novels, *El tálamo y la horca* (1868) and *Venganza y remordimiento* (1869), are set in the Colonial Period. The action begins in Spain and moves to Mexico. If one has a taste for hair-raising incidents, they will do quite well, but there is little else to be found in them. Later on, Olavarría wrote a series of *Episodios nacionales mexicanos* which are more valuable than the earlier novels. Even this value, however, is very limited. They hardly deserve to be called novels, because they are collections of data, which Olavarría tried sporadically and unsuccessfully to place in a framework of fiction. Many of his comments on Mexican customs are interesting but they are not always just. Olavarría was born in Spain and spent his early life there. And in spite of his saying that he considered himself Mexican, I find his comments on Mexico colored with a patronizing impatience that makes his protest sound more quarrelsome than patriotic.

Several authors of historical novels took their first steps in fiction at the moment of victory and later on proved their interest in history. Such was the case with Mateos, and even more clearly with Olavarría. It was also true of Ireneo Paz. His first novel, *La piedra del sacrificio,* published in 1871, was probably written in 1866 or 1867. It is a reasonably well constructed novel of the most astounding coincidences and love relationship. The hero, on discovering that his beloved is really his sister, is delighted to rush to her side, having completely accepted the new relationship at the moment he was informed of it. The same romantically improbable sentiments are present in the author's historical fiction. *Amor y suplicio* (1873) and *Doña Marina* (1883) together, are Paz's account of the Conquest. The sympathy of the author toward both sides is the most interesting characteristic of these two novels, and the presentation would be very convincing if the emotional response of the characters were not so exaggerated. Paz suggests something of the importance of the head-on collision of two civilizations, and appears to understand that Mexican reaction to it needed to be deeper than an emotional choice of sides.

Paz's later work is mainly historical and consists, for the most part, of his *Leyendas históricas,* the last of which was published in 1914. He very often had trouble making fiction out of history, and we are likely to find pages of statistics, legal documents, and the like, which don't fit into a novel at all. But in spite of his faults, Paz may be the best historical novelist of his generation. His historical basis appears to be reliable, his judgment is balanced, and his prose is better than most. I personally am fascinated by the exalted liberalism of Mateos, particularly because it is a part of the truth that is not found in a more objective account. However, Mateos' anxiety is sometimes destructive as in the case of his satire; and specifically in this connection he makes a striking contrast with Paz who shows himself capable of amusing satire in *Amor de viejo* (1874), a *costumbrista* story.

The early novels of Mateos, Riva Palacio, and Olavarría may be taken as the basis for a generalization of what the Reformist historical novel was like, if we take into account their variations in expression of political ideology, in historical authenticity, in Romantic exaggeration, and in the extent to which they involve the reader. It seems to me that all of them moved away from Romanticism as they continued writing, and in one way or another modified their extremist view of reality, whether political or sentimental. One of the early indications of a new direction in literature was Manuel Martínez de Castro's *Julia* (1868) which is a curious mixture of historical detail, exaggerated sentimentality, and Naturalist scientism. The historical background is the Northamerican Invasion, and the author deals with it at considerable length, but has difficulty involving his characters in the historical action. Some of them move in and out of it, involved in the military conflict on the one hand and in a complicated love story on the other. The personal lives of the characters are full of duels, seductions, desertions, deceits, and infidelities—they live in a world similar to that of Pantaleón Tovar. Martínez de Castro is even harsher than Tovar in his pessimistic view of human beings, and he is even more willing to disclose what he considered to be the ugly facts. His characters are not controlled by the inexorable force of circumstances as Naturalist creatures are, but they are revealed in a manner that is not at all typical of Romantic novelists who were less inclined to exploit the details of horror. Martínez de Castro continued in the same direction in his later works. *Una hija i una madre* (1875) tells how a husband punished his unfaithful wife by praising her virtue constantly. Another historical novel, *Eva* (1885), places against the background of the French Intervention, two psychological studies: Eva's hate after her rape by a group of soldiers, and her brother's incestuous love.

Even José Tomás de Cuéllar, who is known as a *costumbrista* novelist, began his career with an historical novel, *El pecado del siglo*

(1869). The novel, which is set in eighteenth-century Mexico, has little to recommend it except its attack on false religious values. The author's social position is the same plea for common sense that is apparent from the time of the Independence. Any attack on institutional religion was, of course, a part of the Reform impulse, but Cuéllar's novel is completely overshadowed by Pascual Almazán's *Un hereje y un musulmán* (1870). Within a sixteenth-century Mexican framework, Almazán took a position on religion which was pertinent to his own time. Although he was not entirely successful in combining history with fiction, he did base the action on a religious question, and so was able to incorporate his ideas without making them seem entirely out of place. Stated briefly, the story concerns a Moor who intended to establish first a Moorish colony and later a Moorish empire in Mexico. For a while he was able to use the Inquisition as his tool, but was later destroyed by it. The author uses this plot to describe religious practices of the sixteenth century.

Against the background, Almazán placed his mouthpiece, Doctor Gutherzig, who had been the teacher of one of the characters when he was studying in Europe. Gutherzig is something of a humanist, but he is even more clearly a nineteenth-century liberal. He rejects any kind of authoritarianism in religion, and he dislikes Calvin and Luther just as much as he dislikes Roman authority. His life has seen a steady weakening of his faith, and at the time of the novel, his position is agnostic. He believes in the intellect, without ever suspecting that it too can exercise its own tyranny. From this point of view, only madness can oppose intelligence. Almazán wrote the novel in such a way that Gutherzig's views are directed against the religious position of the sixteenth century. But only a very innocent reader would leave it at that. The novel is probably the most reasonable attack on the power and practices of the Church that the Reform produced.

Quantitatively, the major fictional expression of the Reform was in the historical novel, but the men who were most concerned about the cultivation of the arts in Mexico thought more in terms of a general artistic revival than in terms of specific kinds of literature or the relationship of literature to the Reform movement. Upon the restoration of the Republic, the optimistic, liberal view was that Mexico was entering a brave, new world. Our retrospective view of the restoration as a moment of brilliance naturally would not have been held by the men of that time. Our view informs us that the Reform had passed its highest point by the time the first issue of *El Renacimiento* appeared in January of 1869. The review was the natural outgrowth of the literary activity of the time and especially of the interest generated by the *veladas* in which almost all the writers participated. Altamirano founded the review with the editorial and financial assistance of Gonzalo A. Esteva, and invited the collaboration of all writers regardless of generation or political faith. The name of the review is indicative of the hope and intent of the founder; but the fact that it lasted only one year characterizes it as a fleeting moment of brilliance. The rededication of Altamirano to politics, after he had left it briefly to follow his literary interests, is one manifestation of the disappearance of the certainty that the Reformists had hoped for. *El Renacimiento* was Mexico's most distinguished literary review up to that time, but the fact is that it was the culmination of a period of interest rather than a stimulus to literary production.

El Renacimiento was a source of encouragement to the writers who anticipated it and worked with it, but it provided little stimulus to new writers. In the novel, the men who belonged to the moment of brilliance kept on writing, and a few new and very minor novelists appeared between 1870 and 1874. Then, from 1875 until 1880, no new novelists appeared. Finally, in the last years of the period, Zayas Enríquez, Castera, and Sánchez Mármol published novels, on the brink of Realism and of a period entirely different from the Reform.

El Renacimiento's short life did not give it opportunity to publish much long fiction. The short pieces it published tended to be rather heavy-handed Romantic pieces on the faithful-lover or similar themes. The brightest spots were supplied by the younger Justo Sierra whose prose forecast the coming symbolism. But Sierra tried the novel only once, in the unfinished *El ángel del porvenir*, a kind of joke dreamed up by some of the editors of the review in an attempt to increase circulation.[8] The review's only complete novel is Altamirano's *Clemencia*. In this novel, the author shows his ideal of patriotism through a young officer who sacrifices himself for decency and love. Altamirano

[8] *Ibid.*, pp. 132–133.

uses two contrasting male protagonists, one attractive and the other unattractive, to show that beauty is only skin deep. The revelation of the men within comes as no great surprise to the reader, but the characterizations are made reasonably, and both men live. The story is set in Guadalajara at the time of the French Intervention, and Altamirano provides a good background of different political affiliations, of the human tendency to see what one wants to see, and of social life in the city. The novel has an authentic ring about it, provided by many circumstances, from the novelty of having a Christmas tree to questions of parental authority. Altamirano's background is always more convincing than his story, and he is at his best in describing a rural or small-town setting. Perhaps for this reason, many people prefer *La navidad en las montañas* (1870) or *El Zarco* (finished in 1888, first published in 1901) to *Clemencia*. But it would be a terrible injustice to deny the excellence of *Clemencia* which expresses the ideas of Altamirano as clearly as anything he wrote. The involvement of personal feelings and destinies in the evacuation of Guadalajara is just one of the aspects of the novel that identify the author as the best Mexican novelist up to that time.

Melancholy is the Romantic note in *Clemencia*. The admirable person and the noble act are always surrounded by it. Apparently Altamirano considered suffering a corollary of doing good. He may have felt this way because of his own humble background, or because he was imbued with Romantic pessimism, or because he considered suffering necessary to the implementation of liberal ideas. It is impossible to know precisely what his thinking was, because his melancholy, which pervades the atmosphere, emanates from individuals.

In *La navidad en las montañas*, melancholy is mixed with nostalgia so it is hard to tell one from the other. A Reformist officer meets a priest who leads him to a mountain village where he spends Christmas Eve. The description of the village and its festivities is outstanding. Altamirano captures the simplicity of life and the meaningfulness that the occasion still has in this uncomplicated society. In doing so, he creates an intense yearning for a particular kind of goodness that is usually associated with the past and always with simple living. And he intensifies the feeling by having a love story turn out happily on that particular occasion.

The author's social opinions are more important in this story than they are in *Clemencia*. He takes a position against the military draft that is used to rid a locality of undesirable citizens, he pleads for a more practical education, he regards worship of saints as pagan, and he denounces members of the clergy who are not concerned for the temporal welfare of their people. He is obviously not entirely against religion, but believes that it should have practical benefits, as should everything else. His attitude is a positivistic plea for social progress. This attitude toward the Church is very similar to Pizarro's, but the literary treatment is quite different. Where Pizarro is militantly optimistic, Altamirano prefers melancholy persuasion. He is much more the artist than Pizarro ever was, but this difference is based on Altamirano's greater ability to re-create visible reality, rather than on the difference in tone of the novels.

The small-town background of *El Zarco* is combined with the story of a romantic young girl who elopes with a bandit. Novels of banditry were fairly common in the last quarter of the century when Altamirano wrote his last novel, and amount to a commentary on the state of things in Mexico. The outlaw bands described in these novels were born of the disbanding of liberal and conservative troops who were unable or unwilling to re-establish themselves in society. They dressed colorfully and lived extravagantly, giving rise to romanticized stories that contained a good deal more glamor than fact. Altamirano, of course, was interested in setting the record straight by showing the girl's disillusionment with the coarseness of the group led by her hero. Contrasted with the bandit chief, El Zarco, is the honest village blacksmith, who is the author's idea of an industrious, valuable citizen. It is important that the blacksmith is an Indian, and again Altamirano coincides with Pizarro in his view of a social problem (both writers made Indians valuable citizens by giving them a trade). I think, however, that one important aspect of *El Zarco* is usually overlooked: the blacksmith-bandit contrast in the later novel is the same as the Valle-Flores contrast in *Clemencia*. The social positions are entirely different, but the message is the same: the value of a solid citizen is overshadowed by the glamor of a rascal. Indeed, it is extremely important that Altamirano chose to show this contrast with two very different sets of men, because it minimizes interest in the fact that the blacksmith was an Indian and emphasizes Altamirano's main point. However strongly he may have felt about some specific social issues, Altamirano's hope for society rested on the same belief in common sense that had been expressed by a number of his predecessors. He maintained a position that was more positivistic than some of theirs, but the basis of it was a hope that people could be made to see the folly of human whims. Herein lies the fundamental difference between the Pizarro-Mateos type of liberalism and Altamirano's. The former were so blinded by reason that they thought its victory inevitable. Altamirano's melancholy has its roots in the doubt that colored his hope.

The conservative position against the Reform found relatively little expression in fiction. However, one novel, José María Roa Bárcena's *La quinta modelo* (*The Model Farm*), is as violent a denunciation of liberalism as Mateos ever made against conservatism. The novel serves as an interesting companion piece to Pizarro's novels and their model communities. Roa Bárcena was one of the most highly esteemed conservatives among the literati of the *Renacimiento*. His honesty was deeply respected, and his collaboration valued. As a poet, his taste was Neo-Classic, and the restraint found in some of his short stories is not at all surprising. When these stories are referred to as "realistic," it should be remembered that they are realistic in the sense that *Astucia* and *El Periquillo Sarniento* are realistic, not *Madame Bovary*. They present a variety of known types and they show a relatively calm emotional response on the part of the characters. This quality is the result of the author's restraint, not of any fundamentally different view of reality. In some other stories he is as obviously Romantic as any writer of the period, and *La quinta modelo* is exaggerated beyond the limits of credibility for the purpose of protest.

La quinta modelo was published in a volume of Roa Bárcena's work in 1870. The novel bears the date 1857. The instigator of the experiment which gives the novel its title is Gaspar Rodríguez, a liberal who returns from exile and is elected to the legislature. There he indulges in eloquent and meaningless oratory which the author satirizes with obvious relish. He sends his son to a secular school and the young man turns out to be a menace to society because his values are so distorted. Roa Bárcena believed that moral values could be taught only by the Church, a position which Nicolás Pizarro would have considered totally unreasonable.[9] The model farm is run on democratic principles, but the workers are not capable of accepting the required responsibility. Unlike some liberals who recognized the abyss between the desirable and the practicable, Roa Bárcena apparently saw no hope of ever treating the working class as anything but children. The result of the experiment is utter chaos, expressed in rebellion and the near destruction of the Rodríguez family. The Church, the only adequate authority, intervenes in time to avert complete disaster.

Roa Bárcena's denunciation is so violent it is hard to understand how he could have been accepted by the liberals even as a collaborator on a literary review. The fact that he was so accepted, and that he chose to participate, is descriptive of the nature of the literary effort behind *El Renacimiento*. Literary activity was understood to be an important aspect of the nation's effort, but it was not related to political ideology. And Altamirano's specific plea for a national literature meant *national,* not *nationalistic.* Although he stated some social opinions in his own works, his emphasis was on more basic considerations. He thought that Mexican literature should take its surroundings into account, and at the same time teach a moral lesson; but the fundamental purpose of literature was artistic, not propagandistic.

Of the numerous writers who came under the direct influence of Altamirano, the one who contributed most to the novel was José Tomás de Cuéllar, one of the most restless men of the Reform period. He was soldier (he put down arms forever when he saw three cadet companions die at the battle of Chapultepec during the Northamerican Invasion), poet, novelist, playwright, publisher, artist, photographer, diplomat. His *modus operandi* was to undertake anything that needed to be done at any time. Following his early historical novel, Cuéllar, perhaps influenced by Altamirano's ideas on the national literature, turned to an entirely different kind of fiction. In 1871, he began publication of a series called *La linterna mágica (The Magic*

[9] Pizarro published a *Catequismo del moral* (Mexico City: Imprenta de J. Fuentes y Compañia, 1868), which based morality on common sense, and which the author obviously expected everybody to believe because the truth was so readily apparent.

Lantern). His photographic intentions make him the forerunner of a kind of novel that developed later and in which reality is a cross section of several lives. Cuéllar was too much under the influence of the ball-of-yarn school of nineteenth-century narration to make the best use of his intentions, but his stories are distinguished from others of the time by the fact that the author does not feel compelled to tie up all the action in a neat little package that accounts for each and every one of the characters. In one of the novels of the series, *Las gentes que "son así,"* he attempted a longer and more traditional novel. In it he shows that he had the necessary imagination, but the short novels are clearer and more realistic.

The novels of *La linterna mágica* are properly considered a series, because one differs from the other only on the basis of the direction of Cuéllar's satire. They are similar in style and structure; and although the characters do not always reappear in subsequent novels, they sometimes do, and they could always be known to each other. Characterization is the basis of Cuéllar's fiction, in spite of the fact that he does not develop characters fully. He prefers to see his people from one point of view and to emphasize what he sees. They belong to the same middle class that most nineteenth-century novelists described, but they are seen in a different light when Cuéllar describes them because he seems to be more intimately involved in their affairs and more deeply concerned about what they are really like. He makes fun of them, and reader and author laugh at their folly. But they are entirely too human to be considered ridiculous, and laughter is mixed with sympathy. Indeed, Cuéllar sometimes shows a conflict within his own attitude: he despises and loves his people at the same time. Tragedy is, of course, a very probable outgrowth of folly. And when tragedy comes to one of Cuéllar's people, he is likely to give up his down-to-earth attitude and become overly sentimental in the Romantic manner. Still, in Cuéllar's novels tragedy is different from typical Romantic tragedy, because the cause of it is clearer.

The unity of *La linterna mágica* becomes apparent after the reading of the entire series. We remember the novels not as separate from each other, but as a related commentary on society. If Cuéllar had written the series as a single novel, undoubtedly his protagonist would have been a *pollo*, the irresponsible young man who was Cuéllar's personification of the people's apathy toward common sense. The *pollo* was both victim and cause of social disintegration, and stands as the clearest possible refutation to Mateos' assumption that the people would accept rational organization of society. Cuéllar describes the *pollo* as the victim of loving but impractical parents who are more interested in the child's immediate happiness than in the development of a socially responsible adult. Indeed, it would be impossible for them to be better parents because they have no concept of social responsibility.

Cuéllar would have surrounded the *pollo* with friends of his own kind, and would have been kindly but sharply critical of their extravagant and superficial tastes. They have illicit love affairs, but also think of marriage. Conjugal fidelity is not an important matter for them. They concern themselves with ways and means of making fast money, but have little thought of profession or vocation. Money is not related to future plans, but is desirable for the satisfaction of immediate interests. A careful distinction must be made between the *pollo* and the more sophisticated *calavera* of Díaz Covarrubias, Rivera y Río, and others. The latter is a dandy, utterly unscrupulous, and somewhat sinister. He knows he is doing wrong. The *pollo* is a more innocent type. He thinks what he is doing is perfectly all right. And if he is not a sympathetic character, he at least commands a certain amount of pity. Cuéllar laughs at his escapades, but is also aware of the inherent tragedy.

Cuéllar would have had his protagonist marry when he was young, with parental consent, but without financial resources and probably against the advice of a German friend who would point out the impracticality of the marriage. As a family man, the former *pollo* would seek employment through any possible line of influence, but would not be capable of holding a job. He might even think of the government as a possible source of income; but civic duty would be entirely foreign to him. Lack of money might well cause the young wife to become the mistress of an older man, for Cuéllar does not idealize women. It is possible that the protagonist might discover the infidelity and defend his honor; but it is equally possible that he might choose to ignore his dishonor. The children born of the premature marriage could expect the same upbringing their parents had, and so would

complete the circle. There appears to be no hope in Cuéllar's society
for the kind of communication between governors and governed that
would have made the Reform successful.

The life history of the *pollo* would be placed against an urban background. Cuéllar would probably have introduced two contrasting elements: the young man with a trade, and the values of rural society.
The young man with the trade could be presented in any sub-plot or
as a minor character in the main plot. He would be allied with the
German friend as an example of common sense. However, the role of
these responsible citizens would not be to influence the majority of
society, but to view its follies with disgust and resignation.

The rural element might well have been introduced by reference to
the family of an ex-soldier. It would be appropriate to have him become a bandit. Cuéllar recognized this social phenomenon, and his
satire is effective because the glamor of banditry impressed him about
as favorably as the *pollo's* innocence. He might have then brought the
bandit's family to the city, or he might have chosen another family. In
any case, the contrast would have been made more effective by Cuéllar's placing them in the city because he was not particularly adept
at re-creating a rural atmosphere. The values he would have chosen to
show are family unity, strong parental authority, and interest only
in the most basic necessities of living and getting along together. The
newcomers would be obvious hicks and would be impressed humor-
ously by the confusion of the city. They would be surrounded by
pollos at various stages of development who would be prepared to
exploit them in any possible way. The innate good sense of the country people would probably save them and they would go back home.

The theme of going back home where safety resides is recurrent in
Mexican literature. But it certainly is not a solution to the problem
of how to make the country progress. The less sophisticated society
has a certain kind of common sense; but it is not the same as the
common sense advocated by the Reformists, whose brand of common
sense was supposed to function in a complicated society. The "going-
back" theme is, therefore, reactionary, unless it is used to discover
basic truths that can be applied to a more complicated circumstance.
Cuéllar's view of rural values emphasizes the absurdity of urban society, but it offers very little hope of changing it.

Along with his principal line of action, Cuéllar would have introduced a number of sub-plots so he could work in as many tragically
amusing characters as he desired. Given the taste of his time, he
would then have had to tie up the threads of action; and it is better
that he wrote mostly short novels, because they saved his panorama
from such an artificiality. There remains about his work a certain aspect of improbability which comes mainly from the occasional shock
of exaggerated sentimentality in characters that have decidedly picaresque characteristics. But it also comes in part from the author's
own ambivalence toward his people. He was sufficiently perceptive to
understand that there was little hope of Reformist common sense being accepted widely, and his reaction was a combination of disgust
and sympathy. His work pointed the way for a continued and even
deeper consideration of Mexican reality, but there were only occasional steps in that direction for many years. As Cuéllar wrote, the
Reform impulse was coming to a halt, and the foundation that the
movement had laid served to support a building that it had not
planned.

During the two years when Cuéllar was publishing the first series
of *La linterna mágica,* only three new names appeared in the history
of the novel. One was Ireneo Paz, who took his place among the historical novelists who began writing a few years earlier. Another was
Francisco Sosa, who more properly belongs to the short story than
to the novel. He could well have extended a few of his *leyendas*
into short novels; but even if he had done so, he would have contributed to the novel only through his relatively smooth prose style.
The themes of his stories turn on Romantic love and he was not interested in searching beyond the outcome of the love affair. The third
was Luis G. Ortiz, whose *Angélica* is a perfect example of moribund
Romanticism. Ortiz found his inspiration in the exotic quality of
travel through Europe, disguised royalty, pure love, and faithful servants. The question of whether or not he saw any kind of reality is
beside the point. He was obviously trying to escape reality, even the
reality of dreams, and to hide himself in the exaggerated world of
his imagination.

From 1882 to 1884, the scene is hardly more encouraging. Vicente
Morales and José Negrete published several novels, for the most part

very bad. Two of Morales' novels, *Silveria de Epinay* and *Ernestina,* are set in Europe, for reasons that escape me since it doesn't matter much where Morales places the action. In spite of a declaration by Juan de Dios Peza that Morales was in a position to describe social evils, the fact is that he sees nothing but personal immorality. Later, when Morales set his novels in Mexico, *Gentes de historia* and *Gerardo,* he might as well have kept the setting in Europe. History has very little to do with the first novel in spite of the implication of its title. It is a novel of the type written by Rivera y Río. *Gerardo* intends to show the evil effects of gambling and carries a laudatory introduction by no less a person than Manuel Acuña. The only interesting thing about the novel is that the protagonist is ruined morally, not financially.

The possibilities shown by Negrete are much greater than Morales', but the fact is that he never wrote as well as he might have. Negrete's narrative ability is considerable; but, except for one book, he never showed any interest in writing anything but what he thought would have the greatest and most immediate appeal. The exception, *Memorias de Merolico,* did not appear until 1880, and even this exception promises more than it produces. If Negrete had continued as he started, he might have written a good picaresque novel, but he forgot he had set out to write a novel, and ended up with a series of sketches. The author's powers of observation are sharp; and it is possible that he was an internationally minded man who might have given a different view of Mexican reality by contrasting it with characteristics of other countries. It is pointless, however, to talk of what he might have done. What we have actually is a truncated novel that is interesting in a few places.

The novels which are most pertinent to the circumstances of the Reform were written by José Francisco Sotomayor and Manuel Balbontín, two writers who offer a direct contrast. Sotomayor, a priest, wrote three novels which exalt Christian virtue and propose to counteract the immorality of other novels: *El solitario del Teira* (1873), *Las ruinas del monasterio* (1874), and *Un santuario en el desierto* (1877). The author's obsession is loneliness and ruins. He was influenced by Lamartine and his own desire for monastic seclusion. His obsession is his idea of beauty, and he bases his novels on the goodness that emanates from concentration on the persistence of Christianity. This procedure has an interesting, and certainly unintentional, effect in that it colors the author's devotion with a kind of yearning for things past. And as a result, the feeling is that Christianity was a fine thing in the past but has little relevance to the present. By creating this attitude in his reader, Sotomayor places himself at a disadvantage from the beginning.

All of Sotomayor's novels have historical backgrounds which are not essential to the narrative. The characters are related to historical circumstance only when they are not moving within the plot. As they move out of history and into Sotomayor's story, each one has a terrible problem which is solved by Christian faith, hope, or charity. The author would have agreed with Roa Bárcena that the Church is the only hope for mankind. And he states with complete clarity that the Roman Church is the only church and only religion. On the basis of reason and emotion, Sotomayor's novels must have been anathema to the Reformist intellectuals, but probably were readily accepted by the vast majority of the people.

Manuel Balbontín's *Memorias de un muerto* (1874) uses the device of bringing a dead Reformist soldier back to Earth for the purpose of aiding the liberal cause. It is never quite clear what he does to this end; but the protagonist's peculiar situation enables the author not only to criticize society but also to suggest ways of improving it. The protagonist has the advantage of knowing both Hell, which is very much like Earth, and an ideal civilization. Father Sotomayor would be shocked by some of Balbontín's unorthodox religious ideas; and even though Balbontín's ideal society would be governed by the Golden Rule, the conservative position would have been shocked by his rejection of authoritarianism. The head of his democratic government would be a "guardian of the law," and would be elected for a term of one year without the right to succeed himself. In expressing this opinion, Balbontín reflected the dissatisfaction of the radical liberals with Juárez's insistence on staying in power after the restoration of the Republic. The *memorias* contain many other tidbits: a condemnation of war, a defense of the intelligence of women, a plea for appreciation of native art; but Balbontín's view of the executive is the most important indication of his position. He was a reasonably good novelist, mainly because he knew how to keep the story moving. And the device he used contributes to the book's interest, because it creates an illusion of objectivity that promises the revelation of truth; and the expectation tends to persist, whether it is justified or not.

Dissatisfaction with the government grew, and a number of liberals, Altamirano among them, who had left politics for the cultivation of letters, went back to the struggle, either in politics itself or in political journalism. In November, 1876, Juárez's successor, Lerdo de Tejada, was defeated by Porfirio Díaz, who assumed the executive power under the motto "effective suffrage, no re-election," and proceeded to have himself re-elected every four years from that time until he was removed by the Revolution in 1911, except for a four-year period early in his regime when he allowed one of his adherents to serve under his direction. The Reform was over. The desire for common sense which would have maintained peace and order along with freedom was perverted so that peace and order were maintained at the cost of freedom. The lower classes were pushed even farther away from the life of the nation, and the proponents of order governed "scientifically." Even the apparent peace and order were an illusion, but the government's scientific instruments were not equipped to reveal the ferment beneath the surface.

The effect of the Reform on the novel, an effect which had all but disappeared by 1874, vanished completely, and not one new novelist of any importance appeared between 1875 and 1880. Some of the established novelists continued to write, but even their contributions were few. Without the sensationalist works of Morales and Negrete, the list would be short indeed. In 1881 and 1882, three new novelists appeared, and they belong to this period rather than to a later one because of their association with Romanticism, although their novels indicate that Realism will soon be dominant.

Pedro Castera published two novels in 1882, one tending toward Romanticism and the other toward Realism. The better known is the Romantic one, *Carmen*, which has often been erroneously compared to Jorge Isaacs' *María*. It is a sentimental novel, but it lacks the idyllic quality that the rural setting makes possible in *María*, and its *costumbrista* episodes are fewer and weaker. The most important aspect of *Carmen* is almost always overlooked: the author's interest in scientific analysis. I should emphasize that it was a question of *interest* in scientific analysis, not of successful analysis. The novel's sentimentalism is based on the hero's love for a young girl who regards him partly as father, partly as lover. Castera writes long passages explaining the nature of this love. He is obviously interested in finding out what it is all about. Since Castera's scientific interest was modified by his Romantic subjectivity, his considerations can get fairly sticky, but there is no doubt about what he was trying to do.

His other novel, *Los maduros*, is the first Mexican novel I know of that deals clearly, specifically, and only with the laboring class. The protagonist, Luis, works in a silver mine, and his living conditions are contrasted with the conspicuous luxury of the wealthy who live in the town, but who do not appear as characters in the novel. The humble people come alive both in their actions and their speech. Luis is a completely honorable man, but he is not improbable. He is the victim of an entirely credible set of circumstances that leave him no desirable alternative. The best he can do is seek the least terrible way to meet his responsibilities. Having gotten his hero into this fix, Castera abruptly resolves the problem by having an epidemic wipe out all the people for whom Luis was responsible, except his sweetheart. The happy ending is tacked on probably because the author was too attached to Romantic resolution of the plot to leave Luis in his dilemma.

Remordimiento (1881), the first novel of Rafael de Zayas Enríquez, shows an impulse toward Realism similar to the tendency seen in the novels of Castera; but Zayas never quite made it, not even in his last novel which was published in 1902. He sometimes achieved genuine dramatic effect from the logical development of emotions, but almost always the probability of the story is lessened by his inventing some very unlikely circumstance with which he intended to heighten the dramatic effect. It is best to regard him, along with Castera, as a writer with strong Realist inclinations who was held back by the persistent taste for Romantic exaggeration. Manuel Sánchez Mármol, who published his first novel, *Pocahontas*, in 1882, is the opposite case. He should be regarded as fundamentally Romantic, and he stayed that way in spite of his making a few concessions to the Realism that surrounded him.

By this time, Romanticism had nothing whatsoever to do with the Reform. Romantic exaggeration persisted because the reading public's taste for tears does not die easily. And it was supported by the fact that the natural realism of the Hispanic tradition obscured further the line of demarcation between Romanticism and scientific Realism, which was none too clear at best.

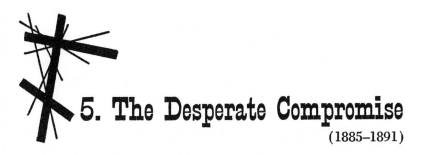

5. The Desperate Compromise
(1885–1891)

It is an apparent paradox that Romantic exaggeration should be related to the hope of social reform. Weeping heroines and fainting heroes appear to have little to do with liberal ideals. Yet the Reformist writers expressed these ideals amidst some of their most sentimentally exaggerated moments, because the tendency to enlarge visible reality through imagination was the basis both of the idealized hero and of the hope of the Reform. The plea for common sense, in itself, was entirely reasonable. It was not a product of the imagination, but of man's consideration of his condition as he saw it. Imagination's role lay in the hope—in some cases, the belief—that common sense, as the liberals understood it, would become the norm of human behavior. As Romantic exaggeration diminished, so did the force of the Reform impulse. In a way, common sense served as its own hangman, because it was an aspect of common sense that informed its advocates of its impracticality. What remained of Romantic exaggeration was mixed with a more objective view of reality, and served not as a social force but as an outlet for the reaction to tragedy. The overstatement of emotion in Martínez de Castro's *Eva* (1885) is objectionable to the sophisticated reader because he has other ways of facing tragedy. In Zayas Enríquez's *Oceánida* (1887) the heroine's insatiable desire for vengeance and her resignation to a religious life are equally improbable. Neither the one nor the other has anything to do with a particular period in history, because the historical rele-

vance of overstatement had vanished. They are intended to satisfy
the requirements of the reader who needs an *obvious* means of facing
tragedy. Life is lived in terms of what we commonly call tragedy,
though perhaps a better term would be "unwanted circumstance."
We are forever facing or avoiding this circumstance, and its happening is the only real event. The consequent anguish, whether of
realization or of anticipation, finds its easiest outlet in an exaggeration of emotional response which, at a certain stage of cultural development, acquires characteristics that appear to be insincere or
trite to people who are not at the same stage. But as long as there is
such a stage, the required response will be reproduced in some kind
of literature. So tears did not disappear with the coming of Realism,
but their significance was modified.

Of course, it is also reasonable to think that novelists who had been
writing earlier would not be very likely to shed all the characteristics
of an earlier period just because a different tendency was in fashion.
Manuel Payno, for example, published another serial novel, *Los bandidos de Río Frío*, from 1889 to 1891. The subtitle even states that
it is "naturalistic," but it has much Romantic overstatement that identifies it with an earlier time. Taking the theme of banditry that had
by that time become very popular, Payno wrote another essentially
costumbrista novel. Payno's understanding of the new kind of fiction
is apparent in a comparison of this, his last novel, with *El fístol del
diablo*. His understanding is limited to incorporating revolting scenes
into the later novel. It would be easy to say that Payno and Zayas
and Martínez de Castro are "novelists of transition." But if we say
so, we must also include Inclán in 1865 and Lizardi in 1816.

What we are dealing with is not a fundamental change in men's
attitude toward life, but a slightly altered view of reality and how to
deal with it. There is no basic conflict between romanticism and realism (it is best for reasons of clarity to use lower-case "r's" here). The
fundamental conflict in literature is between classicism and romanticism, between authoritarianism and individual freedom, between
the general and the particular. Both forces are always present in culture—not just in literature, but in all aspects of life—and their relative intensity varies. At a particular time, one may so overbalance the
other that it identifies a period, in which case it is appropriate to capi-

talize the name, as in the Romantic Period. But the literature of that time contained a great deal of realism (re-creation of visible reality), which is amply evident in Hispanic *costumbrista* prose that existed side by side with the most exaggerated emotional expression. There was no fundamental difference between the two because they were both rooted in individual freedom and insistence on the particular. Their common intent is not altered by the fact that one laughed at man's foolishness while the other exalted his virtues. Both honored man profoundly and looked for his improvement.

The identification of Realism (spelled with a capital) rests on the use of a technique of writing rather than on a fundamental change of outlook. The Realist does, of course, try to restrict himself to visible reality; but what is more important is that he wishes to enhance his objectivity by remaining outside the work. The matter of objectivity, which is often discussed in connection with Realism, is frequently misunderstood and leads to the expectation of some special revelation that comes from the author's superhuman ability to be outside himself. Realist novelists never demanded so much of themselves. They did not intend to enter the novel for the purpose of instructing the reader as to how he should react.

The high incidence of tragedy (unwanted circumstance) in the novels of the Romantic Period is partially an expression of the anxiety that arose from fear that the ideal could not be achieved. When the ideal was abandoned, the reality that remained was visible reality. In Mexico, where visible reality seemed to demand protest on the part of the conscientious writer, it is remarkable that the Realist novelist could make peace with a regime that ignored the needs of the country. Perhaps it was sheer fatigue. The promise of enough social stability to allow the cultivation of letters would be very appealing in a country where the cultivation of the arts had been hampered by social upheaval throughout the national history. However, the position taken by most writers was that the official structure was not in communication with the people, and that social improvement depended on individual improvement. Revolution was regarded as counterproductive, even by such liberal oppositionists as José Ferrel, in *Reproducciones* (1895). It is far less remarkable that more conservative men should have taken a similar position.

The six years with which we are concerned here constitute the period when Realism became the dominant influence in the novel, and the Díaz group established itself as the dominant power in the political life of the country. Speaking in very general terms the vision of the Independence and Reform was forgotten. The "possibility" of incorporating all elements of society into the national life was amended to read "impossibility." The Indian came to be regarded officially as a burden to be borne with the least possible effort. And extraofficially, the working class, far from being ignored, was mercilessly exploited. It is not easy to respect the opinion of an honorable man like José López Portillo y Rojas, who, in *Nieves* (1887), said that the unfortunate would be better off when they wanted to be. But we have to remember that his opinion was based on a common nineteenth-century assumption that individual man could improve himself. The great mistake that is often made is the assumption that the novelists of the Díaz period did not see the need for social improvement. They did, but their attitude had lost the vigor of the Reformists and did not envision the possibility of a social upheaval that would be great enough to change the social structure.

If we consider together all the novels published between 1885 and 1891, inevitably the sharpest impression is of the worst kind of class distinction. The classes are not just sharply distinguished, the damning fact is that the more favored people have utterly no respect for the rights of members of a lower class. The writers disapprove of this fact, but they didn't do much to change it. Undoubtedly the strongest condemnation is Arcadio Zentella's *Perico* (1885). Zentella was an ultraliberal who later expressed strong, if inaccurate, Marxist ideas. In *Perico*, he is concerned with defending the rights of a peon against the brutality of the *hacendado* (hacienda owner). The author uses scenes of unmitigated horror to show that the *hacendado* considers the peons to be certainly no higher than animals, and probably somewhat less estimable. In addition to mistreating him physically, the owner takes Perico's betrothed to work in the house where he intends to use her for his sexual satisfaction. There is no intention on his part of making her his mistress; she is too humble a being to aspire to that status. Perico kills the *hacendado*, and escapes with the girl to another hacienda where they are exploited even more than is usually the case, because they are fugitives. They are finally caught—not by the apathetic defenders of justice but by the *hacendado's* brother—and tried in a court where a man of Perico's social status has absolutely no chance. Everyone regards them as troublemakers from whom society should be protected. One matron even remarks that such people would be less of a nuisance if they were not educated at all. The two lovers escape from prison, and manage to cross the river into another state before they can be caught. This ending, obviously, is no solution to the problem; nor does Zentella mean that exactly the same thing happens in the life of every peon. However, he does mean for Perico to be understood as an exemplary case, even if his resolution of the problem could not serve a similar purpose.

Zentella was an indignant novelist. There is no doubt that his work was a crusade. And I suppose that its bitter denunciation of the existing order may be the reason for its publication in San Juan Bautista, Tabasco, rather than in Mexico City. The Díaz regime never took kindly to such boat-rocking, though official disapproval was more rigid in the middle years of the regime than it was at either end. No novelist of the period expressed himself as vehemently as Zentella, but class distinction is amply apparent in novels by López Portillo y Rojas, Delgado, De Campo, and Eligio Ancona. In *La mestiza* (1891), Ancona based class distinction purely on racial grounds, without paying much attention to the economic differences that complicate the issue in the novels of Zentella and López Portillo. In the works of Delgado and De Campo, class lines are drawn by implication more than by direct description. Their settings are urban, and the circumstances of the characters make clear the prestige or scorn they suffer because of their social position.

López Portillo's *Nieves* (1887) is a close relative, thematically, of *Perico,* but the author's view of the problem is much more typical of the period. It reflects vividly the compromise with conscience made by well-intentioned men, and the reasons with which they justified their position. López Portillo was an honorable traditionalist who saw in the supposed stability of the Díaz regime a means of protecting values that he held dear. Among these were a number of old-fashioned social customs and a set of ethics that required decent behavior and respect for the authority of tradition. This attitude incorporated a de-

fense of the Church, which he regarded more as a moral agent than
as a mystic one. In this respect, his attitude was much like Altamirano's, although his proposals for social reform were more conservative. López Portillo's position shows how the Church was able to
ally itself with the positivism of the Díaz political group, in an alliance
for mutual preservation. There was really nothing unreasonable about
López Portillo's position since it must have appeared to him to be
based on common sense. But we must notice that this common sense
was based primarily on what seemed to be practicable; it excused
society from undertaking what appeared to be impossible.

Nieves is rich in examples of conscience and compromise. Writing
in the first person, López Portillo recalls the weekly payday on the
hacienda. Externally, the scene is similar to payday in Gregorio López
y Fuentes' *Tierra* (1932). However, the description in *Nieves* is not
a protest of injustice; rather, we sense the author's uneasiness beneath
his picture of the happy peasantry. He speaks patronizingly of the
respect shown the *hacendado* by the peons and of their innocent astonishment at seeing so much money.[1] His tone of paternalistic concern indicates that he is trying to convince himself that all is well
in a situation where he knows much is wrong. He does indeed openly
admit that evil exists in the hacienda system. But his protest is directed at certain unjust people, not at the system itself.

Unfortunately, in Mexico, a country of free institutions, where the
little people have been declared free from the tyranny of the great, there
are many landholders who still hold in their possession the ancient rights
of the lord over his servants, as if the latter were still serfs. They
administer justice by their own hand, they subject the unfortunate to
torment in the stocks, they lower their wages, they pay them with corn,
with script, they oblige them to use what the landowner sells them at
prices set by the latter, and heaping injustice upon injustice, they dishonor their daughters or wives, bringing misfortune into the bosom of
the family and into the depths of the peons' hearts.[2]

López Portillo suggests no program for improving the situation, but
he registers no objection when Juan, Nieves' betrothed, takes ven-

[1] *Nieves*, in *Cuentos completos* (Guadalajara: Ediciones I.T.G., 1952), p. 12.
[2] *Ibid.*, p. 23.

geance on the offending *hacendado*. Don Santos, who is the author's example of the evil *hacendado*, is determined to take advantage of Nieves' inferior position; and when the author tries to dissuade him, he replies that Nieves was born to an inevitable life of misfortune. The author tries to tell Don Santos that he should be concerned for the improvement of the girl's condition; but the *hacendado* is so far from understanding that point of view he can only accuse the author of being jealous.In this conversation, López Portillo seems to be taking a position against his own argument that progress can be made on an individual basis, but he continued to maintain the position even in his last novel, *Fuertes y débiles* (1919). We may assume that the role of the Church was to show Don Santos the difference between right and wrong. An exemplary priest is present in *Nieves* as well as in other works of López Portillo.

The author's insistence on the particular case applies to the evaluation of the peons as well as the *hacendados*. Nieves and Juan are admirable people, but many of the peons are not. Petra and Analco, who are presumably responsible for Nieves' welfare, are censured for their immorality and for their obsequiousness toward Don Santos. Still it is difficult to see how else they might have acted, in view of the author's description of the evil *hacendado*. It is clear from the description of Don Santos that if his peons had become unruly, they could have been saved by the Church only if the good priest had been ubiquitous. López Portillo asks himself why some people seem to be born to misfortune, which suggests a particular interpretation of the meaning of Christianity. He is distressed by poverty, but believes that its presence is caused by the lack of ambition or will.

The misery in which the country people live is truly astonishing. They work without respite, they have little to eat, they go about nearly naked, and have neither necessities nor pleasures except those of animals.

Necessity has fostered progress; where there is no need, there is no stimulus, or improvement, or civilized life. Our workers will come out of the abject condition in which they are vegetating when they aspire to eat well, to dress decently, and to acquire the comforts of life. As their moral level rises, the republic's will rise with it.[3]

[3] *Ibid.*, p. 41.

At the end of this quotation, López Portillo expresses an idea that is most unusual for that time: that the nation's progress was related to the improvement of the lower class. The more common tendency was to regard the middle class as the hope of the future.

Even the concern for the relevance of the law to the life of the people was based on the middle class rather than the most humble people. Representatives of the civic structure were members of the middle class, but their adherence to the government was representative of professional allegiance rather than class allegiance. The middle class in general did not identify itself with the governing structure. The novels of the period demonstrate an almost complete lack of understanding, on the part of the middle class in general, of what the Reform had intended. The main point of Emilio Rabasa's novels was precisely this abyss that yawned between the intent of the law and the requirements of the people. In his four *Novelas mexicanas* (1887–1888), he spelled out the problem, and then brought it to a concise climax in *La guerra de tres años* (1891).

Social problems would not likely be resolved by the nation's politicians, as they were seen by Rabasa, because they were at worst opportunistic in their outlook, and at best were involved in ideologies that had no practical application. *La guerra de tres años* illustrates the difficulty by describing the conflict between a politician who wishes to enforce the Reform Laws and a town that wishes to maintain its traditional religious practices. The author has the good sense not to draw a firm line between two diametrically opposed forces, so the novel shows varying degrees of liberalism, and different attitudes toward the conflict. But the town is not in accord with the law; and the will of some of the townspeople is strengthened by the apathy of others, since apathy tends to support established custom rather than reform. The politician is removed from the town and sent to another place by his superiors who know that his obstinacy will accomplish nothing.

The *Novelas mexicanas* are four rather short novels that deal with four different aspects of public life. *La bola* and *La gran ciencia* were published in 1887, *El cuarto poder* and *Moneda falsa* in 1888. The word *"bola"* is used to refer to a local political skirmish in which an ambitious politician establishes himself as the local boss. Property is damaged, lives are lost or endangered, and the only result is that one man has increased his power over other people. The bandits that are described in several novels of the late nineteenth century might become involved on one or both sides of a *bola*. Such a political procedure was clearly antagonistic to the law, and did not encourage confidence in the winner as a representative of established authority. It was, however, what the novelists of the Díaz period understood "revolution" to be, and they saw nothing to be gained by it. Rabasa is effectively satirical in *La bola*, emphasizing the meaninglessness of the struggle by laughing at the provincial isolation of the town where it takes place. Although the people of the town have some sense of belonging to the nation, its seat of government is far removed from them; and although their customs are somewhat related to those of the larger world, they are content in their old-fashioned and makeshift interpretation of how things are done. The *bola* has significance for them only on a local level, just as the "revolution" in *Nieves* serves only as a means of escape for Juan.

When the local political boss calls on the people to defend the town against "revolutionaries," in *Nieves*, a voice from the crowd informs him that the defense of the town is the responsibility of the authorities, not of the people. The anonymous voice also says that the people defended themselves earlier against the bandit Lozada because he would have killed them, not because of any particular political belief. López Portillo says the voice expresses a minority opinion when it says, "The truth is, we don't care much whether Dick or Tom gives the orders, so long as we enjoy our security, and we don't have much interest in running the risk of getting killed defending the government—let the government defend itself any way it can, if it can."[4] We cannot help being suspicious of the author's statement that this is a minority opinion, since it would serve no apparent purpose if it were. It is far more likely that López Portillo's sense of propriety made him wish it were a minority opinion, but that his sense of reality, as a novelist, made him reflect the same condition that Rabasa describes. The concern of the people was for their own interests, and on this point they were in closest communication with the politicians.

[4] *Ibid.*, p. 85.

There is no doubt that López Portillo, on the intellectual level, understood revolutionary action to be anti-social. Yet it is extremely significant that it provided the only possible salvation for Juan, one of the characters whom he defends. The author does not condemn Juan for administering his own personal form of justice, nor does he condemn the authorities for putting him in jail. Yet he lets the "revolution" free him, and regrets that Juan's only chance for freedom is to join the revolutionary band.

Not surprisingly, the *bolas* took place in the more isolated sections of the country. In the city, social disorganization and even class lines were seen in a different way. The city had no specific institution quite as vulnerable as the hacienda system, but the characters of the novels are held as rigidly within their circumstances as are their rural counterparts. In some of the urban fiction, the possibility of genuine revolution is seen more clearly than in the rural novels. Angel de Campo's *La Rumba* (1890), for example, without any reference to revolution, shows a segment of society which must necessarily be the spawning ground of social upheaval. The rigidity of the society feeds discontent. And, although De Campo never speaks of revolt, his description of the people is characterized by a persistent, detailed examination of their condition that is more deeply convincing than an obvious argument. A similar insistence is present in "Vendía cerillos," one of the stories from Federico Gamboa's first book, *Del natural* (1889). Running entirely contrary to the proposition that the individual can improve his situation, Gamboa describes a protagonist whose improvement could be effected only by a change in the circumstances that surround him.

Society in the provincial cities of Rafael Delgado's novels is somewhere between the complicated society of De Campo and the small-town isolation of *La bola*. In *La Calandria* (1890), Delgado borders on the lower class, but he never quite leaves the middle class. When these people suffer at the hands of the wealthy or the sophisticated, their reaction resembles envy rather than resentment. They are brothers in misfortune of the middle class of Juan Díaz Covarrubias. The heroine's wish for a more exciting life is the only attempt by any character to change his status, and the author describes her as the victim of her own folly. Delgado was much more conservative than either López Portillo or Rabasa, because he never suggests that there is anything wrong with society. He judges people on the basis of their morality, but always in terms of the existing social circumstances. Society is static and complacent. It is hard to imagine an attitude that would be more in keeping with the interests of the Díaz group.

Active politicians were not inclined to bridge the gap between the law and the people. Their opportunism is the point of criticism in Rabasa's *La gran ciencia.* The "science" is the ability to stay in power. Rabasa's view may be slightly more cynical than the general attitude, but its basis is the same. Political activity is a way to make a living, and the politician's concern must be with methods of promoting himself. He cannot stand still, and he must be sharp enough to use all the people around him for his own purposes. The cultivation of the right people is, therefore, more important than the welfare of the public or the exercise of justice. Zentella was particularly insistent on the latter point as it applied to peons, and López Portillo took a similar position.

One of the more interesting aspects of Rabasa's novels is the complicated motivation of Juan Quiñones, who appears in all four of the *Novelas mexicanas* along with Mateo Cabezudo, the politician. Quiñones is never above trickery, but he also possesses a streak of idealism. However, in his struggle with Cabezudo, neither trickery nor idealism will win for him. His animosity toward Cabezudo is sharpened by the latter's disapproval of Quiñones' love for Cabezudo's niece; and finally Quiñones finds himself in a position of some power as a newspaperman in the capital where his enemy is a member of the national congress. In *El cuarto poder,* Rabasa attacks the press with some of his heaviest irony. He pulls the rug from under the profession by having Quiñones discover that much of the "news" is invented by the newspapermen for personal reasons or simply for the purpose of attracting readers. Therefore, Quiñones feels perfectly free to attack his enemy even though the main reason for the attack is personal animosity. The political complexion of a newspaper depends on the will of its supporters; all are susceptible to official influence. Quiñones' newspaper takes an oppositionist position because official support is withdrawn; but given the proper circumstances, it starts to support the government again. The two-faced nature of journalism is shown by the case of an oppositionist paper that is secretly supported by another paper of the opposite persuasion. What little idealism Quiñones has left is destroyed, though not without his own assistance.

The politician and the journalist manage to destroy each other in spite of the momentary success that each enjoys in the large and complicated world of the capital. The author, in *Moneda falsa*, faces them with the possibility of a common personal tragedy, at which point they decide to go back where they belong—the *moneda falsa* (counterfeit money) returns to its point of origin. It is not quite clear why Rabasa thought they ought to return, though presumably it was because their careers had been destroyed. Certainly they had been anything but a blessing to their home town; and if they had changed in any way, it must have been to assume that provincials should not venture forth from their isolation. However, the general tendency of Rabasa's criticism was against dishonesty in the middle class. As he saw it, the world would function well if the middle class could be improved. In such a situation, Quiñones and Cabezudo could serve adequately and not become the victims of others or of themselves. He was, in other words, advocating the same kind of morality that Altamirano had thought the novel should teach. This kind of morality would improve the society without changing its basic structure. The possibility of fundamental social change is implicit in Rabasa's works only if one assumes that the changes he recommends are impossible without social upheaval.

Although Rabasa was unusual in his attack on the press, his general message is essentially the same as that of other novelists who were writing at the same time. The picture they present during the early Díaz period is one of intense dissatisfaction, if we except Delgado's holier-than-thou smugness. Politics was personalistic, journalism a farce, class lines inhumanly rigid, workers exploited, justice for the humble nonexistent. The generous assumption by López Portillo that injustice was the exception rather than the rule does not jibe with its prominent place in the novel of the time, including his own work. In many ways, the world they describe is the same as the network of conspiracies that Manuel Payno saw, and we are impressed by how man's vision changes while the facts remain the same. Still, in spite of the fact that the new novelists did not in any case recommend change by force, their books are far more convincing than the works of the preceding generation, because the techniques and attitudes of Realism and Naturalism breathed life into visible reality.

The new tendencies in literature were inclined to place the novelists in conflict with the complacency of their society. We have seen, however, that in Mexico the novelists suffered a certain ambivalence: they saw social ills, but at the same time wanted to preserve social stability. Therefore, they modified the new influences that tended to place them in a position directly opposed to existing social circumstances. We cannot understand their novels unless we accept a certain amount of Romantic sentimentality along with a basically Realist approach, and remember that Realism and Naturalism were terms used interchangeably in Mexico. It is also desirable to examine the nature of the change in fiction, rather than evaluate each novel's degree of adherence to a literary definition.

As for Romantic sentimentality, it is present to some extent in the works of all the novelists of the period, for reasons that have already been discussed. And its presence is hardly surprising in a society where José Rafael Guadalajara's *Sara: Páginas de un primer amor* (1891) offered the reading public a series of juvenile love letters whose single characteristic is "sensitivity." Even Rabasa's heroine, Remedios, is a frail creature in spite of his unkind comments about sickly Romantic heroines. Zentella's Perico may be somewhat improbable in the conflict presented by the knowledge that the *hacendado* is his real father. But the degree of *probability* seems to me to be more appropriately a question for sociologists and psychologists than for artists. Delgado argued that sensitivity was a part of reality and refused to regard it as inappropriate to Realist-Naturalist fiction. I suspect the crux of the matter is whether the effect of Romantic exaggeration alters the author's intent. In the case of Remedios, for example, it certainly did not, because the character has nothing to do with the failures that are the main point of the novel. In the case of Perico, on the other hand, the resolution of the conflict could alter the course of the novel, and the reader must decide for himself whether or not Zentella offered the more probable resolution. But it is hardly within the province of the average reader to decide whether or not the author was re-creating reality as he saw it.

In general, Mexican writers accepted Realism-Naturalism with certain reservations concerning what they considered to be in good taste and what they considered to be the whole of reality. Realism-Naturalism seemed to them to eliminate a spiritual element that they considered an essential part of reality. Many people have observed that such a point of view was related to traditional religious ideas; but the fact is that the basis of the objection was as humanistic as it was religious. The matter of good taste had a similar basis. Mexican writers believed that the methods of Realism-Naturalism could produce the opposite of reality,[5] by confining the novelist to the treatment of visible circumstances, and by making life appear to be more horrible than it really was. They did not react against the new kind of fiction in a categorical way; rather, they used what they wanted of it, amending the methods of their French masters to suit their own ends.

For reasons which are not at all clear to me, many literary critics and historians enjoy being tyrannized by their own definitions, and feel compelled to set up some kind of standard for Realism and Naturalism by which novelists may be measured. In this way we can show that López Portillo was not a genuine Realist because he enters his work to explain a position, or that Gamboa is not a genuine Naturalist because of certain redemptive forces in his works. These measurements seem to me to obscure the function of the novelist. Saying that Gamboa is not a Naturalist is like saying a lamp is not a piece of furniture because you can't sit in it. The importance of Realism and Naturalism cannot be confined to the adherence of fiction to a particular standard. What really matters is how the new ideas in the novel made writers look at the world they sought to re-create.

The realism of Emilio Rabasa is by far the most "native" of all the novelists of the period. He is much more clearly related to the *costumbrista* realism of Cuéllar and Lizardi than to any of the novelists of intentional Realism. Rabasa is less inclined toward explanatory

[5] The position of Mexican writers is discussed at some length in my article, "The Mexican Understanding of Realism and Naturalism," *Hispania*, XLIII, 4 (December 1960).

digressions than Lizardi, or even Cuéllar; and in this respect, his
novels probably show the influence of French Realism. But the author is indeed present in causing both action and characters to express his ideas. He makes them and breaks them with the assurance
of a man who knows what he wants to accomplish. In some cases like
Quiñones and Cabezudo, Rabasa's character development is detailed
and complicated; but other characters are brought in, already formed,
for a specific purpose, and dropped after that purpose has been served.

The small town that Rabasa chose as the scene of *La bola* and,
indeed, as the essential background for his series of novels, is characterized by anonymity but not by objectivity. The isolation of the
town, both geographical and cultural, is needed for the development
of the two main characters. The description of its customs, its small-
mindedness, its attempt to stage a grand celebration, all contribute
to the feeling that the town does not have the resources needed to
make it what it wants to be. Rabasa's setting is not lifted specifically
from visible reality, though there is no doubt that the town's characteristics are probable enough. It is a town created by the author to
serve his novelistic purpose, and its identity is more general than
any specific town could be. The presentation of the town is as subjective as the description of its individual inhabitants.

Toward the setting of the novel and toward the characters, Rabasa's
attitude is patronizing although humorous. He understood that the
people and their circumstances were something less than ideal for the
good of the nation. But his work is not a studied crusade for improvement. It is primarily critical, and the manifestation of his critical
attitude is the picaresque tone in which he wrapped his disapproval
of corruption and personalism in politics and in journalism. Rabasa
appears to be asking whether anything can be done about such a
hopeless situation. The basis of this effect is a casual style that exploits
common speech and makes the novels sound very Mexican and, therefore, very real. Juan Quiñones says, "*Yo tenía veinte años, una novia
que me requemaba la sangre, y un trajecillo flamante . . .*"[6] The sense
of this nearly untranslatable sentence is that the speaker is recalling
a time when he was twenty years old, had a girl friend that set him

[6] *La bola y La gran ciencia* (Mexico City: Porrúa, 1948), pp. 3–4.

afire, and owned a flashy suit of which he was very proud. Several linguistic elements give the sentence special meaning. The verb *"tenía"* (I had) expresses possession of the twenty years, the sweetheart, and the suit. The prefix *"re"* in *"me requemaba la sangre"* adds humorous intensity to the idea that Quiñones' sweetheart "burned his blood." The diminutive suffix on *"traje"* (suit) expresses the owner's particular pride in it. *"Flamante"* is something like "flashy," used to describe a new car, for example, and in Quiñones' statement implies sartorial splendor beneath his present state of sophistication. Rabasa enhances the humorous reaction by selecting and enumerating these three possessions as if they were inextricably related to each other, although they are three entirely different kinds of possessions.

With Quiñones' description of himself, Rabasa established the basis for his characterization which is quite complicated. But we must not let the intricacy of the Quiñones characterization obscure a fundamental quality: at the very beginning, the author creates a revolving-door identification between the reader and Quiñones, a relationship which the reader can enter or leave as he pleases. The generalization of active and impatient youth in Quiñones is intended to evoke memories of similar times in the reader; but the tone is sufficiently scornful to allow the reader to withdraw from the relationship and look down on the young man. The quality of this relationship seems to me to be a fair example of what happens to the reader's—and the author's—commitment throughout Rabasa's novels. We can participate in the author's concern for the wrong he sees, or we can withdraw from the circumstance and see the wrong as funny or hopeless, or both.

Rabasa's procedure as a novelist began with a clear idea of what was wrong with society. And this idea was bolstered by the conviction that improvement of the middle class was the great promise for the country. The lower class really has no role in Rabasa's work. He then set out to expose the evil that he saw. But his method was far from a hard-driving re-creation of visible reality. Rather, he chose to select detail and distort visible reality so it would come out as a picture of life viewed subjectively. The often humorous result does not mean that Rabasa was a frivolous novelist. Indeed, beneath the humor, there is a very somber picture. Possibly the author's tone indicates some doubt on his part as to whether the situation could be improved. He certainly does not compel his reader to pay attention to the problem. Any reader who opposed the suggested reforms could support his own point of view simply by taking a round-trip through the author's revolving door. His consequent position would be a conservative one with a pessimistic view of the people's ability to participate in public life.

The similarity between Rabasa and Cuéllar is particularly apparent if we consider the pieces that Cuéllar wrote during this later period: *Baile y cochino* in 1886, and *Los fuereños y la nochebuena* in 1890. In these works Cuéllar gave up the attempt to weave his observation of middle-class life into an intricate plot. Stripped of improbable coincidences, his sketches are much more realistic. Like Rabasa's stories, they tend to suffer from the ambivalence of satire, and they are developed on the basis of the problem rather than on the basis of the people. In *Los fuereños* we find the idea of rural people returning to their first environment, which is also the outcome of Rabasa's *Novelas mexicanas*. In Cuéllar's story, the outcome has nothing to do with public life; and this fact makes the two books complementary rather than opposite, because the two authors together are saying that simple people cannot adapt to any aspect of sophisticated society.

The novelistic procedure of José López Portillo y Rojas was entirely different from Rabasa's: rather than use characters to demonstrate a given problem, López Portillo began with people in whom the problem became evident. His writing is sober and careful. As in the case of Rabasa, Realism freed López Portillo from the need to develop an intricate plot, so what happens in his work is entirely possible, though we may question his interpretation of the hacienda system. His great difficulty as a novelist was that he never found a way of expressing his objections to social evils without generalizing those evils in a way that he did not believe to be realistic. The only way he could balance the generalization was to enter the novel and explain. *Nieves* contains numerous intrusions through which the author explains that while injustice is all too common, it should be understood as the exception rather than the rule. This kind of intrusion, however, is a very different thing from the intrusion of the Romantic novelist. López Portillo does not instruct the reader as to how he should react. Nor does he really digress from the main point. Rather, his entrances into the work are intended to explain further a circumstance that could not be presented clearly in the story itself.

The effect of López Portillo's intrusions is fairly apparent: they distract the reader from the thread of action, but not disagreeably so. Without them, *Nieves* would be a strong condemnation of the social structure, which is not what the author intended. In his second novel, *La parcela* (1898), López Portillo is less inclined to enter the book; but his criticism of society is correspondingly less apparent. It had to be that way, or he would have misstated his case. A person who reads *La parcela* without reading *Nieves* and *Fuertes y débiles* (1919) will grossly misinterpret the social position of the author and probably assume that he regarded the society of his time as close to the ideal. The negative side is present in *La parcela,* but emphasis is on the positive. Its generalization was, therefore, more acceptable to the author than a negative generalization would have been; but the point is that no generalization could have been entirely satisfactory for López Portillo, since reality for him was not generalized.

López Portillo's novels are based on people rather than on principle because such was the nature of his concern. Yet his characters are not quite independent of their creator. Once the problem has presented itself in the life of the character, the author is inclined to deal with the character in such a way that the problem will be emphasized. As the story of Nieves unfolds, she becomes a little more honorable than we might have expected her to be at the beginning. But López Portillo did not intend to make her an exemplary case; the slight idealization is the natural outgrowth of his interest in describing a worthy individual.

Arcadio Zentella's Perico is, like Nieves, a flesh-and-blood person who captures the author's sympathy and then serves as an example of the author's complaint. The difference in the two authors' views of reality rests on the question of generalization of the accusation of society. There is not the slightest doubt that Zentella, unlike López Portillo, intended to make a general accusation, so his use of fiction is quite different. Zentella sees his character as the victim of circumstances that stand between him and happiness, even between him and a decent human existence. No action on the part of Perico can save him from the vortex of tragedy that he is sucked into. Zentella informs the reader of this situation by careful analysis of Perico's reactions and by vivid description of the inhuman treatment of the peons. He is a Naturalist; and even though he uses a contrived, individualized ending, the force of the novel depends on the use of Naturalist techniques.

Some effects of Realism-Naturalism are apparent in a number of novels without having any real importance except with regard to the dates and extent of French influence in Mexican fiction. The horrifying scenes of Payno, the abnormal psychology of Martínez de Castro, the study of vengeance in Zayas Enríquez, all are interesting as steps in the development of the Mexican novel. But we feel, on reading these novels, that the new techniques are not quite understood, that they are used as tricks to attract the reader, rather than as a means of seeing reality. And I suspect that a similar opinion might be expressed of Federico Gamboa if only his earliest work were considered, and even of Angel de Campo.

Gamboa's *Del natural* (1889) is a collection of short stories which represents his entry into fiction. His later work gives a much more complete view of the author's reality, but the Naturalist basis of the first work is important to an understanding of how these several authors saw their world. "Vendía cerillos" is perhaps the most typical of the stories. Its protagonist is kept from becoming the person he wants to be, by a series of circumstances quite beyond his control. His suicide at the age of fifteen seems improbable to some readers. I can think of few acts more likely than the suicide of a boy who is effectively dead already, since he is separated from all apparent means of self-realization.

"Vendía cerillos" is typical of Gamboa's later work also in its portrayal of a sentimental hero. These heroes are romantically sensitive and, in the opinion of some readers, keep Gamboa from being a Naturalist. Such an attitude is all right if one wishes to toy with words. What is important is not whether you call Gamboa a Naturalist or don't call him a Naturalist, but the fact that he saw, as a part of reality, a number of people who could not be what their wills would have made them. It matters little whether they were sentimental or not. The pessimism of this view limits the possibility of individual improvement and even casts doubt on the efficacy of fundamental social change.

Angel de Campo, like Gamboa, dealt with life in the city; and in both novelists, we find a new presentation of the world of Díaz Covarrubias and Pantaleón Tovar. Gamboa and De Campo went deeper into the lower class and discovered a group of people effectively cut off from full social participation. De Campo's technique was to restrict his novel to a particular neighborhood and to examine it carefully and intimately. *La Rumba* has an air of authenticity that can come only from an author's knowing whereof he speaks. He is lovingly satirical, gently indignant. Although he is capable of laughing at his characters, he is never against them. He reveals them through his intimate knowledge of them, and he suggests through the same use of detail, that they are a potentially explosive force. *La Rumba* comes closer to having a collective protagonist than any other novel of the period. The reality that De Campo saw was the visible daily life of insignificant people. But to him this life was very meaningful, and he leaves his reader with an impression of the neighborhood rather than of individuals.

Rafael Delgado shows something of the same interest in detail in his description of life in a provincial city. The effect of his novel is quite different from De Campo's because he created an atmosphere of dull complacency as contrasted with the potential explosiveness of De Campo's world. We may speculate that both authors re-created accurately what they saw, and that the difference in effect is a reflection of the difference between life in a modest neighborhood of a large city and life in a provincial town. But I think that the complacency in Delgado's fiction reflects the attitude of the author primarily, and we may speculate on the extent to which this attitude may be an indicator of the nature of the town.

Delgado selected a protagonist who serves as a contrast to the customs of the town. We might expect the author to complain about the stifling atmosphere. But what he does in fact is to warn against any attempt to disturb the way things ought to be done. In *La Calandria*, the background to the main action is convincing enough as a picture of small-town life. But against this background, the characters that move the story are stereotypes of good, evil, and folly. The heroine's vivaciousness makes her something of a nonconformist. Quite innocently, she yearns for a more exciting life than the humdrum town affords. She finds it, and with it tragedy. Although the reader would like to sympathize with her, she is such an artificial creature it is difficult not to despise her. Delgado is very clearly saying that anyone who does not act as nice people ought to act will surely get his come-uppance.

Delgado objected more strongly than the other novelists to the influence of Realism-Naturalism. Undoubtedly it constituted a threat to the nice, stable world of middle-class convention that he thought was real. The idea that ugliness might exist in this world was abhorrent to him; and within his novels he uses ugliness as a kind of threat to his characters in case they should misbehave. Although the new tendencies in fiction enabled him to describe the social background with a fair degree of objectivity, he really did not understand the rigorous examination that they proposed. Therefore, he insisted on a kind of idealization of characters that preserved the decorum of a world he was afraid to destroy.

Looking at the changes in the Mexican novel during the years when Realism-Naturalism became established, perhaps the most outstanding is that the novelists got outside the capital city, something which had rarely happened in earlier years. They understood that the re-creation of Mexican reality—even if it were limited to visible reality—must include the whole country. Then, separated from the cosmopolitanism of the city, life in the novels took on characteristics that were particularly Mexican. The exploitation of these characteristics was entirely possible within the *costumbrista* tradition, even without the influence of the objectivity and analysis of French fiction. But the latter was not ignored, and it contributed to the formation of a literary mood that produced a considerable amount of social protest. The protest was indeed not in accord with the general tendency to ignore problems that could not be solved easily. And for the most part, the very novelists who saw the problems sought justifications for ignoring them. We may regard this attitude as cynical if we wish;

but we are also obliged to see it as the product of that desperation that emphasizes the possible at the expense of the desirable. The world that this mood produced was artificial, because it saw reality and denied reality at the same time. And for some years after, it was much easier to keep on the same path than it was to change course.

6. A Certain Elegance
(1892–1906)

The years of the "establishment" were elegant years, a period of splendor, of prosperity, of security, of apparent progress. Porfirio Díaz and his group of *científicos* reigned supreme, giving Mexico the outward appearance of a modern nation. They controlled the army (even used it as a safe place for malcontents), increased the national income, stabilized the economy, and imposed a system of law enforcement that administered summary justice to any who proposed upsetting the peace and order that were the official goal. Bandits, strikers, and occasional rebellious Indians were a constant denial of the reality of the "porfirian peace"; but they were held in check and, insofar as possible, their activities were hidden from the orderly elements of society. These were the years of stability, and not much attention was paid to the inevitable question of the presidential succession.

The improved economy was beneficial to perhaps a fourth of the nation; the remainder lived in circumstances that were several centuries behind the rest of the country. But if satisfaction was the state of the wealthy, resignation was the state of the poor, who were assured by the Church that they would be rewarded later. Human dignity was the birthright of a few. There was no longer just an abyss between the people and the law, there was a wall between the society and those who did not belong. The civic structure had relevance only for the fortunate; for the rest, authority was the paternalism of the master.

Somewhere, far away, there was a Don Porfirio whose eminence made thousands of peons his namesake (in Gregorio López y Fuentes' *Tierra*, the many Porfirios are identified by nicknames), but he belonged to a different world. If from time to time, a peon wondered why he had no land, or opportunity before the law, or freedom to choose his employer, he was likely to be silenced by custom or by his neighbors. And if he did not remain silent, there was always the army, or worse.

The hacienda was the scene of elaborate fiestas for the master's friends from the city, and the peons could look on and enjoy a handout that would get them drunk. In the city, the rich built great town houses along Reforma and Londres and Liverpool and other fashionable streets—houses that were comparable to their counterparts in Europe. Indeed, many were little bits of France, placed in Mexico to prove that the country was a land of cosmopolitan sophisticates. Turrets, stained glass windows, designs in brick, mansard roofs, great courtyards, servants' quarters that look like small hotels, luxurious decoration emphasized the superficiality of an already limited reality. Gentlemen stood in the doorway of the "Jockey Club"—now Sanborn's House of Tiles—and watched the elegant ladies pass in their carriages. Great balls were held in great rooms under great chandeliers. And the beggars on the streets were considered a disgrace, but not much was done about them.

The regime was respected both inside and outside Mexico. Even those who saw the festering sores of the society were disinclined to blame them on the regime. After all, it was the regime that had brought progress and order, and the opportunity for Mexico to enjoy a cultural life it had never known. The progress that the nation enjoyed, partial though it was, represented a step toward maturity; and this maturity was strangely married to conservative traditionalism in art as well as in the civic life of the country. It is as if Mexico wanted to move ahead while holding on to its past, thinking that any other way would lead to disaster.

As late as 1902 a new edition of Florencio M. del Castillo's *Hermana de los ángeles* appeared. And in 1900 Aurelio Luis Gallardo's *Adah, o el amor de un ángel* was published for the first time, though it had been written more than thirty years earlier. These two novels are so obviously Romantic and old-fashioned that they appear to be entirely out of keeping with the time. Yet neither novel was good enough or old enough to have been published for its antiquarian charm. The only possible reason for their publication is that the public still nourished a taste for Romantic sensitivity, and probably found a considerable amount of personal comfort in stories where happiness and tragedy were limited to individual experience, and neither promised nor threatened anything outside the novel.

These two novels by no means stand alone. Altamirano's *El Zarco*, though written many years earlier, was not published until 1901. The simple moralization of this novel, if the factor of race is left aside, could be very acceptable in a society that placed a high premium on conformity with custom. The position of Altamirano, superficially considered, is not very different from that of some later writers, particularly López Portillo as he expressed himself in *La parcela* (1898). The general effect was to create the impression of stability, to give the feeling of tradition deeply rooted in history. In this way the reader was assured that his support of an orderly society was justified.

Both history and legend were capable of contributing to stability because they offered material either for the evocation of the good old days or for the assurance that the years of uncertainty were past. In a society where reality was compromised for practical purposes, almost any interpretation of past, present, or future was possible. And there is no doubt that some of the old liberals who continued writing had lost much of their fire. Even Juan A. Mateos came to an agreement with the semireality of the period. He no longer believed that human perversity was the only obstacle to the realization of liberal principles. The practical questions of administration became apparent to him; and although he did not exactly change position, his protest was muted. In any case, his historical novels could always be read with the accent on patriotism rather than liberalism. And indeed, there never was any objection to giving lip-service to liberalism, provided no one rocked the boat. Even Don Porfirio himself claimed to be a man of the Reform, though in practice he used only those parts of the law that suited his purposes. Another historical novelist of the period, Ireneo Paz, was less of a threat to the public conscience, because he had never been as declamatory as Mateos. Together they

presented the past in the glorious perspective of victory; and to this
the *porfirista* mind was able to add progress, and respect for Mexico
among the nations of the world.

The tellers of legends were even more numerous. In 1892, Carrillo
y Ancona published *El rayo del sol*, which is exactly like his earlier
work—a very poor novel showing the inevitable victory of Christianity, in a legendary setting, and one that would delight the hearts of
religious traditionalists, especially if they were not discriminating
literary critics. But even more appropriate were the tales of Roa Bárcena, Riva Palacio, and José María Esteva. In *La campana de la
misión* (1894), Esteva tells a shipwreck story with a light touch of
mystery. It is restrained Romanticism, but gives us no reason to believe that the author ever heard of either Realism or Naturalism. A
few comments in the book—particularly regarding high tariffs and
contraband—relate it to the political life of the time, but these comments are far less interesting than the story, are not given any particular importance by the author, and probably were ignored by most
readers. The novel has the same qualities as some of the stories of
Roa Bárcena, particularly in *Noche al raso* and *Lanchitas*. Each is designed to tell a good tale, and in addition to provide the stimulating
effect of a mysterious circumstance which could have a supernatural
explanation. These stories seem to me to be important for two reasons. In the first place, they exist for their own sake, since they
are in no way committed to any political or social ideology. They
are written with considerable care, and their popularity reveals an
interest in literary craftsmanship. But in the second place, and in
partial contradiction, is the fact that their persistent though subtle
assumption of the goodness of things past made them especially acceptable to the *porfirista* mood.

I suspect that Riva Palacio's *Cuentos del general* must have contributed even more directly to conservative traditionalism because
of their strongly Mexican identification. Even some old stories are
retold by the general in a very satisfying Mexican framework. And
a number of them have a regional, folk flavor that calls for reminiscence. Riva Palacio wrote them as if he had been telling an anecdote
about an old friend, and the tone makes the reader belong to the situa-

tion. The traditionalist character of the stories is much like the novel of customs that praises the way things used to be, with the implication that people used to live closer to reality and were consequently better people. There is much of this feeling in some of the younger novelists of the period, like Delgado in *Angelina* (1893) and Manuel Sánchez Mármol in any of his novels, all of which seem to have been written for his grandmother. Sánchez Mármol always wrote in praise of good clean living; and rather than relate goodness to progress, the author chose to hang on to what was desirable in the past. His position in the novel of his time was similar to María Enriqueta's some years later, during and shortly after the Revolution.

Angelina has a particular value in its portrayal of small-town conservatism. And although Delgado tends to be "old-womanish" in this novel as in his others, his description of life in the town rings true, and provides a picture of a certain aspect of life which was one of the characteristics of porfirian society, but which is not always clear in the setting of a larger city. The love story that provides the thread of action—and it is a slight thread indeed—is colored by a fair amount of Romantic misfortune and renunciation; but against the background of the town, it is not unrealistic. The very life of the town was artificial because it denied reality.

The town of Córdoba, called Villaverde in the novel, had a population of about eight thousand when Delgado described it. It would be hard to find a better example of a provincial, defensively proud city. The people gossip about each other as one of their main sources of recreation, but they all get along together socially. Many complain about the backwardness of the town, but the same people resist change. Most of the young men leave because they must look somewhere else for a challenging future. And many of the young women look forward to becoming spinsters, partly because the young men leave, and partly from a kind of inertia that pervades the whole town. One of the characters is an inordinately proud lawyer whose personality, added to the general circumstances, has doomed his two daughters to spinsterhood. They know it, accept it, and take their vengeance in gossip. The schoolteacher, convinced that general ignorance is the inevitable result of the substitution of French for Latin, is opposed by two young liberals who have no real chance of changing the basic conditions. The respectable but penniless aunts of the hero accept help from a former servant.

It is hardly surprising that Rodolfo dreams away his possible happiness in a fog of indecision. Anyone would suffer melancholy in such an environment. The interesting thing is that, while Delgado creates a stifling picture of Córdoba's stagnation, he never really says it is bad. Rather, he persistently emphasizes the goodness in the very conservative physician, the honesty of the conservative teacher, the pleasant surface that hides the gossip. I think we cannot be quite sure whether Delgado is trying to maintain objectivity, or whether he too is hanging on to superficial security, but I'm inclined to believe the latter. This closed town could never come alive without an explosion. Essentially, it is the same as Yáñez's town in *Al filo del agua*, ready for the storm that it must have known would come—somewhere in its innermost being—but not prepared to let go its hold on what was known and accepted.

Although the traditionalism—or at best, caution—of the golden years of the establishment is an important factor in understanding the period, the most spectacular literary production grew out of the particular progressivism that stability fostered. This literary manifestation was the collection of interests that is called *modernismo*. This term, which is hardly descriptive at all when used by itself, becomes one of the most meaningful "isms" in literature when it is understood in the context of the period. *Modernista* literature was modern in two ways. It was a searching for new ways of expression that would replace the tired literature of an earlier period whose residue was dominated by mediocrity. But it also was modern in its desire to know and understand the latest trends in literature and to bring those influences to Mexico. To an extent, *modernismo* was like the great French houses that Mexicans built to prove that they belonged to the larger world, and often the *modernista* writers have been accused of having no more serious intent. But the truth is that *modernismo* was profoundly national, profoundly progressive, because it took the writers through a period of aesthetic searching and artistic discipline that Mexican writers had not known before, creating a feeling of confidence that could come only from such a professional experience, and relating Mexico, at the same time, to the culture of the western world.

Modernismo was a manifestation of the whole Spanish-American world, rather than of Mexico alone, and part of the artistic confidence that it generated can be attributed to the fact that its influence was felt in Spain. The relationship of *modernismo* to certain characteristics of the Díaz period gave it a special importance in Mexico, and it was here that two of its most important reviews were published. The *Revista Azul*, established by Manuel Gutiérrez Nájera and Carlos Díaz Dufoo, lived from 1894 to 1896, and its lifetime, generally speaking, may be said to correspond to the parnassian phase of *modernismo*. The most notable characteristic of this stage was the preoccupation with form, with the most beautiful description of the external. The *Revista Moderna,* whose guardian angels were Amado Nervo and Jesús Valenzuela, lasted from 1898 to 1911. Again speaking very generally, its span corresponded to the symbolist phase of *modernismo*, which is the more subjective expression of the artist's self-centeredness.

It should be quite apparent that *modernismo* was primarily concerned with poetry. Indeed, one of its characteristics was a reaction against the ugliness of Realism-Naturalism, and was really an antifiction position. One of the interesting facts of literary history is that both *modernista* poetry and Realist-Naturalist fiction have been accused of ignoring reality in order to support the Díaz regime. The truth is not so simple. Poetry, in its search for beauty, undertook not an escape from reality, but an adventure into discovery, and a foundation was laid for the understanding of art. The novelists had their own struggle with reality, as we have already seen, and it is probably true that the aesthetic awareness of the *modernistas* may have tended to make them think of themselves more as artists than as defenders of social justice. They were restless because they were constantly searching for new forms, themes, images. They were at once an extension of Romanticism (melancholy, rebellion) and a reaction against the tired and wordy songs of their predecessors. The *modernistas'* search for new expression interested them in virtually all poetry, of the present and of the past. Certainly their renewed interest in Classicism contributed to their reaction against the too abundant triteness of late Romantic poetry. Still, the melancholy remained, and toward the end of the century it combined with Realism-Naturalism to produce a body of decadent prose whose characteristics are studied boredom, thrill seeking, and artistic snobbishness. Such fiction could not possibly come from anything but deep dissatisfaction with the state of the world.

A period of genuine artistic awareness had come. Even the traditionalist novelists were more concerned for artistic value than any of their predecessors had been. López Portillo's *La parcela* is one of the most artistically conscious novels written in Mexico. However we may judge the result, there is no doubt at all that the author wrote it with the intention of creating a work of art. Probably for this very reason it is not as good a novel as *Nieves* or *Fuertes y débiles*. So much attention to structure, to balancing the elements of the book, to maintaining a highly literate style, destroyed the author's spontaneity. Not many people find fault with the literary values of *La parcela*; its critics content themselves with blaming the author for painting a picture of rural Mexico with benevolent master and contented peasantry. Their accusation has some merit, because in this novel the author presents the positive side of the society whose negative characteristics constitute the themes of *Nieves* and *Fuertes y débiles*. The reader who is forewarned by either the earlier or the later novel will find in *La parcela* certain objections to the administration of justice and the unreasonable desire to own more and more land. But López Portillo's main purpose was to show how men can get along with each other, and the general impression left by the novel is of a happier society than was probable at that time. It also makes sense to assume that his artistic self-consciousness, at a time when writers were keenly aware of artistic discipline, imposed restraints that would not allow him to explain his position. It is a fact that he enters this novel less than any of his other works. We may suppose that he chose not to enter because he preferred to follow the principles of Realist fiction, or because the pressure of the society discouraged him. Probably both factors influenced his writing. Certainly there is no doubt of his artistic awareness which is seen in many ways. The chapters are balanced in a description-action sequence; the two *hacendados* are neatly antithetical; the popular is balanced with the sophisticated, though the two are not in conflict; love and workaday problems get the author's attention on a turnabout basis. Such an extremely deliberate novel must almost certainly appear to be smug, and for this reason it has been all the more bitterly attacked by those latter-day critics who thought that López Portillo should have been a revolutionary.

La parcela is, as a matter of fact, one of the most significant novels of the Díaz period, because it shares with the life of the time all of the important characteristics that identified the period: stability, tradition, artistic impulse. In contrast to *Nieves*, it also reflects the establishment, the years when the Díaz regime was practically beyond criticism. The unrest that lay beneath the surface was apparent in fiction during the earlier years of the regime—in a special perspective—and again in the later years; but during the years of glory, evidence of unrest in fiction is almost entirely the result of hindsight.

I don't doubt for a moment that, for the public of its own time, the *costumbrista* aspect of *La parcela* was the most interesting. But it is important to note that these customs were of a special kind, based on Christian ethics and Hispanic tradition. Joaquina Navarro believes that López Portillo was the inspiration of a large number of novels, written around the turn of the century, that favored the same specialized view of Mexican customs.[1] She may well be right, though I believe it might be more accurate to limit the influence of López Portillo to that of two of his works, *La parcela* and *Los precursores* (1909), and to extend the presumed inspiration to include the novels of Rafael Delgado.

One of the novelists Navarro has in mind is Rafael de Ceniceros y Villarreal, whose *La siega* (1905) is a rather complicated story of love and proper behavior in a provincial city. The book is of particular interest because López Portillo said that "it is filled with the national life, it is the fruit of truth and of observation and a new, triumphal note of our progress."[2] What the novel actually does is show the pettiness of small-town ambition, and tell a story in which injustice threatens but Christian morality triumphs. We must assume

[1] Joaquina Navarro, *La novela realista mexicana*, p. 237.
[2] Rafael de Ceniceros y Villarreal, *Novelas*, tomo I of *Obras* (Mexico City: Victoriano Agüeros, n.d.), p. xxii.

that the progress noted by López Portillo is the victory of good over evil. And few would deny that this is indeed progress; but we know from other works by López Portillo himself that he didn't really believe that any such progress was reality. He held fast to the possibility, and it is possible that wishful thinking may have deceived him during a particular period of his life.

At that particular moment, or in that particular mood, he was very close to Ceniceros, to Delgado, and to the nearly frantic traditionalism that was for many the best source of security. The stodginess of the position is pathetically disturbing, and distracts the reader from the obvious artistic improvement of the novel. Delgado's *Los parientes ricos* (1904) is much more in tune with its time than his earlier works, but it still holds the threat of disaster over all who think of altering the circumstances into which they are born. We come to believe that we are witnessing not just a stagnant town, or a hidebound family, but a whole society that views unreality as real and whose only reality is what does not exist.

In a way, then, the *modernistas* were the genuine realists. Their adventure may have separated them from sociological fact, but it also led them away from sterility. Because of their predominant interest in poetry, the prose of the *modernistas* generally gets little more than the most cursory mention. Of course, some of its characteristics make it more closely akin to poetry than to the other prose of the time: brevity, unbalanced character emphasis, symbolism, preciousness. But its awareness of psychology, frequently abnormal, shows that there was no real line between *modernismo* and Realism-Naturalism. If sometimes the *modernista* tendency withdrew from the ugliness of prose fiction, the act was just one manifestation of a restless movement that had many facets and no definition. The techniques of Realism-Naturalism are apparent in the stories of the *modernistas*, just as their interest in literary refinement is apparent in the Realist-Naturalist novels.

Amado Nervo was, beyond question, the best writer of fiction among the *modernistas*, and one of the very few capable of producing novels. Yet even his tended to be short. His first, *El bachiller* (1895), concerns a young man's struggle between worldly and spiritual love. Trained for the priesthood, he is faced with the temptation of physical love. In a dramatic moment at the end of the novel, he castrates himself to avoid being seduced. This ending is described in the literary histories as horrible, revolting, and improbable. Indeed it is so unacceptable to most people that one has to read the novel to find out what happens. Not surprisingly, it created quite a furor in 1895. The resolution of the problem is indeed sensational, but those who criticize it do not give the author enough credit for the psychological development that creates the protagonist's impasse. If it is not entirely credible, it at least shows the author's willingness to probe human reactions.

The second novel, *Pascual Aguilera* (1896), is a considerably more sophisticated effort of the same kind. It uses the same theme of the "*hacendado's* privilege" that is found in *Nieves* and in *Perico*. But Nervo's novel is psychological rather than social. Pascual—to keep the record straight—is the son of the *hacendado* rather than the master himself, but he assumes the right to take his pleasure with the peasant bride. Nervo develops the character of Pascual with extreme care. Sometimes his explanation of the basis of his protagonist's actions becomes positively textbookish. He omits no detail that will support the case, and the frankness with which he treats sex must have been earthshaking in the world of Delgado. Pascual is unsuccessful in his plan to possess the young bride, but he loses control of himself so completely that he rapes his stepmother. Nervo, not satisfied with having exploded this bomb under the chairs of his complacent contemporaries, then reveals that the stepmother enjoyed the experience and explains why.

The impact of *Pascual Aguilera* cannot be appreciated fully unless we recall that it was published just three years after Delgado's *Angelina*, and before *La siega* and *Los parientes ricos*. Nervo's book is always a surprise too for readers of his gentle, and frequently soporific, poetry. The motivation behind the writing of *Pascual Aguilera* was not a desire for sensationalism, but an interest in investigation. Nervo's was one of the most searching minds of his time. He explored everything, was interested in everything. Scientific discoveries particularly fascinated him, and in many stories he tried interpreting them in human terms. Every piece of information seemed to move him to speculation, with the human condition always the laboratory.

There is always something of the poet in Nervo's prose. His adjectives show the influence of symbolist poets; his descriptive passages were born of an imagination that could make them as compelling as the action. But the surest sign of the poet is his thematic concentration. All the detail—and especially in *Pascual Aguilera* there is much of it—is pertinent to the central theme which, in this novel as in *El bachiller*, amounts to a problem. Nervo gives no panoramic view of society, or even of physical surroundings. He bores in toward the problem and develops what is necessary.

Nervo's only other piece of relatively long fiction is *El donador de almas* (1899). In this book, he moved into the same world of fantasy-philosophy that provided the material for many of his short stories. *El donador de almas* tells the story of a physician who is a competent man of science, but who, at the beginning of the story, has no soul. He would like to have one, however, and a poet friend finds one for him. The novel then describes the relationship of the physician and his soul.

Nervo's imagination never leaves him stranded. His intense interest in both the positivistic and the spiritual functioned as a rewarding source of ideas for his consideration of the human estate. His story moves easily from natural to supernatural, and the reader is not disposed to resist the author's lead. Obviously, *El donador de almas* is far removed from the novel of customs, but it certainly is not art-for-art's sake. It is a deeply committed novel. Of course, it is possible for the reader to withdraw from involvement; and when he does, he may well regard the novel as a kind of intellectual toy that has no relationship with reality.

The highly imaginative works of Nervo seem to me to be related to the decadent, sensationalist novels that appeared around the turn of the century. Nervo's works are distinguished by their sound philosophical base. But they have in common with the other works a constant striving toward the new, the strange, the unexperienced—a striving born of disillusionment with the ordinary world that stands in the way of hope. Not many of the *modernistas* wrote long fiction, and it is really not surprising that their high-pitched, intense longing could not be sustained over many pages. And when it was, as in the case of Rubén M. Campos' *Claudio Oronoz*, it becomes very tiresome.

The aesthetic neuroticism of Campos' protagonist is unbearable. He cannot do anything, cannot make a decision, cannot assert himself. He can only suffer from his yearning. His unhappiness rather than his inertia is typical of his fellow protagonists, because the thrill-seeking of some of them took them into the most bizarre situations, and we discover all sorts of abnormalities, including necrophilia and aesthetic homicide.

Actually, *modernista* prose does not lend itself to definition any more easily than *modernista* poetry does. The apparent influences and directions were many and varied. We may include in the group, in addition to Nervo and Campos, Efrén Rebolledo, Bernardo Couto Castillo, Ciro Ceballos, and perhaps even José Juan Tablada. We have to remember that these writers were not in some strange way separated from the world they lived in. They were very obviously present and affected by what was around them; but their interpretation of what they knew was controlled by an artistic point of view that represents a particular kind of radicalism. Their works show the influence of Realism, Naturalism, Romantic melancholy, artistic yearning, the science of psychology, disgust with the commonplace, boredom. These characteristics do not appear in the same proportion in the works of all the authors, but they can serve as a kind of group identification. In another generality, we may say that they were similar in spirit to present-day "beatniks," with one extremely important difference—their nonconformism was always expressed within a framework of elegance, both personal and literary. Above all, they were not escaping from the world. They wanted to change the world—there is even some direct social protest in their works—and even if they most often resorted either to unproductive sensationalism or to boredom, their world was considerably less static than Delgado's Villaverde.

The *modernista's* most important contribution to fiction was not in their own works, but in their influence on the works of writers who normally are not considered members of the group. We see it generally in the literary awareness of the late 1890's. It is more specifically evident in the works of some writers. Angel de Campo, for example, shows in his sketches (*La Rumba* was his only novel) a refinement that could have come from no other source. Federico Gamboa, in spite of the fact that he is commonly and erroneously regarded as Mexico's only Naturalist, frequently shows a choice of adjective that suggests the symbolist manner. Indeed, the careful writing of Gamboa and López Portillo, which is often considered overly correct, is a result of the artistic awareness that the *modernistas* promoted.

The whole question of style is something of a barrier to consideration of Gamboa's novels. This man, who was the best novelist Mexico had produced up to his time, has often been underrated because of repeated criticism of his style, described as academic, dull, pretentious. The criticism is not entirely without justification, because Gamboa's careful writing occasionally creates the impression that he was trying too hard, and the popular elements that he injects from time to time are surprising rather than unobtrusive. But for reasons that are hidden from me, adverse criticism of his style has acquired prominence in commentaries on his fiction that is entirely out of proportion to its real importance.[3] Really there are far more good things than bad to be said about it. It is clear, accurately descriptive, and appropriate to his theme. There is nothing about it that inhibits participation in the novels, nothing that removes the reader from the world in which the author wishes to place him.

Following the stories of *Del natural*, Gamboa published his first novel, *Apariencias*, in 1892. His only advance over the stories was to write a longer work. *Apariencias*, which combines a story of the French Intervention with an almost separate story of adultery, is a failure because the author simply did not have enough to say. Gamboa was just learning how to surround his protagonists with society and to give them backgrounds that justify their actions. He shows his interest in creating an identifiable Mexican setting; and he reveals the mixture of Christian hope and Naturalism that has made many people say he could not possibly be a Naturalist. The fact is that neither his Naturalism nor his Christianity is strictly orthodox, and his novels are the more probable for that very reason. His characters are controlled by circumstances which frequently could be altered by

---

[3] Recently, Seymour Menton made a careful analysis of Gamboa's style that should have a healthy corrective effect, in "Federico Gamboa: un análisis estilístico," *Humanitas*, No. 4 (1963).

Christian concern; but that concern, like the hope that is its corollary, is not always present.

Gamboa's first mature novel, *Suprema ley* (1896), is one of his best, though it is overshadowed by the tremendous fame of *Santa* (1903). Since its characters are more "average" than those that frequent Santa's world of prostitution, it gives us a somewhat better idea of how Gamboa viewed life. The story is the fall of Julio Ortegal, an unimportant court clerk. Ortegal married less for love than because it was the thing to do. His conjugal bliss gradually gives way to the boring exigence of family responsibility. At court he meets a woman who is accused of murdering her lover. Although she is acquitted, she is friendless and is taken into the home of the Ortegal family. At first, she saves this family that was already on the brink of disaster. But later Julio seduces her, and the ensuing adulterous affair destroys Ortegal's family, and eventually Ortegal himself.

Suprema ley deserves several amplifying comments concerning Gamboa's approach to fiction. The surrounding circumstances for the plot are provided by his detailed description of the court and its employees, and by a similarly detailed description of theater life, when Ortegal takes a backstage job in order to supplement his income. The two sets of circumstances offer a remarkable contrast to each other. The court employees represent a struggling middle class shrouded in dullness; the theater offers glitter, but no more genuine happiness than the contrasting drabness. Both groups are dishonest. Ortegal bribes the jury; success in the theater has no direct relationship to talent. Ortegal's home life is based on common sense, but it is ruined primarily by the fact that there is no common sense in his financial situation. The home, the court, and the theater form a triangle which Gamboa uses as a means of taking the reader through the life of the city. He makes it a good experience because his accurate view catches the reader up in the contrasts that are typically urban.

Both the reader and the characters are involved in life. Neither withdraws to consider the circumstances. For example, even before the coming of Clothilde, Julio and his wife, Carmen, are struggling to keep their marriage in good working order. Without knowing what is happening, they sense that an extra effort is necessary. Gamboa's description of their reaction to the problem is pathetically human. Before and after Clothilde's coming, Julio is only partly aware of what is happening to him. In the first stages of his relationship with Clothilde, he is apparently moved only by human compassion. His later obsession does not kill his paternal concern. It is as if he were suffering from an illness. Clothilde is never in love with him, although she accepts him as a lover. When finally she is forgiven by her family and leaves the city, death is the only course available for Ortegal, although he dreams of rehabilitating himself and his family.

Obviously, *Suprema ley* is Naturalism rampant. Gamboa took a middle-class situation similar to many other novels, and based the action on the common sense and conformist attitude that were so dear to the time. He supplemented the situation with commendable human concern, and then let circumstances destroy the whole thing. In a way, *Suprema ley* was even more shocking than Nervo's novels, because the fundamental setting was so familiar.

Metamorfosis (1899) is like *Suprema ley* in most matters of technique, but the theme of the novel is even farther removed than *Santa* from commonplace living. It deals with the transformation of a woman from religious commitment to the male protagonist's lover. Gamboa's careful development, of course, makes the metamorphosis reasonable, and the nature of the change reveals the author's understanding of what love means. Unfortunately, the change takes place at an irregular pace; that is, the change in Sor Noeline appears to move too slowly at one point and too fast at another. The effect is to remove the reader and make him critical of the process while it is going on. The nature of the theme also makes it hard for Gamboa to maintain the general movement of the novel. The hero abducts Sor Noeline and hides her in the house of a friend. Once this mission is accomplished, there is no way to involve her in action going on outside the house. So we are taken from her presence to more or less extraneous happenings, and then brought back.

One rather long section of *Metamorfosis* takes place on a hacienda, where Gamboa's detail is interesting enough, but the episode doesn't have much to do with the rest of the novel. Among the characterizations, Gamboa makes very interesting use of the hero's young daughter, who is Sor Noeline's pupil, and an unwitting catalyst to the transformation of the woman.

Gamboa's best novel, *Santa,* has had an odd critical fate. It has had an exceptionally wide reading, which it deserves because it is an excellent novel, but which it has gotten largely because of its reputation for being risqué. The critics, as a result of a kind of reflex negativism, have tended to concentrate on its faults—a difficult task, because its faults are few.

Santa, a dishonored country girl, suffers rejection by her family and comes to Mexico City where she becomes a prostitute. She starts at the top and goes to the bottom, with interludes as the mistress first of a *torero* and later of an unhappy husband. In spite of some inclination to reform, she is never quite able to do so; indeed, she even deceives the *torero* who is the provider of at least a semirespectable life. Finally, she is rescued from the gutter by Hipólito, who has loved her from the beginning, but she is near death when this happens. She is, in fact, redeemed by Hipólito's love—an outcome that displeases many of Gamboa's readers. Incidentally, this may well be the only case in Mexican fiction where a woman has been redeemed by a man —usually it is the other way.

The honest care with which Gamboa wrote *Santa* is the novel's greatest asset. Perhaps some of the scenes may be regarded as risqué, certainly many are repulsive; but Gamboa must be respected for his wisdom in writing details that contribute to the impact of the novel and omitting those that are unnecessary. He might have been able to omit some of the uglier details if he had used narrative techniques more complicated than objective statement. But given his technique, he was compelled to use the details. Still he chooses his words carefully, and avoids pornography—except for those who can make pornography of any mention of sex—by adopting a clinical attitude toward sexual matters.

Hipólito has always been a highly controversial character because many regard him as being too "sentimental." He is an ugly, blind pianist who worked in the brothel where Santa lived. At the very beginning he fell in love with her, partly because she was kind to him, partly because he recognized her fundamental decency. The picture is completed by a description given Hipo by his guide. This is a fine, poetic piece—perhaps a little too elegant for its source—but an appropriate way for Santa to be seen through the "eyes" of Hipo. His love endures even after Santa's fundamental decency has changed to fundamental immorality, because Hipo's picture of her does not change. I suspect Hipo is an example of what Delgado and some others meant when they spoke of the reality of sentiment, a better example than Delgado was able to create.

The changes of mood throughout the novel are interesting and extremely convincing. The intransigent family honor of Santa's brothers is felt as keenly as a raucous celebration at the brothel. One particularly good episode is the coming of the brothers to inform Santa of her mother's death, when Santa is the toast of the town. Into the glitter and gaiety stride the brothers, somber, deliberate, hermetic. Gamboa does not push his reader in either direction, but lets him feel the reality of the contrast. He was capable also of catching the simple goodness beneath the flamboyance of "El Jarameño," the *torero*. The jealousies and intrigues of the women are equally real, as are Santa's moments of happiness and her gradual decline. We may well argue about the matter of Santa's will power and whether or not she could have changed the course of her life. I think Gamboa's purpose was not to present an air-tight case for the dark powers of destiny, but to show a situation in which Santa's possibilities for choice were limited. A Mexican student of mine has noted, regarding the change in Santa's character, that she, like Mexico, followed a particular course until, having reached a point-of-no-return, she found it easier—almost necessary—to go the wrong way rather than to turn back.

The comparison of Santa and the nation suggests that Gamboa was one of the few writers, if not the only one, of his time who wrote beyond himself. That is, he actually said more than his original design intended. López Portillo may have done so in *Nieves*, but Gamboa did so more generally. His novels suggest a revision of values because the basis of common sense doesn't work. It is a risky thing to compare specific characters to general conditions; but there is no doubt at all that these novels, written during the years of the "establishment," are novels of questioning unrest. This general mood is communicated to the reader who, at the end of each novel, has a feeling of vague uneasiness that the world is not turning as it should.

As a matter of fact, things were not going very well. The Díaz society of peace and order was fundamentally without either quality, and the *científicos* had to maintain the brilliant surface by an increasingly intense suppression of liberty and by encouraging the "haves" to stay within their own small world. Naturally, the novelists who belonged to the establishment were inclined to cooperate insofar as their consciences would allow them. But there was some opposition to the regime, particularly in the newspaper *El Demócrata*. One of its collaborators, Heriberto Frías, published a novel, *Tomochic*, that brought the *científicos* up from their leather chairs and made them commit an entirely obvious act of injustice. Before the affair was over, *El Demócrata* had been closed, Frías had faced trumped-up charges of revealing military secrets, and had been saved by the cloak-and-dagger action of a friend who stole into the offices of the closed newspaper and destroyed evidence that might have been used against the author.

Actually, only the wildest imagination could find military secrets in *Tomochic*, but it is not difficult to find some serious doubts about the stability of the regime. Frías did not belong to the establishment. He came from a prominent family that was in poor financial circumstances. In the process of getting an education and establishing himself in a suitable position, Frías saw a good deal of life on many social levels in Mexico City, and he took a dim view of society's false glitter. Part of his education took place in the national military school, and though he did not graduate, he found himself involved in the third Tomochic campaign as a junior officer. The novel, which was published serially and completely by 1895, is his novelized report of the campaign.

Tomochic was a small Indian village in the northern part of Mexico, inhabited by a few hundred strong-minded people. The *tomochitecos* first ran into trouble when the civil authorities removed from their church some paintings that they cherished. Their protest was to no avail. The problem was aggravated by their adherence to a religious cult that had grown up around a neurotic young woman who was called "The Saint of Cabora." This heretical group had counterparts to the Holy Family and indulged in a number of fanatical activities which are extremely interesting, but not to the point I am making here. The *tomochitecos* were moved to rebellion by a combination of injustice on the part of the local officials and their own fanaticism. The government sent troops to put down the revolt and the government troops were soundly defeated. A second expedition suffered the same fate. Finally, the government, in desperation, sent a regiment which, by sheer force of numbers, systematically and ruthlessly destroyed the town, house by house, man by man. Heriberto Frías took part in this third expedition.

Frías' novel is similar in many ways to the lineal accounts of the Revolution that are somewhere between a real novel and a report of personal experience. He describes the military action with concern for the success of the expedition, but he does not hide the ruthlessness of the government's intent. The author is a protagonist, who is called Miguel Mercado, Frías' alter ego in several novels. Mercado's character is clearly seen, and many other characters are presented, either developed fully or by selection of outstanding qualities. Frías weaves in a love story of sorts which really doesn't have much effect on the novel one way or the other. But it is important that he was careful to re-create the feeling within the army toward the campaign, the ethos of the *tomochitecos*, and the attitude of the people of the region toward the federal troops.

Objectively, Frías has nothing but praise for the federal forces; but beneath the praise, we feel a considerable amount of uncertainty on the part of the troops about attacking this indomitable village that has twice defeated federal forces. And there is certainly an implicit question about the glory of wiping out a village of brave people. The soldiers face silent resentment on the part of the inhabitants of the general area. They are really considered an invading force. Frías seems to identify the northerners as real people, contrasted with the world of hypocrisy that the army has come to defend.

The most obvious link between *Tomochic* and Frías' later novels is his attitude toward the *soldaderas* (camp followers). His consideration of these women was part of his search for something basic in society. The women have a redemptive function. Their sole concern is for the men, and they care for them even in defiance of regulations. They are the point to which the men return, because they are a basic reality and in active opposition to cultivated society. Yet Miguel Mercado is repelled by their filth and coarseness, and finds himself in the position of belonging neither to basic reality nor to cultivated society.

Naufragio (1895), later published as *El amor de las sirenas,* is a story of student life in Mexico City, where the author again searches for basic values and tries to find the woman who will be the proper redemptive agent. Even in *El último duelo* (1896), which turns primarily on the custom of duelling—a burning subject at the time—the same search is apparent. Many years later, he described redemptive woman with a fair degree of success in *Aguila o sol* (1923), though he never was able to see his personal masculine condition as the object of redemption. His effort was motivated by a reason much more profound than the ordinary man-woman relationship; it was an attempt to discover, within a society where individuals obviously had to associate with each other, some relationship that was indestructible. Frías was in an unusual social position. He did not belong to the group that supported and profited from the regime. Yet he was not one of the forgotten. In this middle position, he saw that the dominant society of the time was a shell of pretense. His career was an attack on that pretense, but he also looked carefully for reality. Frías' protest was the most vigorous of the years of the establishment. Within the limits of the period he found no better solution than the *modernistas* found for their anxiety, or than the traditionalists found for the improvement of individual man. But there is no question that he was more aware of the protest that he was making.

Very early in the twentieth century, there was a revival of the kind of satire written by Emilio Rabasa, in Porfirio Parra's *Pacotillas* (1900) and Manuel H. San Juan's *El señor gobernador* (1901). I use the word "revival" in connection with these novels because they are more than ten years away from Rabasa's, and there is no connection running through the intervening years.[4] *Pacotillas* is a criticism of dis-

---

[4] The only possible link would be José Ferrel's *Reproducciones,* which is a minor novel, and somewhat tangential to the Rabasa viewpoint. Ferrel de-

honest journalism; *El señor gobernador,* of political opportunism. Pacotillas, the nickname of the first novel's protagonist, is similar to Rabasa's Juan Quiñones, but he is more idealistic. His criticism of the government leads to his death. It is possible that Pacotillas' journalistic purity is a reflection of the author's insistence on a stricter understanding of positivism than that represented by the compromise which the regime had made with traditionalism.

El señor gobernador is more obviously satirical, but it is not as good a novel. The people are typed as clearly as the author could make them by using every trick available, including names that suggest the misuse of their offices. I really doubt that San Juan was much interested in writing a novel. His book is more like a political cartoon in words. There are similarities to Rabasa's politicians; but if Rabasa was using them to illustrate the lack of communication between the law and the people, San Juan is saying that the politicians offer nothing that is worth the people's attention.

It seems to me that these two novels and Rabasa's novels represent two distinct stages of the Díaz regime. Rabasa wrote before the years of the establishment, when the compromise with conscience was being worked out. The following years were a period of conscious calm and subconscious anxiety. *Pacotillas* and *El señor gobernador* are cracks in the wall of the establishment. There was already some talk of who would succeed President Díaz, and discussion that was basically political occasionally spilled over into social considerations. The literature from this time to the Revolution is a pathetic mixture of a holding action accompanied by a not-too-daring look forward.

---

scribes revolutionary action as serving only selfish interests. This view agrees with Rabasa and several other writers of the period. Ferrel's book is satirical, but it is neither as amusing nor as biting as Rabasa's.

7. The Hope of the Past

(1907–1912)

These few years, when the planned reality of the *científicos* disappeared and Mexico moved into the Revolution, were agonizing times of searching for solutions that were hidden behind the wall built by the establishment. In the world of ordinary knowing—that is to say, the information that we would get from the newspaper— there was a curious mixture of stability and discontent. Mexico planned to celebrate the centennial of its independence, basking in the world's esteem and telling itself, somewhat uncertainly, that Mexico had become a modern nation. On the other hand, there were more strikes and more violent suppression; more and more people were wondering who would succeed Díaz; there were even some searching questions asked about ownership of the land. The uncertainty of the time had two aspects: one purely political, the other political and social. The question of who would be Don Porfirio's successor was not raised only by the opposition. Even the regime's most ardent adherents were aware that Díaz could not last forever, and there was no generally accepted heir apparent. So the political aspect of the matter concerned both sides. The social consideration was important mainly to those who believed that no real social progress had been made during all the years of the Díaz regime. No progress, in a country that had become a modern nation. This pessimistic view was taken, for the most part, by a few members of the lower middle class, like the Flores Magón brothers, who had syndicalist ideas.

Finally, the political issue was brought to a head when Francisco Madero challenged Díaz on the matter of the succession. Most unwisely, Díaz had Madero put in jail, and started a cold war between the government and the Madero family. Francisco Madero was one of the sons of a very wealthy family that owned an enormous amount of land, so his position was far from weak. After a series of maneuvers by the Maderos and the government, the Revolution began in November, 1910. The fundamental weakness of the Díaz regime became apparent very quickly. Díaz went into exile and Madero became president.

Obviously, Francisco Madero was not a lower-middle-class radical. He was a very wealthy man who believed in democratic institutions. Ideologically, he was close to the men of the Reform; but we must remember that during the administration of Díaz, Reformist progressivism had given way to expediency.

The agony of uncertainty is amply apparent in the novel. Some of the writers—López Portillo, Ceniceros y Villarreal, Cayetano Rodríguez Beltrán—held fast to the hope of man's individual improvement. While this improvement was associated with Christianity, it was really morality that concerned them; and the morality they advocated is more sensibly associated with traditionalism than with Christian faith. The *costumbrista* element of their novels serves as more than an interesting picture of customs. It is the basis of morality. They show how people acted, differentiating good from evil, and they propose that these traditional customs be a standard of conduct. The example of good conduct may also be an exponent of Christian faith; but the implication that Christianity and morality are equal to each other is just another example of the manufactured reality of the period.

The novels are extremely thin. Ceniceros' *El hombre nuevo* (1908) is the not very convincing account of an act of redemption on the part of a young woman. Rodríguez Beltrán's *Pajarito* (1908) is even less substantial in its account of the inevitable triumph of justice. The simple fact is that these novels are not about anything of importance. The customs and the language can be evaluated for their authenticity, how Hispanic or how Mexican they happen to be. But custom-for-custom's sake is unrewarding; and when we consider the apparent purpose of the customs, we must confess that the authors' desperate hope is not genuine optimism.

It seems that the anxiety of moral concern distorted traditionalist thinking so that it was incapable of producing good fiction. López Portillo's *Los precursores* (1909) is the worst thing he ever wrote. It is reactionary in two ways: first, because he forgot all about Realism and wrote a novel which is pervaded by the most saccharine and improbable sentimentality; second, because he yearns for the good old days when goodness was really goodness. López Portillo is even more conservative in *Los precursores* than in *La parcela,* and we can only conclude that anxiety drove him to a position at the opposite extreme from his early position in *Nieves* or his later position in *Fuertes y débiles.*

Los precursores is a semihistorical novel that deals with the expulsion of the Sisters of Charity and the struggles of a young musician. With apologies for discussing such an inane book, I think it is important to specify the attitude of the author. Joaquín, who is an orphan, and Berta, who is the daughter of a courtesan, grow up in an institution run by the Sisters of Charity. The sweetness and light of this refuge is such that we must wonder why any child chose to stay at home. Mexican children might well have established a new custom of running away to the orphanage. Supported by the solid training that the good sisters have given them, Joaquín and Berta become model man and woman. He becomes a pianist-composer, she becomes a singer. They marry. Joaquín struggles unsuccessfully for recognition as a composer. Finally, he gives up and gets a job as choirmaster, which will enable him to provide for his family. The exodus of the Sisters of Charity brings deep grief to all, especially Joaquín and Berta, who have always lived close to the institution which was the source of their joy.

Admittedly, this is a very silly novel. The juxtaposition of López Portillo's two propositions—that the Sisters of Charity were a good influence, and that Mexicans ought to appreciate Mexican art—is awkward enough. It is made even worse by the author's tearful evocation of goodness in its sweetest form. Few characters come alive, because they are mired in the author's sirupy intent. In short, *Los precursores* has no artistic merit. But it has several noteworthy ideas.

The Sisters of Charity can do no wrong. They are examples of perfect goodness, individually and collectively. They are universally loved, and no one favors the law that requires them to leave. This cleavage between the law and the interest of the people is the same point that Rabasa made in his novels, particularly in *La guerra de tres años*. The products of the Sisters' moral education are a drab lot. Joaquín, for sound moral reasons, gives up his creative dream and settles for a modest living, an unspectacular career, and security. He realized that the "good" thing to do was to attend to his chores and not upset anybody. López Portillo wasn't happy about the lack of appreciation of Joaquín's genius, but he decided that even genius must reconcile itself with the facts of an immature society. Another child of the institution, Paulina, makes no attempt to rock the boat at all. Early and eagerly she marries an elderly man for his money and lives securely ever after. Paulina, however, is the soul of honesty and makes perfectly clear to her husband the circumstances under which she accepts him in marriage. The author was not entirely happy about Paulina either. She is the contrast to Berta, the life and laughter of the institution. Apparently at this point in his life, López Portillo thought everybody ought to have just a little spark, but not enough to start any fires.

López Portillo says that these "precursors" were responsible for the Mexico of his time, upon which the world looked favorably.[1] If I read him correctly, he is saying that Mexico's stability was based on the absence of initiative. To a considerable extent, this evaluation was accurate, though I doubt that he understood his judgment in the way an oppositionist would have taken it. Lack of initiative, as it was seen by López Portillo, was moral behavior; that is, it was good, it was what people were supposed to do, it was recognition of the apparent facts of life. His opinion that Mexico was an immature society seems to be in contrast to his pride in the country's progress. But the probable explanation is that he did believe he saw moral progress in a situation where that progress would be placed in jeopardy by strong objection to the existing situation. We know that in both his earlier and later works, he was far more critical of society, but his solution was always an individual one. However, he saw clearly that the individual

[1] In the author's preface to *Los precursores*, López Portillo makes this point as well as his point about the lack of appreciation of Mexican art. His anxiety would not allow him to let the novel speak for itself.

solution was not working. It is entirely reasonable to suppose that, when he wrote *Los precursores*, he sensed the danger of a radical upheaval, and wrote somewhat desperately in the defense of traditional values. Indeed, the insistence of the traditionalist view at that particular time probably represents the anxious hope that, somehow, out of the past would come the salvation of the present.

Federico Gamboa's last two novels, both published during this period, are somewhat different from the traditionalist position and also from his own earlier works. They have many of the characteristics of Naturalism, and the style is still much the same; but they are inferior to the earlier novels because Gamboa wrote under the compulsion of solving his protagonists' problems. He fell into the trap of direct moralization, and he bent his characters almost to the breaking point to make them turn out the way he wanted them. It is interesting that he now felt the need of solving the problem, something that didn't bother him in his earlier novels. It is interesting also that the problem of the protagonist is related, in both novels, to a national problem. This fact, by the way, supports the idea that Santa's life can be associated with the circumstances of the Mexican nation. In the two late novels, there is a great deal of social protest. The national problems are not resolved, in spite of the author's vague discourses on the meaning of patriotism and the soul of Mexico, and in spite of the resolution of the problems of individual characters.

Reconquista (1908) deals with the spiritual rehabilitation of a gifted Mexican painter. Because he is a freethinker, his personal problems nearly destroy him. He loses both his professional job and his inspiration. He talks a lot about the soul of Mexico, which he proposes to discover among the poor and miserable. When he is asked by a magazine in the United States to paint a series of pictures of Mexico, he decides to paint the real Mexico, which is, in his opinion, the misery of the underprivileged. He believes only in the committed artist, saying that art for its own sake is of no importance. However, he is never really successful in capturing the soul of Mexico until he formally accepts the Church.

There is never any question of the artist's concern for social justice, though he is no moralist in his personal life. Gamboa apparently did not base his hope for a better society on personal morality. Indeed his

closest approach to the traditionalist position is his assumption that
the painter cannot discover the soul of Mexico until he has professed
his Christian faith. And in this regard, no half measures would do.
The act of conversion is not a dramatic, single moment in his life, but
a gradual change. He is impressed by the persistent faith of another
person, and moves toward Christianity. But his artistic inspiration
does not come until after his definitive confession of faith. However,
the meaning of Christianity in *Reconquista* is quite different from its
meaning in *Los precursores* and the other traditionalist novels. Gamboa is less concerned with its moral values than with the quality that
feeds the artist's inspiration. The mystic quality of this inspiration is
not entirely clear. From one standpoint it seems that Gamboa considers Christian faith to be the source of the painter's creative power.
From a slightly different point of view, he seems to say that commitment to Christianity is necessary before the artist could really comprehend the soul of Mexico. The second assumption makes more
sense in view of the author's obvious interest in social justice. It also
means that Gamboa was probing into Mexican reality, trying to discover what was meaningful to the Mexican people and to relate that
meaning to the social circumstance. His choice of Christianity as a
means of understanding was somewhat different from the traditionalist approach, because it was an act of looking beyond visible reality
rather than settling for superficial morality.

La llaga (1910) is the story of another kind of rehabilitation, this
time of an ex-convict. Gamboa is likely to please and to annoy his
reader alternately in this novel. It is full of preaching that makes one
want to tell him to stay out of the way; on the other hand there are
many fine novelistic touches that are typical of Gamboa at his best—
for example, when Eulalio leaves prison, one of the first things he does
is buy some flowers, without having any idea of why he wants to buy
them. The act is a symbol of his re-entry into the world. And that re-
entry is far from simple. He finally makes a place for himself in an
entirely different social situation from the one he had known before.
Gamboa finds the opportunity to praise manual labor and to study
the living conditions of the working class.

Gamboa speaks of the absence of patriotism in Mexico; and what he seems to mean is that genuine patriotism demands less personalism in the national life. He complains of economic and moral injustices on the part of the *hacendado*, and says that the Mexican peon is prepared for insurrection rather than for civic responsibility. He is not educated as a child. Later, the insurgents tell him the government is always bad, and the government tells him all insurgents are bandits. In the end, he discovers that insurrection does nothing to help him, whether he participates or not. For the national dilemma, Gamboa's only solution is gradual enlightenment, and he expresses his hope in Eulalio's becoming a father.

The *llaga* (sore) is apparent in several different forms. Eulalio bears it psychologically as a result of his imprisonment. He bears it physically as the result of mistreatment in prison, and of a later accident. It also exists nationally in the social rejection of Eulalio and in the nation's inability to cure its ills. There is no suggestion of revolution in Gamboa's novels, unless we presuppose the rejection of gradualism. In both *La llaga* and *Reconquista*, he struggles to find a ray of hope within the existing situation, but the result of his efforts could hardly be satisfactory to him or to anyone else. There is not the slightest doubt that by the time Gamboa wrote these novels, he was acutely aware of the dichotomy in Mexican society, and convinced that different circumstances should prevail. In a way, his hope was also based on the past, but it seems to require a deeper change in individuals than would be required by the *costumbrista* morality of the traditionalists.

The conflict and confusion in urban life that Gamboa portrays so well, are apparent also in Salvador Quevedo y Zubieta's *La camada* (1912) and Heriberto Frías' *El amor de las sirenas* (1908), a revision and enlargement of *Naufragio*. *La camada* is a clear and violent protest against social and political corruption; *El amor de las sirenas* does not concern itself with politics, though Frías certainly loathed hypocrisy there just as he did in any other situation. The scenes of *La camada* are similar to Gamboa's. The principal one is a clinic. But the plot is based on an attempted assassination of President Díaz, and the action moves all over the city. Quevedo y Zubieta had a low opinion of mankind's actual state, though he apparently had faith in its potential. The decent people in *La camada* serve as a contrast to the others, but offer little hope of dominating them. He was certainly no traditionalist, because he was inclined to blame the social defects of his time on the disorderly process of Mexican history. He took a rather "practical" view of what should be done, advocating less dreaming and more work—an attitude that recalls the common-sense approach of the early nationalists.

El amor de las sirenas is less violent than *La camada*. In his search for stability, Frías shows the depraved life of the city. His protest takes a different form from that of any of the other novelists because its basis is the author's personal need for identification with some social fact that will not change. As in his other novels, he looked for this stability in the redemptive role of woman. The heroine of *El amor de las sirenas*, however, is too passive a character for the role Frías wishes her to fill. He is left without the answer he seeks. What he shows of society is a discouraging shell of falsehood. It is a society that doesn't believe in anything but the preservation of its self deception. Frías was not interested in López Portillo's traditionalist values, but continued to look for the values of a different level of society which was more primitive than the society of the capital. He was seeking the honest, essential human relationship which is not perverted into pretense.

In *El triunfo de Sancho Panza* (1911), Frías—or rather, Miguel Mercado—is the victim of omnipotent hypocrisy. The novel is called a sequel to *Tomochic*, but it is so only in the sense that it follows Frías' career and provides another setting for his alienation from the society to which he might have belonged. Mercado, now a journalist, goes to Mazatlán where he exposes some political chicanery. He is forced to leave the paper and the city. The novel contains references to the writing of *Tomochic* and to Mercado's earlier bohemian life, all of which are autobiographical. Frías presents Mercado as an idealist, but not as a moralist. In the society that he describes, there is no possible way for honesty to prevail, since dishonesty and power feed each other.

Mariano Azuela, the most important novelist of this period and for many years later, was even farther removed than Frías from the world of the crumbling establishment. He was completely outside the literary circles of the time, and his work was hardly noticed.[2] Indeed, the military phase of the Revolution had been over for several years before his novels were given much attention. Azuela had published *Los de abajo* (*The Underdogs*) in 1915, during the heat of the Revolution, and this fine novel had to wait for attention until the Mexican people became interested in considering what had happened to them. As for the earlier novels, interest in them grew after Azuela had become an established novelist. He was a physician, the son of a modest, middle-class family, and owed nothing to the establishment. His pre-Revolutionary novels deal sharply with the society of his time, but there is nothing in them that advocates revolution.

The first novel, *María Luisa* (1907), deserves mention only because it is the first novel of a great writer. It was written ten or twelve years before it was published, when Azuela was a medical student. He was impressed by a clinical case and composed a novel around it. It is a fairly standard story of a student's mistress who suffers illness, desertion, and death. *María Luisa* is obviously a first novel, and probably should never have been published, since it was one of Azuela's earliest attempts at prose fiction. When he wrote the novel, he had not mastered style or structure, nor had he cultivated his ability to observe society. What little he does show us of his world is similar to what we find in many novels of the mid-1890's. It is somewhat like the world of Heriberto Frías, but Azuela's concern does not go beyond the tragedy of the young girl. His sympathy for her is apparent, but her tragedy is in no way related to Azuela's understanding of the social reality or of his own reason for being.

Azuela took enormous strides toward literary maturity before writing his second novel, *Los fracasados*, which was published in 1908. Still under the influence of his reading of Naturalist novels, Azuela had liberated himself to the point where other writers helped him say what he wanted to say. Their influence no longer restricted his expression. In many ways, *Los fracasados* is a compendium of novelistic attitudes of the Díaz period. The setting is a small town that has the

---

[2] Among the few notices of Azuela's early novels were Heriberto Frías' articles in *El Correo de la Tarde* of Mazatlán, the paper that was edited by Frías and José Ferrel. I have been unable to find the issue in which these works were discussed. See Mariano Azuela, *Cien años de novela mexicana*, p. 211.

smug hermeticism of Delgado's Villaverde. The treatment of its people, however, is more like Rabasa's satirical characterizations. The defeat of idealism recalls Heriberto Frías. These similarities should not be taken to mean that Azuela was imitating other writers, but that he belonged to a period when these characteristics were likely to appear in the novel.

Azuela did not concern himself much about the construction of a neat plot. If his subject indicated the need of careful narrative development, he was capable of providing it, but his main concern was to move his characters about enough to make a picture of what he saw in them. One rarely thinks of an Azuela character as being particularly well projected. Sometimes they grow, sometimes they are static. Always he makes clear the role of the character within the circumstance. And circumstance is really the basis of his novel. Apparently Azuela saw a set of general conditions first, then placed his characters and moved them to show what he saw.

There is really not much hope for change in the town of *Los fracasados*. The ambitions of its inhabitants vary a great deal, but most of them can be achieved without changing the fundamental structure of their closed society. Azuela discovers foolishness, egocentric power, passivity, and idealism among his characters. Sometimes he laughs at their foibles, but he is not amused by the selfish use of power. Reséndez, the idealist who might have set the town in motion, is completely defeated by local conservatism, a fact that made the novelist react by letting satire become sarcasm. I doubt that Azuela's protest, when *Los fracasados* was published, would have appeared to be any stronger than Frías', or even Gamboa's. And even if the novel had been widely read, it wouldn't have been much of a surprise, because the town he describes is not very different from small-town life in many other novels. As for probing into Mexican reality, Gamboa was far more ambitious in *Reconquista*, which was published the same year as *Los fracasados*, and in *La llaga*, which was published two years later. Azuela's militant identification with his characters was equalled only by Frías during this period, but Azuela was a wiser novelist than Frías and did not often let his personal interest modify the reality of the re-created world.

What distinguishes *Los fracasados* from the several novels that are more or less similar to it is the author's attitude regarding change. Even Frías tried to make sense of his world by looking toward a more primitive society, which is really looking backward. Azuela was looking ahead through Reséndez. The idealist's defeat does not change the direction indicated for improvement of society. Later on, Azuela, who always enjoyed taking the opposite position, started looking backward when most people were looking ahead; but in 1908, the suggestion that society should move forward without reference to conserving the past, was a unique proposition. Indeed, it suggests that however similar his visible reality might be to that of other writers, his vision of a deeper reality makes his town different from its counterparts in other novels.

Azuela's sharpest protest against social conditions, in the early novels, is his treatment of the *hacendado*-peasant girl plot in *Mala yerba* (1909). He is less satirical than in *Los fracasados*, and so his complaint has a more serious tone. The basis of the story, and of the protest, was by no means new. At least three other novelists—Zentella, Nervo, and López Portillo—had dealt with it during the Díaz period. The difference between *Mala yerba* and the other novels on the same theme comes from the author's characterization of power and weakness. Using the same basic facts, Azuela saw a slightly different society.

Marcela, the girl in *Mala yerba*, is no Nieves. She is sensuous, tantalizing, aware of her own particular kind of power. Julián Andrade, the son of a wealthy, land-owning family, is ruthless in his assumption of his right to do anything he cares to do in his relationship with the peons. These two forces are set against each other, and the power that enables Julián to prevail is the power that comes from his social position, not from his personal strength. Azuela's treatment of Julián is different from Zentella's or López Portillo's description of the *hacendado*. Zentella simply assumed that his power was a given condition. López Portillo lets his reader know the *hacendado's* rationalization of his attitude, but he does so by explanation that is rather external to the characterization. Andrade, on the other hand, is perverted by the power that he knows he has, and the reader feels this power as a part of the characterization. The result is that the *hacendado's* power does not seem to be an immovable object. At the same time, since Marcela is not idealized, Azuela avoids a simple conflict of individual good versus evil. The society is corrupt, and the social blight has affected not just one group but all groups. There is no idealist in *Mala yerba* to point toward the future; but the circumstance of general corruption is enough to suggest movement in that direction, rather than improvement on the basis of the past. Indeed, Azuela left nothing of the past on which a hope for change could be based, because he sees the triangle formed by *hacendado*, government, and Church, as the antagonist to the peon. But the profound importance of Azuela's observation is not in the identification of offending institutions. Rather, it is the recognition of what corruption of a human relationship has done to both sides of the conflict.

Mala yerba is Azuela's best novel before *Los de abajo*. Although it has a number of faults—some inauthentic characterization, and some action that might well have been omitted—it is apparent that the author was finding his way, learning from his French models, and adapting what he learned to his own needs. Throughout his literary career, Azuela started with what he wanted to say, and then found a way to say it. He was never a man of letters, either in the scholarly or artistic sense. He was a physician who wrote novels. Sometimes this highly personal approach produced art, sometimes it did not.

In 1911 Azuela published a short novel, *Andrés Pérez, maderista*, which may well be considered the first novel of the Revolution. We should be quite clear that it is a novel *of* the Revolution, not a revolutionary novel. That is, it deals with the period of the Revolution, but does not defend it. A journalist goes from Mexico City to the northern part of the country to cover the Madero revolt, and becomes involved in it somewhat against his will.

The novel is an utter failure artistically. It does not have even one genuine character. The people who move in and out of the very slender plot are intended by the author to exemplify types who took part in the revolt for reasons which were not satisfactory to Azuela. The heart of the matter is that everybody was trying to save his own skin, an attitude that is less surprising to some people than it was to Azuela. He is disgusted by the officials who switch sides when they sense the direction of the wind, and by a *hacendado* who can save his wealth only by adherence to the Madero cause. The list of such people is fairly long. But the length of the list does not complicate the circumstance, it just provides more examples of the same thing. We can join the author in his disgust, but his astonishment is somewhat surprising in a man who knew the world as well as Azuela did.

I don't question for a moment the accuracy of Azuela's observation. The objective facts of history show that the Madero movement was full of Díaz opportunists and, indeed, of other opportunists too. It is hard to imagine that anything else would have happened. The novels of the Díaz period describe a society in which political opportunism was almost a profession, and revolution was regarded as a means of furthering one's personal ambitions. The world had not changed overnight, and the magnitude of the change that grew out of the Madero revolt could not possibly have been apparent at the time. The world that Azuela describes, if we allow our imagination to supply the development that the author omitted, is exactly what would happen in the society described by his predecessors.

Andrés Pérez, maderista is a fairly good introduction to Azuela's treatment of the Revolution, in spite of the fact that its artistic value is slight. Since Azuela had already shown that he could write better novels, I suspect the artistic failure of this one should be blamed on an overly intense reaction to his theme. Attempting, as he always did, to find the most adequate means of expressing his ideas, Azuela's indignation overcame his artistic sense. The same thing happened in some later novels; but in others, his indignation is controlled and the novels are more convincing. In these cases of controlled indignation, disillusionment is apparent and, in a sense, Azuela's novels, even *Los de abajo*, are antirevolutionary. It seems to me that *Andrés Pérez, maderista* is essential to an understanding of the author's disillusionment and his general attitude toward the Revolution. The point is simply that he raised no objection to the intent of the Madero revolt, but to the way it was used by selfish people. He was repeatedly disappointed by people and could not forgive them for not living up to his ideal of what they should do. He judged his contemporaries and his precursors on this basis. And yet, in his best novels he saw beyond what individuals did and understood the change that was taking place in Mexico. *Andrés Pérez, maderista* set the stage for the extended vision of *Los de abajo*.

At the end of this period, the form that the change would take in the long run was by no means clear. But a bridge had been crossed and burned. In 1911, the year of Azuela's disillusionment in *Andrés Pérez, maderista* and of Heriberto Frías' defeat of idealism in *El triunfo de Sancho Panza*, an old Reformist fire-eater, Juan A. Mateos, exultantly published his own version of the end of an era in *La majestad caída (The Fallen Majesty)*. It is not a very good novel, but there is a certain poetic justice in the appearance of the vehement old liberal's account of the end of Porfirio Díaz's regime.

8. The Gradual Tempest
(1913–1924)

In one of those coincidences that delight a literary historian, Juan A. Mateos and Ireneo Paz, both novelists of the Reform, witnessed and wrote about the fall of Díaz and the beginning of the Revolution. *La majestad caída* was Mateos' last novel, and Paz ended his career with *Madero* (1914). Far less happy is the memory of the tragic murder of Madero that is evoked by Paz's account of very recent history. By the time Madero became president, the Revolution was well under way. The middle-class revolt had touched off a popular reaction, and it was not going to be stopped until a clearly new, and clearly dominant, government was set up.

It is not surprising that very few novels were published during the years of revolutionary turmoil. The only important novel published before 1918 was Mariano Azuela's *Los de abajo* (1915) which is the best account written of the popular Revolution. However, *Los de abajo* is a special case, because Azuela published it in El Paso, Texas, where he had gone after the retreat of the forces of Pancho Villa, and it was hardly known in Mexico until the mid-1920's. Meanwhile, Carlos González Peña (*La fuga de la quimera*) and José López Portillo y Rojas (*Fuertes y débiles*) wrote novels that deal with phases of the Revolution prior to the action of *Los de abajo*. Both novels, published in 1919, were probably written earlier and kept by their authors until a more serene society made their publication practicable.

The intellectuals' transition from the Díaz period into post-Revolutionary Mexico finds very satisfactory expression in Carlos González Peña and his novel—both the man and his work. The author, a man of letters in both the creative and the scholarly sense, grew up in the traditionalism of a disappearing society, deeply respected European culture, recognized the importance of Mexican cultural growth, and looked forward into the post-Revolutionary world. These characteristics describe a static position, not an evolution. González Peña was always the same.

La fuga de la quimera is a story of adultery in the middle-class society of Mexico City, at the time of the Madero revolt. Although all the characters belong to the middle class, there is a considerable range of wealth and customs from the lower to the upper spheres of the middle class. The social life of the poorer people is simpler, tending toward neighborhood or family parties, gossip, and a brave pretense of belonging to a wealthier group. The wealthy pretend in the same direction, but in a more sophisticated fashion, and are more inclined to look for their entertainment at the theater or at large parties. Both groups are ambivalent with regard to imitation of the foreign and defense of Mexican customs. Among the more modest, a francophile may be limited to uttering French phrases at inappropriate times while his wealthy counterpart may express the same inclination by buying a European-style house in a new section of the city. The lower middle class resembles the people of Rafael Delgado's novels; the wealthy are the hypocrites that Heriberto Frías despised. González Peña shows a great respect for the kind of moral behavior that both Delgado and López Portillo y Rojas regarded as the basis of modern civilization.

La fuga de la quimera can be most properly described as a novel of customs, because a wealth of detail provides background for the story of adultery. The characterizations, done mainly through direct description rather than through action, fit together nicely to give a picture of the society. There are a few people of intelligence and humility who are blessed with good intentions, good taste, and good sense. The others are victimized by their own small ambitions. Caught up in the stability of the Díaz period, they think only of more money, more power, more elegance within the framework of that society. When the news of the Madero revolt reaches these people, they are inclined to push it aside as something of no consequence. It is just another small-time rebellion that can be put down easily by a detachment of troops. As the rebellion grows, a few people start to take it more seriously, and generally they are disposed to defend the Díaz government. One lonely voice attacks Díaz, and its owner has personal reasons as well as political ones.

Jorge Bazán, the principal male character, is a young lawyer with few ambitions until the Madero revolt gives him a good political opportunity. Although he has been a supporter of the Díaz regime, he remembers that his father was a liberal and decides he should follow the paternal lead. He expresses to the people a sympathy he could not possibly feel, and promises improvements he could not possibly produce. When the revolutionary forces actually enter Mexico City, the middle-class characters of the novel are repelled by the popular reaction. These lower-class people, shouting "viva Madero" and "abajo Díaz" through the streets of the capital, are stepping out of their place. Bazán, witnessing such a demonstration with a conservative friend, silently acknowledges that the friendship is at an end. It is important that González Peña sees no reconciliation between the two political extremes, yet he does not divide the people into two definite groups. He obviously means that some conservatism will continue, and that various degrees of liberalism and compromise will appear.

From the standpoint of structure, *La fuga de la quimera* has one very obvious fault: the facts and opinions concerning the Revolution are not well related to the plot of the novel. That is, the action of the Revolution doesn't have much to do with what happens to the people. This fact may well be a fault from the standpoint of conventional literary criticism; but in this particular novel, it seems to me that the lack of articulation adds a great deal to the reality of the circumstances. The fact that the Revolution in the north is unrelated to the lives of the people of Mexico City is probably an accurate reflection of the actual case. And it is probably also true that, in those early days of the Revolution, even when the action reached the city, the people felt that it was a hardship brought upon them by outsiders. Certainly, the people in González Peña's novel have no sense of participation in a great national movement.

The political atmosphere of *La fuga de la quimera*, like that of *Andrés Pérez, maderista,* promises rather poor support for the Madero government. And that is exactly what it got. Old Díaz men were everywhere in the government. Madero innocently thought they would support him. He was unable to put into effect the reforms he advocated, and the revolutionary elements became dissatisfied. He was blamed by both right and left for what he did do and for what he didn't do. Some foreign elements became uneasy about their interests in Mexico. A group of conservatives, aided by these foreign interests and especially by Henry Lane Wilson, the ambassador from the United States, plotted the overthrow of Madero and the substitution of Victoriano Huerta, a Díaz general who was supposed to be the strong man who would restore order to the country. A battle between the two opposing forces broke out in the heart of Mexico City. This terrible affair is generally called "The Ten Tragic Days." The martyr-heroine of *La fuga de la quimera* is killed during this battle, not because she was in any way involved with the plot, but simply by accident. With a war raging outside their house, González Peña's characters continue being concerned about their personal intrigues as if they belonged to an entirely different world. At this point the novel ends.

The closed society of the city was naturally less responsive to the revolutionary movement than the rural society was, because the *hacendado* system was immediately sensitive to uprisings by the peons or to incursions by bandits. José López Portillo y Rojas related the urban and rural situations by moving the protagonist of *Fuertes y débiles* (1919) from one scene to the other. Juan Nepomuceno Bolaños (Cheno) is the last male of a distinguished family whose more responsible members cling to their Mexican interpretation of Hispanic tradition. Cheno is a black sheep whose positivistic education has separated him from religion, and therefore, in the author's opinion, from morality. Cheno has a certain sense of justice which makes him see that his peons are well paid, but his concern for them does not keep him from sleeping with their wives and daughters. Indeed, the central theme of the novel is a repetition of *Nieves* within the new framework of the Revolution. Cheno takes as his mistress the wife of Chema, a jealous but cowardly peon.

Cheno's friends in the city are divided into two groups: his traditionalist relatives and their friends, and his fiancée's circle of *nouveaux riches*, sophisticated francophiles and anglophiles. It is in the home of his fiancée that Cheno becomes involved in a plot to overthrow Madero. He wants nothing to do with it because he says there is no trouble in the rural areas. But finally, weak-principled fellow that he is, he allows his girl friend to tease him into agreeing with the others. After Huerta assumes power, the fiancée and family find that conditions are worse than they were under Madero, and decide to go to Europe. The traditionalists remain, of course, and do not appear to be greatly affected by the Revolution.

Cheno finds that on the hacienda there is now a great deal of unrest. The author was not writing a historical novel, so he does not give a general picture of the course of the Revolution after Madero, but focuses on the impact it has on one hacienda. The fact is that the nation's turmoil increased considerably. Pancho Villa was the principal leader in the north, although Alvaro Obregón had a more lasting influence on the movement. Emiliano Zapata, in the south, gave the movement its most genuine popular character through his demand for redistribution of the land. These leaders and others of lesser renown fought against the government and sometimes against each other.

The unrest on Cheno's hacienda gives López Portillo the opportunity to discuss the attitude of the *hacendado* and to restate the position that he had taken many years earlier: some *hacendados* are evil, some are not. He was still not inclined to attack the system itself. The attitudes of Cheno's peons vary a great deal. Many are quite satisfied with the status quo, especially since on this particular hacienda they have plenty to eat. Others side with Cheno because they are personally attached to him. And still others oppose him for personal reasons. Poli, an exceptionally intelligent peon who has been an overseer, leaves the hacienda and recruits a band of revolutionaries. Poli knows that he is fighting for freedom, but he is the only one of the revolutionaries who understands what he is doing. López Portillo presents Poli favorably, and makes a point of distinguishing between rebels and bandits. The rebels are men who are fighting for their rights, under responsible leadership. Bandits are social misfits who take advantage of the situation to pillage.

The disintegration of the hacienda is gradual. Finally, the revolutionaries attack, and Cheno, left with only a few supporters, is attacked and captured. He is condemned to death; but since many people believe he deserves special consideration because of his policy of paying fair wages, the revolutionaries agree to ask their general to commute the death sentence. Poli chooses Chema, the aggrieved husband, as messenger to the general. Chema's trip is one of the finest things López Portillo wrote. Knowing that his enemy's life depends on his arriving on time, Chema never makes a decision, but lets his conflicting inclinations control his speed, and finally arrives a moment too late.

The action of the revolutionaries is a much more important part of the story in *Fuertes y débiles* than in *La fuga de la quimera*, but López Portillo does not describe it as a movement of the whole society. Much of the novel, especially the first part, is a *costumbrista* contrast of the two elements of urban society: traditionalist and sophisticated. The main concern of both groups with regard to the Revolution is how they can avoid it. While these contrasting groups contribute something to the picture of the time, they also cause the author to preach. The novel is, therefore, rather diffuse. But it is still a good novel—perhaps the author's best—because it grows with the Revolution, as the movement becomes more intense. As the story progresses, *costumbrismo* becomes less important and the Revolution gets more attention. It is as if López Portillo wrote it during the course of events, when the fact of the Revolution became more important than the static society that preferred to ignore it.

None of the early novels of the Revolution pretends that the movement incorporated the whole society. Even *Los de abajo*, which presents the most sweeping picture, recognizes that the revolutionaries were often regarded as a phenomenon exterior to regular life. Sometimes they were a threat, sometimes a blessing, but never ordinary people. The difference between *Los de abajo* and the two novels I have been talking about is a matter of the author's point of view. González

Peña and López Portillo presented established society as the norm, and saw the Revolution as something that would change it. Azuela accepted the Revolution as the established fact, and saw static society as an obstruction. *Fuertes y débiles* really moves from one viewpoint to the other during the course of the novel.

Mariano Azuela subtitled his novel "Pictures of the Revolution," and it is a good description of the book. Using large strokes of his literary brush, he painted the types that assembled around one revolutionary leader, Demetrio Macías, and the ambitions that Demetrio came to have. The words "large strokes" describe Azuela's technique. *Los de abajo* is the best example of the author's independent interpretation of techniques he had learned. Firmly rooted in the tradition of objective observation, Azuela perfected a technique of selection that suggests more than words could say. His descriptions of nature are superb. A mountain is a cathedral. He suggests, without detail, and nothing more is needed. When Demetrio walks with his wife after a long absence, they stand under a tree during the rain, and the white blossoms are stars. A morning can be a "wedding morning" and the mountain mist is a veil. His descriptions are never long, always suggestive. Each image leaves the reader looking forward to the next one. What Azuela does in his description, he does also in action. There is no intricate plot of complicated details, but the movement of the story is clear. He leaves episodes without resolving them, but the reader knows exactly what is going on. The barking of Demetrio's dog signals the coming of the *federales*. It also means a dramatic change in Demetrio's life, and it means fear, desperation, and loneliness.

There is some justification for saying that the Revolution itself is the protagonist of *Los de abajo*. In a large sense it is. But Azuela was too canny a novelist to make an abstraction of something as intensely human as the Revolution. Demetrio Macías is the protagonist even though he does not take on the heroic proportions we might like a revolutionary protagonist to have. Macías is propelled into the Revolution as a means of defending himself. In animal fashion, he recoils and strikes back. He thinks—or doesn't think—only in these terms until the "slicker" (*curro*), Luis Cervantes, tries to educate him in revolutionary ideology. Demetrio does not accept Cervantes' grandiose ideas readily, but he doesn't turn down his flattery. And as the

Macías band marches from success to success, and joins a larger force, Demetrio is delightfully ingenuous in his awareness of his new eminence. As his importance increases, he becomes less and less concerned for individuals, and only defeat is able to rekindle his concern.

It is very fitting that Demetrio should be more susceptible to Cervantes' flattery than to his ideology. Flattery was a more characteristic expression in a man whose ideology was only a cover for his opportunism. Cervantes believed that a small group of men would benefit spectacularly from the Revolution. Perhaps he even regretted it, but he had every intention of being one of the group. Solís, another city man and an acquaintance of Cervantes, is disillusioned, but not cynical. The opportunism of men like Cervantes, and the inhumanity of the others, combine to make Solís consider the whole movement a disgusting spectacle. Yet he is caught up in it. Solís probably comes closer than any other character to expressing the author's view of the Revolution. But I am not certain that Azuela intended to use him as a mouthpiece, because the Revolution, in *Los de abajo*, exists on two levels. It is a discernible, social action that can be discussed in terms of how men act and what they expect as a result of what they do. But on another level, it is the movement of a people in which individuals participate not because they know what they are doing, but because they cannot resist the force that puts them in motion. The fact that men like Demetrio Macías did not know what they were fighting for is not a condemnation of the Revolution; rather, it is a reflection of its essence, and such men were more authentic revolutionaries than the ones who could spell out an ideology. *Los de abajo* says all this, whether or not the author intended to say it.

The outstanding characteristic of *Los de abajo* is movement, and movement is revolt against a static condition. The troops move. We often feel they are out for a stroll, rather than on the march. Women go with them, cook for them, forage for them, fight beside them, suffer with them, and carouse with them. These are the *soldaderas* of *Tomochic*. But the popular Revolution sometimes preserved family unity along with the fighting. Trains have a special role. They transported troops, but sometimes they transported whole families that belonged to a society which, at long last, was in motion. The train itself, because of its importance to movement, became a kind of supernatural ally. Brutality and orgies are movement too, disgusting perhaps, but movement away from domination, from stagnation. The troops destroy, not knowing what they are creating, not even caring whether they are creating anything. They sack a pretentious house and go away carrying draperies, furniture, paintings, books. One soldier carries a typewriter. When he gets tired of carrying it, he sells it to someone else. And so the typewriter, becoming more and more a nuisance, passes from hand to hand, always at a lower price. Its last owner buys it for twenty-five *centavos*, just for the experience of throwing it against a rock and seeing it break.

Azuela relates the incident of the typewriter as if it were a daily occurence. If it symbolizes the destructiveness of the Revolution, the reader must make the assumption, because the author does not indicate that he intends it to be an example. He tells the story, drops it, and moves on. Azuela's narrative technique contributes spectacularly to the feeling of movement. His ellipses carry the story forward, expectantly, creating a more complete world in motion around and between the episodes.

The movement of Demetrio Macías is circular: geographically, psychologically, and materially. He and his men are ambushed at the scene of their first victory. Demetrio is the last; and as he watches his friends die—the ones who were with him from the start—he becomes again the man he was when he assembled them around him for their protection and vengeance. Each one is important. Once a subordinate told Demetrio that some of his men had been killed in a friendly brawl. Demetrio matter-of-factly ordered that they be buried, and brushed the affair aside. But now the names matter, the men matter, and Demetrio is back where he started. His career no longer has significance. It doesn't matter that he has been called colonel. Now he is just a revolutionary. And the circle almost closes, but not quite. We might say that it closes on the first level, but not on the second. Azuela never tells us that Macías dies. He tells us when he is shot, and then he says that Demetrio keeps on aiming his rifle forever. If on one level there is the silence of death, on the other there is endless movement.

In the world of newspaper reality, the forces of Alvaro Obregón entered Mexico City after the fall of Huerta,[1] but were forced to withdraw by Pancho Villa and Zapata. Then Obregón began a show-down fight with Villa which ended with the latter's defeat and retreat to the north. Azuela pictures this retreat in *Las moscas*, a short novel published in 1918.

Las moscas is one of several short pieces published by Azuela in 1917 and 1918; and although the book is, in my opinion, a failure, it is important in the trajectory of his works. Azuela used exactly the same techniques that he used in *Los de abajo*. The novel is composed of flashes of narration and deft character sketches, showing Villa's men and the hangers-on (*moscas*—flies) who are interested in enjoying every possible advantage from association with Villa, then moving over to the other side at the first opportunity. The pictures are vivid, revolting, and bitter. The author's disillusionment is much more apparent than it is in *Los de abajo*, and it is not surprising, because he was dealing with humanity at its worst.

Las moscas is a failure because it has no Demetrio Macías. It is exactly the kind of novel that *Los de abajo* would have been if Azuela had made a protagonist of the Revolution abstracted. As vivid as his pictures are, they lack the power to draw the reader into them. *Los de abajo* is different because the human quality of the Revolution is seen in and through Macías. Because this human quality is lacking, there is no promise in *Las moscas*. In many of Azuela's novels, notably *Mala yerba* and *Los de abajo*, the author's pessimism is accompanied by a suggestion of movement toward an improved future. In *Las moscas*, there is no such suggestion, and it reaches a dead end. It is not a picture of the Revolution, but of defeat. It is not a convincing novel, because the lack of a protagonist separates it from reality except for readers who are prepared ahead of time to join Azuela in his disgust.

Venustiano Carranza, a Díaz politician, was able to organize a constitutional convention late in 1916. His own ideas tended to be counter-revolutionary; but more liberal elements prevailed at the

---

[1] U.S. foreign policy changed when Woodrow Wilson was inaugurated. His administration refused to recognize Huerta, and arranged to furnish supplies to the revolutionaries.

convention, and early in 1917, the present Mexican Constitution was adopted. It is based on the Reform Constitution of 1857, but makes more radical and specific provisions for revising the social structure of the country. Most notably, it laid the foundation for the redistribution of lands, declared the principles that were to provide the basis for expropriation of the oil companies, and granted rights and considerable power to labor. Carranza became president.

Azuela's *Las tribulaciones de una familia decente* (1918) makes an interesting companion piece to *Los de abajo* as a picture of Mexican society during the period that reached into the administration of Carranza. It is the story of the troubles that beset a distinguished family during the Revolution.[2] The family belongs to the static, traditionalist society of the earlier period. But now traditionalism can no longer be a way of life. Azuela describes their plight in a manner that is more reminiscent of *Mala yerba* than of *Los de abajo*. The more traditional approach to the novel is appropriate since *Las tribulaciones* is not a novel of motion. A number of interesting character studies make it a good novel. Unfortunately, Azuela committed one grave error: the first part of the novel is narrated autobiographically by one of the characters; then the narrator dies and the author takes over as narrator. I am at a loss to explain this unusual procedure. It contributes nothing to the intent of the book, and has the effect of putting the reader at odds with the author, since there is no apparent reason for the change.

Rather than a novel of movement, *Las tribulaciones* is a novel of shock. With their way of life destroyed, the members of the family must make their way, and with little money. They must decide whether to work or to try to bluff. And they find themselves victimized by the opportunists of the new order. They have to decide which of their traditional values can be preserved, and whether it is better to accept those values as an ethical basis or reject them and become new people in a new society. Perhaps the most significant of the char-

---

[2] Some readers may note a striking similarity between this book and a novel by Alice Tisdale Hobart, *The Peacock Sheds His Tail* (New York: The Bobbs-Merrill Company, 1945). Miss Hobart tried to include a larger segment of Mexican history, and made some bad mistakes. But her account of what happens to the family is quite similar to Azuela's.

acters is Procopio, who has never had much of a voice within the family and has been somewhat retiring because he does not control the money. With the money gone, Procopio finds himself on a level with the rest. Without sacrificing his decency, he discovers assurance in working for a living. The family has not become a part of the Revolution, but it will gradually disappear as a family, and different members will find their places in the new society. Some will forget their traditionalism, others will cherish memories of the good old days and perhaps even pass on a futile snobbishness to another generation.

As the nation's president, Venustiano Carranza's main job was restoring order to the country. Emiliano Zapata was not content with the course of events, and kept on fighting for immediate redistribution of land. In 1919, he was treacherously murdered, and, without his leadership, his army disintegrated. Carranza showed no strong inclination to implement the more radical provisions of the Constitution, nor did he seem inclined to give up the presidency. His opponents caused him to leave Mexico City in 1920, and he was murdered between there and Veracruz. Alvaro Obregón became president in November of the same year and began implementation of the social reforms called for in the Constitution. It is probably fair to date the political expression of the new Mexico from that time, though it should be clearly understood that the country was still far from stable. It should also be noted that the radical side of the Revolution was modified, from the very beginning, by a conservative element that was more interested in political than in social change. And while the popular element in the Revolution was strong, so was the influence of the middle class.

The three novelists discussed so far in this chapter belonged to three different worlds. López Portillo y Rojas belonged to the Díaz period. His vision, apparent even in his early works, helped him accommodate himself more or less to new circumstances, but he really belonged to a past age. Azuela belonged to his own world and to no literary group. González Peña belonged to a group that straddled the two periods. He was one of a group of young intellectuals who were called the Ateneo de la Juventud (Atheneum of Youth). From this group came some of the most productive men Mexico has known:

Alfonso Reyes, José Vasconcelos, Enrique González Martínez, and several others. These men were, in a way, the intellectual side of the Revolution. Although not related directly to the revolutionary movement, they were themselves revolutionary. Their aim was to move the country out of the nineteenth century philosophically and artistically. Julio Jiménez Rueda, a critic and creative writer who studied under several members of the Ateneo, gives an excellent short analysis of the group in an interview with Emmanuel Carballo.

The Ateneo marks a moment of transition in the life of Mexico: it attends the burial of *porfirismo* (the Díaz regime) and the advent of the new regime. Most of the members of the Ateneo did not understand the political and social Revolution although they revolutionized the cultural life of the country. They were, basically, aristocrats, withdrawn from the people. The Revolution came along to disturb the world of their childhood, of their industrious adolescence. In a way, it was uncontrolled barbarism breaking academic harmony. The Revolution was a middle-class movement. The members of the Ateneo were middle class, but middle class with their hair combed carefully. The theorists of the armed movement were dishevelled middle class.[3]

What the members of the Ateneo intended to do called for awareness of what was going on in Europe, and an evaluation of Mexico in terms of its allegiance to European culture. The tendency toward national introversion that came after the Revolution, made their work look antinationalistic to some, but one of the expressions that grew out of the Ateneo was the so-called "colonialist" novel which was, at least in part, a nationalistic expression. Jiménez Rueda, in his comments on the Ateneo, says that many of the characteristics of the colonialist novel were present in the works of Mariano Silva y Aceves, Genaro Estrada, Julio Torri, and Alfredo Cravioto.

Actually, the men who wrote colonialist novels—Jiménez Rueda, Francisco Monterde, Artemio de Valle Arizpe, Ermilo Abreu Gómez —were not a completely distinct generation from the members of the Ateneo. The latter were trying their wings at the time of the fall of Díaz. Monterde published his first colonialist novels in 1918. From

---

[3] Emmanuel Carballo, "Julio Jiménez Rueda," *México en la Cultura*, No. 484, Supplement to *Novedades* (22 junio 1958), 3.

that time until 1924, this kind of novel was the most cultivated among the writers of the literary circles of Mexico City. The authors looked at the past in much the way an antique-hunter looks at a beautiful old table. It was a new view of the past in Mexican fiction. Nineteenth-century historical novelists obviously preferred dealing with the Independence and later events. When they looked back into the Colonial Period, usually at the Inquisition, their purpose was to judge it on the basis of their own liberalism. The twentieth-century *colonialistas*, however, were interested in re-creating artistically a past which held for them an obsessive, antiquarian charm.

The colonialist novels all have the same general characteristics and can probably be defined as a group better than as individual novels, although the problem of definition is complicated by the vague line between historical novel and historical account. Some of the works of the *colonialistas* stay close to historical fact without remaking it into fiction. But even these works are written in the affected style that was characteristic of the novels. The authors cultivated an overly archaic style which they supposed would enhance the atmosphere of the past that they wanted to create; but they tended to overdo it, and the result is often more precious than convincing.

The motivation behind the colonialist novels is fundamental to their literary characteristics. The basic question is whether these novels, which constitute the first literary trend after the Revolution, were an attempt to escape the confusing reality of their time, or were the expression of a new nationalistic interest. I suspect that these apparently conflicting motivations actually worked together. The authors were upper-middle-class intellectuals who were artistically oriented. It is not surprising that they sought the security of a time so far past that its disturbing specifics were hidden by interesting generalities. In re-creating the specifics, the novelists were in control, and could remake them to their own taste. On the other hand, the fact of the Revolution was apparent enough to lead them to a new national awareness which kept their interest in Mexico. Their particular view of the past deepened the perspective of the national tradition and made it quite different from the *costumbrista* traditionalism of the preceding generation.

In addition to the basic question, there are two secondary considerations that have to do with *colonialista* motivation. One is Jiménez Rueda's opinion that this type of novel is related to a larger movement, in other literatures and in the other arts. He sees a relationship with the works of Enrique Larreta, D'Annunzio, and Valle Inclán, among others. He also sees the same tendency in painting and in mission-style architecture. The second consideration is one of attitude, rather than influence. It involves the incredulity a person feels when he stands on a historical spot, when he is acutely aware that this place was the scene of a past that affects his present. This reaction can be even more intense if he "discovers" this place, more or less accidentally, in the midst of a modern world, or in the midst of modern confusion. Then he becomes, in a sense, the owner of the place. It seems to have a special relevance to him, and he is inclined to think of it in familiar terms. The discovery may even evoke a gentle laugh —not because it is funny, but because he feels there is something incongruous, yet delightful, about the identification of the place with himself. I think it was this feeling that led to the *colonialista's* mannerism. The techniques they used to re-create the intimacy that they felt made their novels appear superficial. They succeeded, to a considerable extent, in "re-hispanicizing" the language which, in artistic usage, had moved toward French. And this linguistic influence is part of the different perspective in which they saw Mexican tradition.

Judging the colonialist novels from the standpoint of reading pleasure, the only just statement is to say that a little is delightful, but a little goes a long way. Any one of the novels makes pleasant reading, but its preciousness is likely to become annoying by the end of the book. My own taste would select Jiménez Rueda's *Moisén* (1924) as one of the best. I suppose we might regret that the authors allowed their preciousness to modify their possible influence on Mexico's awareness of itself; but I also think that what might have been gained in one direction would have been lost in another equally important direction: the conscious cultivation of artistic prose. The *colonialistas* were the intentional literary artists of their time, and the continuation of Mexico's literary tradition depended as much on them as on the spontaneous genius of Azuela.

The picture of what happened in the novel during this period can be distorted by too much attention to Azuela's novels of the Revolution. If we except his works, the novels that deal with the Revolution are very few. The nation was still not ready to examine the phenomenon of the Revolution, probably because it was still not aware of its depth or breadth. The colonialist novel was more cultivated than the novel of the Revolution. Mixed with the two were a few *costumbrista* traditionalist novels that were as out-of-date as a moustache cup, but which probably appealed to people who used moustache cups.

By 1923, Heriberto Frías had reached the only solution he was ever able to find to the problem of social stability. In *Aguila o sol,* he portrays redemptive woman in the person of Gaudelia: mestiza, long-suffering, self-effacing, heroic, optimistic, feminine, and aware of her redemptive role. Opposite her, he places three men who are in need of her redemptive action. Miguel Mercado, Frías' *alter ego,* is not one of the three; but he solves his personal dilemma through Gaudelia's inspiration rather than redemption, and asserts himself by speaking against the Díaz government. Using a symbolic approach to his description of Mexican reality, and telling the story objectively, Frías came very close to writing a great novel. He failed because he could not synthesize Gaudelia's opposite, and so presented a three-headed reality which owes its existence as much to the author's wishful thinking as to his vision. The society that Frías sees leans toward Revolution, but is not totally committed. His people include many who are humbler than those of *La fuga de la quimera,* but it is clear that even among them, the Revolution will not have immediate and complete acceptance.

In the same year, Azuela published *La malhora,* the first of three novels that the author and some critics like to regard as hermetic, or *avant-garde.* Azuela changes his theme from the Revolution to life in one of the extremely poor sections of Mexico City. Like Heriberto Frías, he was both fascinated and repelled by this social class. *La malhora* is a pessimistic novel because it is hard to see how the lot of these miserable people can be improved. Their subhuman values intensify the misfortune into which they are born. This disheartening picture is the first of its kind in the Mexican novel. It leaves no doubt that the Revolution has much to accomplish, and its successors are expressions of dissatisfaction with the Revolution's failure to remove the problem entirely.

Azuela's manner of writing *La malhora* is an intensification of the techniques used in *Los de abajo* and *Las moscas*. He took greater liberties with chronology, depended more on imagery, made more use of eliptical narration, demanded more of his reader's imagination. Azuela and some of his critics have said that *La malhora,* along with *El desquite* (1925) and *La luciérnaga* (1932), is a reaction against the lack of attention given his earlier novels. He is supposed to have written the so-called hermetic novels to suit the taste of the time which, presumably, tended toward surrealism and other literary "isms" of the 1920's. We cannot take this position seriously, in view of the technical similarities between *La malhora* and two of his earlier works, and in view of the fact that there were no *avant-garde* novels published in Mexico prior to 1925, except Azuela's own. He deserves to be considered an innovator, and a particularly important one because of his combination of social concern and art in the novels that some people prefer to disregard as atypical of the author.

In the years following, the nature of literary commitment became the subject of a debate which grew out of the conflicting tendencies toward introversion and extroversion. Writers disagreed, often violently, on the question of attention to the immediate social problem versus consideration of the deeper reality of man. The issue, which was fundamentally confused, was complicated by uncertainty concerning the ultimate goals of the artist. In *La malhora,* Azuela shows a comprehension of integral reality that might have resolved the conflict. Unfortunately, *La malhora,* although it points out the direction, was not a really excellent novel, and was not strong enough to act as the necessary guide.

9. The Artists' Intent

(1925–1930)

Mexico City in 1925 was change set on change, confusion within confusion, the heart of a nation discovering itself in a larger world that was bursting its cocoon. The movement of the Revolution was in the city. Its streetcars, rolling over the same tracks, no longer carried three-dimensional inertia to its predestination. They rushed now, imbued with life, to mystery, hope, despair, on an endless trip of discovery. The city was alive, and there was meaning in every human movement, in every flicker of a light. The definition of destiny, delayed by the exuberance of the moment, awaited its statement.

The Revolution struggled toward implementation. Alvaro Obregón began it; then grim-faced Plutarco Elías Calles became the *caudillo*, determined to be the strong man, to retain the power. Agrarian reform moved faster under Calles than it had before, but still not fast enough to change the social structure radically. Many social reformers demanded faster relief for the underprivileged masses, and thought that all the nation's energy should be directed toward that end. They saw little value in any activity that was not for the sake of the people. Calles attacked the Church and provoked a religious war —or better said, a series of religious rebellions—that were more brutal than decisive. The *caudillo*, working within the provisions of the Constitution, proved once again that the people were not in complete agreement with the reformers who had set out to redeem them.

The first post-Revolutionary tendency in the novel, colonialism, lasted only a few years. Genaro Estrada's *Pero Galín* (1926) marks its end, in much the way that *Don Quixote* marks the end of the novel of chivalry. The colonialist novel fell victim to its own preciousness; its more fundamental qualities were not substantial enough to maintain it. The novelists turned to other kinds of fiction, with the exception of Artemio de Valle Arizpe who cultivated his extraordinary relationship with the past throughout his lifetime.

The members of the Ateneo de la Juventud were scattered by the Revolution, and they did not leave an intact, instructed group to succeed them. The cultural revolution that the Ateneo had begun was revived in the mid-1920's by the young men who constituted the group associated with the review *Contemporáneos*: Carlos Pellicer, Bernardo Ortiz de Montellano, José Gorostiza, Jaime Torres Bodet, Salvador Novo, Xavier Villaurrutia, Enrique González Rojo, Gilberto Owen. Since the association was entirely informal, it is not always possible to say whether a particular writer belonged to the group or not. Indeed, many critics and even the writers themselves have discussed at great length the question of whether they were or were not a "group." They certainly show a high degree of individuality in their works, but they had in common the intention of renovating Mexican cultural expression, of bringing it up to date with the rest of the world. Although they were inclined to deny their similarity to the *modernistas*, they obviously had a similar interest in knowing the latest trends in artistic expression.

The *contemporáneos* were revolutionary in three ways: theirs was part of the ebullient, sometimes explosive expression of the youth of the 1920's, they seriously intended to inject into Mexican literature the characteristics of European literature of the time, and they were dedicated to the proposition that the creative act is revolutionary by its very nature. The first of these revolutionary postures appears to be the most frivolous, but may in fact be the most profound. From this feverish attitude, at once explosive and searching, came the many literary "isms" of the 1920's. They had primary reference to poetry, and frequently produced manifestoes of what literary art should be. Invariably, the great writers grew beyond the manifestoes, but these proclamations served as necessary explosions which enabled the artist to assert his radical intent and begin his writing. Then he was able to develop in his own way. This process was particularly appropriate in Mexico because it became the literary means of expressing the movement of the Revolution.

Far more explosive than the *Contemporáneos* group were the *estridentistas* (stridentists) who gathered around two reviews called *Horizonte* and *Irradiador*. To some extent their poetry resembles Italian futurism because of their interest in the artistic use of machinery and speed. It is, for the most part, abrupt poetry, consciously modern, too aware of technology and the social problem. Indeed, *estridentismo* tended to degenerate into political propaganda. The group produced only one novel, Arqueles Vela's *El café de nadie* (1926).[1] It is very short, as are most of the *avant-garde* novels of that period, and there is some doubt as to whether it ought to be called a novel or a short story. However, there is no doubt that these highly imaginative works contributed substantially to the development of the contemporary novel.

"El café de nadie" (the cafe of no one) was the way the *estridentistas* referred to their favorite haunt. Although their references to it make it sound like a purely imaginary place, it actually was a real restaurant. It was located in a residential section of the city, at that time far removed from the center of activity. It is not hard to imagine that few people went there. The reference to it as "nobody's cafe" probably began as a humorous allusion to the fact that there were few customers. Beyond that, the reference became a matter of identity. The place was both real and unreal. People who were actually there appeared to be imaginary, and imagined people appeared to be real.

The door of the Cafe opens toward the most populous, most sunnily tumultuous avenue. And yet, crossing its threshold which is like the last stairstep of reality, it seems that you enter the subway of dreams, of ideation.

Any emotion, any sentiment, is made static and parapeted in its atmosphere of a ruined and abandoned city, of a city laid waste by prehistoric catastrophes of incidental customers and merrymakers.

---

[1] The author published some fiction later which may have been written quite a bit before the date of publication, but the *estridentistas* were only a memory by that time.

Everything becomes hidden and patinaed, in its alchemist atmosphere of retrospective irreality. The tables, the chairs, the customers are as if beneath the mist of time, cloaked with silence.[2]

Arqueles Vela's imagery is effective. It is poetic imagery, carefully chosen to create just the right effect. It requires the reader's creative participation, since his own imagination must reach out to meet the author's in order to make the imagery effective. Much of the external imagery can be effective without being difficult.

The trees, awakened violently by the course of the automobile, were stumbling over each other along the whole length of the rapid perspective.[3]

But when the author moves inside a character, the reader has to work harder and is sometimes thrown off by the use of technological or scientific references that would not ordinarily be associated with the circumstances.

While Mabelina was hearing his phrases, she was feeling frenetic impulses to kiss him, to embrace him, to exalt him. But that defenseless attitude that he always assumed obliged her to be still, frightened, as if in the electric chair of love, as if in a clinic where they were testing the effects and variations of a class of ultraviolet rays that were breaking down her spirit and subjecting her body, transmigrating it to all the shadows where it contemplated itself and abstracted itself, recognizing its immoderate movements that were tapestrying the room with decorations of dreams.[4]

I think it is fair to say that part of *El café de nadie* is a serious expression of the author's attempt to comprehend reality, and part of it is sheer youthful extravagance. For him and for many of his contemporaries, the world (life, relationships, physical surroundings) was something to be explored, evaluated, and remade. The novel, not surprisingly, offers no earth-shaking conclusions. Its principal suggestion is that people do not really see (know) each other. The reality *of* a person—that is, his essence—is as elusive as is reality *for* a per-

---

[2] *El café de nadie* (Jalapa: Ediciones de Horizonte, 1926), p. 11. These are the first three paragraphs of the novel.
[3] *Ibid.*, p. 25.   [4] *Ibid.*, pp. 22–23.

son—that is, his existence. But joined with this serious concern is a kind of joy of freedom that can belong only to youth. He is threatened by his ignorance of reality, and his defense is outrageous statement, which he makes with the sure knowledge that it can do nothing but shock the reader.

Before going into this description of *El café de nadie*, I mentioned three revolutionary postures of the *Contemporáneos* group. The first was the explosive characteristic of the youth of the 1920's, which was even more apparent among the *estridentistas* than among the *contemporáneos*. They also shared the second posture, which was the belief that Mexican literature needed to be brought into the twentieth century. The writers of both groups knew that the literature of a static society would have to change when movement replaced inertia. Both groups were influenced by European literature, but the *contemporáneos* were more critical. They were not so inclined to accept the new simply because it was new, but to consider its artistic validity. It was this acute awareness of art that supported the third posture: the tenet that the act of artistic creativity is in itself revolutionary because it necessarily transcends existing circumstances.

To a certain extent, of course, the *estridentistas* understood the relationship of art and revolution, but they joined it with sociological and political concern. The *contemporáneos*, on the other hand, were committed to art as more basic than either sociology or politics, and they guarded art jealously against the intrusion of propaganda. They were bitterly criticized by writers who wanted to use literature as a means of promoting social justice. Many of the same writers condemned the "Europeanism" of the *contemporáneos* and demanded literature that dealt with themes that were clearly Mexican. Both sides went to extremes in defending their positions. The *contemporáneos*, for example, preferred Azuela's *La malhora* to *Los de abajo*, a completely indefensible critical opinion. Their opponents, on the other hand, greatly exaggerated what they considered to be the apolitical attitude of the *contemporáneos*. And some of them even went so far as to say that any literature that was inaccessible to the people was unacceptable. To these writers, even the socially oriented *estridentistas* were of no value. In making these generalizations, I am consciously indulging in a kind of inaccuracy. Since neither side of the issue was an organized group and neither had a stated policy, I am attributing to each side opinions that may have belonged only to some individuals. This extremely complicated argument involved many opinions, not always clear, on nationalism and cosmopolitanism, art-for-art's-sake and social commitment, hermeticism and easy accessibility, reality and imagination, even masculinity and effeminacy. What made the discussion so complicated is that the poles of the argument kept changing. At one point a discussion might be of nationalism versus cosmopolitanism, at another art-for-art's-sake versus social commitment, but at still another cosmopolitanism versus social commitment, and so on. Undoubtedly the argument grew out of Mexico's dual and contradictory tendency toward introversion and extroversion after the Revolution. That is why the discussion has never ended, and also why it is better understood now than in earlier years —in the last fifteen years or so, Mexico has taken giant strides toward reconciliation of its introversion and extroversion.

The *contemporáneos* were poets. The amount of prose fiction they wrote was slight, but it dominated the fiction of the last half of the 1920's, and plays a role in the Mexican novel far out of proportion to its quantity or even to its intrinsic quality. The novels are weak in narration and in structure. They are rich in style and in sensitivity. Obviously, the authors were interested in probing the human condition in order to see a deeper reality than was visible in their social environment. It might be said with some justification that the *contemporáneos* who ventured into fiction—Owen, Novo, Villaurrutia, Torres Bodet—were novelists without a novel. An exception must be made in the case of Torres Bodet, the only one who persisted as a novelist, because he eventually found his novel in *Primero de enero* (1934) and *Sombras* (1937).

As a group the novels may be described as psychological. However, the use of the word is quite different from its application to nineteenth-century novels in which characters were analyzed. In these *avant-garde* novels of the 1920's, the authors enter the characters in a kind of soul-participation. They use a great deal of imagery, much of it based on unusual associations that approach synesthesia. They use free association, dreams, and the displacement of time. Partly technique and partly theme is their persistent interest in things of their own time: advertisements, movie stars, makes of automobiles, and the like. They show a swaggering certainty in the permanence of the amazing symbols of a brave new world. Some of these symbols have lasted; others have long since disappeared and, if they are remembered at all, it is with a significance that is quite different from what the author intended. An allusion to Zasu Pitts, for example, may be completely lost on many present-day readers. If they recall her at all, it will be with much the same feeling that they recall a Star sport coupe. It was only in this respect that the novelists did not achieve universal appeal.

Gilberto Owen was the first of the group to publish a novel. *La llama fría* (1925) is a provincial love story reminiscent of Ramón López Velarde's poetry.[5] The woman, Ernestina, like López Velarde's Fuensanta, is older than the boy who loves her, and is a love-object rather than a sweetheart in the conventional sense. The lover seeks his identification in Ernestina by responding to his idealization of her. But this response is not just to the woman; it is a response to the provincial ethos, in the sense of basic identification with tradition, rather than of acceptance of established custom as the standard of conduct. For this reason, Owen's provincialism is not restrictive, but provides a basis of security on which he can enlarge his vision.

La llama fría is better described as poetic than as *avant-garde*. The characteristics that differentiate it from a conventional novel are mainly the result of Owen's poetic concept of reality and communication. The novel is all *feeling*—a more exact word in this case than "atmosphere." Owen suggests, and the reader responds. The sense of the novel grows outward from the love relationship. Neither characters nor situation are fully described. What we know of them develops from the central theme, and the novel probably is highly unsatisfactory to a reader who waits for the author to come to him with clearly described people and circumstances.

Of course, all the *avant-garde* novels demand the kind of participa-

[5] Readers who are familiar with the nuances of this kind of provincialism will be interested in Rojas Garcidueñas' opinion that Owen is closer to González León than to López Velarde. "Gilberto Owen y su obra," *Cuadrante* (San Luis Potosí), III, No. 1–2. Offprint bears the date 1954, but the author says it did not appear until 1956.

tion that we are more used to associating with poetry, but they also use specific techniques that help transpose the reader into a reality beyond the visible. In the case of Owen, the step outward from the security of his first novel was natural and easy. *Novela como nube* (1928) anticipates an almost unbelievably wise and clever audience. Its base is mythological. ". . . before Ixion, Hera was transformed into a cloud; the goddess is woman and woman is like a cloud, so also in this novel, this *Novel Like a Cloud*."[6] Owen uses his artistic sense and intellectual background just as he pleases. The novel sparkles with suggestion, and the author assumes that the slightest gesture on his part will bring the reader right along with him. It doesn't work that way. The lyric quality of *Novela como nube* is so powerful that the reader finds himself reading eagerly and gradually moving away from the author. Then he realizes suddenly that he has wandered too far, and he must go back and work for meaning. The novel is neither philosophical nor psychological, unless philosophy and psychology can be impressionistic. The characters, like the circumstances, are real only within the limits of Owen's particular reality. It is a partial reality, and it is open. Owen knows that he sees only a part of reality; and instead of fabricating a substitute for the rest of it, he leaves the door open to the possibility of truthful completion.

Gilberto Owen certainly could have written a good novel of a more traditional kind. Many sections of *Novela como nube* show the necessary insight into people and suggest the ability to round out a novel to the average reader's taste. One memorable sentence shows his ability brilliantly: "Now all the men who get off at that corner will have, for Ofelia's hope, the body of Ernesto, his way of walking, his slightly exaggerated gestures of weariness."[7] I think he chose to write as he did because he believed it was the only road to reality. It is typical of the novelists of his group to use a combination of intellect and artistic sensitivity in the search for elusive truth. Perhaps it was this elusiveness that suggested titles like *Novela como nube* and *Margarita de niebla* (*niebla*—mist) which Jaime Torres Bodet published in 1927.

[6] *Ibid.*, pp. 14–15.
[7] Gilbert Owen, *Poesía y prosa* (Mexico City: 1955), Imprenta Universitaria, p. 158.

Torres Bodet's novels are more clearly psychological than Owen's. However, Torres Bodet never made a complete and clear analysis of person or problem. Rather, he deals with the inner confusion that his characters experience because of the impossibility of really knowing another person.[8] Like Owen confronting reality, Torres Bodet left the relationship incomplete rather than substitute a falsehood. In *Margarita de niebla*, Carlos decides to marry Margarita, a cultivated girl of German parentage, rather than her friend Paloma, an authentic Mexican type. Carlos' agonizing plight of confusion and indecision is very carefully treated by the author. Indeed, it is treated so carefully that I am afraid the reader loses interest in Carlos and wishes only that he would do one thing or the other, for any reason whatsoever.

Margarita de niebla, since it contrasts foreignness with nativism, and culture with something we might call homespun charm, cannot escape interpretation as symbolic of the cosmopolitan-nativist controversy that, in various guises, was a burning issue of the time. Carlos, a young teacher, chooses the cultured and sophisticated Margarita. In terms of the cosmopolitan-nativist controversy, he chooses cosmopolitanism. But stated in terms of matrimony, I think the novel does not really express the author's attitude toward the contrast. Since the story involves marriage, Carlos has to choose one girl and reject the other. So he appears to choose cosmopolitanism and reject nativism. However, if we ignore marriage as the goal of the man-woman relationship, Carlos does not actually reject Paloma, but finds in her the basis upon which he can build communication with Margarita. In other words, nativism provides the basis on which cosmopolitanism can exist. The symbolism is unfortunate because, stated in terms of social custom which makes Margarita the "winner" and Paloma the "loser," Carlos' growth outward becomes a crass misuse of another person.

La educación sentimental (1930), Torres Bodet's second novel, is even weaker than the first, but continues the same agonizing study of the attempt that individuals make to know each other. He wrote four more novels by 1937, and in his last two, he found the way to express

[8] For a number of interesting observations on the novels of Torres Bodet, I am indebted to Merlin Forster who was kind enough to let me read the manuscript of his essay on these novels, still unpublished when this book was written.

the same form. It seems to me that much time could be spent uselessly discussing whether one or another of many books about the Revolution is or is not a novel. The important thing is that, if they are not novels, they took the place of novels, just as the chronicles took the place of novels early in the Colonial Period. The novel plays a role in society, and we are concerned with its presence, its absence, or substitutions for it. The role is more important than the form taken by the agent that fulfills it.

El águila y la serpiente is an account of the author's relationship with several revolutionary leaders. Guzmán is a very literate man, and his style combines ease with accuracy. He is admired throughout the Hispanic world as one of the best prosists of the century. He also has remarkable powers of observation and the ability to describe what he sees. His ability—or perhaps, inclination—to re-create the observed is inconsistent. His descriptions of the men he knew are always interesting, but some are photographic and others are interpretive. Undoubtedly the best is the character of Pancho Villa, who was Guzmán's obsession. He is a marvellous combination of ingenuousness, brutality, and strength.

The Revolution in *El águila y la serpiente* is not the people in motion, but the manipulation of power. It doesn't matter very much whether the men like Demetrio Macías ever find out what the Revolution is all about. In this book, the decisions that control the nature of the Revolution and what it will accomplish are made in circles far removed from the people. Guzmán's view of the Revolution does not mean that he was *against* the common people, but that he simply did not communicate with them. So far as he was concerned, the people were related to power only insofar as they could be used to implement the will of a leader. His view might be described as administrative, because it was concerned only with the master plan and the personalities of key figures.

Guzmán's position was a perfectly honorable one, but it did not comprehend the full meaning of the Revolution. His ignorance of the role of the people was as serious a mistake as Azuela's assumption that the leaders perverted the intent of the movement. As a background explanation of the political implementation of the Revolution, following the military phase, *El águila y la serpiente* is more ac-

curate than *Los de abajo*. The post-Revolutionary governments up to
the administration of Lázaro Cárdenas, although they made some attempts to implement the principles of the Revolution, were clearly
more concerned with the position of power than with the welfare of
the people. Many revolutionaries became disenchanted, and Martín
Luis Guzmán was one of them, though I think his disenchantment
came less from identification with the people than from disapproval
of the way the master plan was working out.

When Calles arranged the re-election of ex-President Obregón in
1928, the latter was killed by a religious fanatic, but the power of
Calles was not broken. Although his ruthless use of power was quite
apparent, the will of more idealistic men was of no avail. In 1929,
Guzmán published *La sombra del caudillo*, a condemnation of Calles'
virtual dictatorship. It is a political novel in which most of the characters are identifiable. The only one of importance who is not identifiable is Axkaná González, who is also the only really honest man in
the book. Guzmán was not basically a novelist and, I think, had no
real desire to create fictional characters. It is quite a commentary on
the Calles regime that, when Guzmán needed an honest man, he had
to invent him.

The novel is probably an accurate picture of personalistic politics.
The absence of social responsibility among the leaders is revolting.
And the people are real enough, in spite of some awkwardness in the
description of social relationships. Because Guzmán was writing the
account of a political plot, he paid attention to the narrative as a
whole, rather than to isolated scenes, and so he has re-created more
than in *El águila y la serpiente*. The book is almost a great novel, but
falls short precisely because the author, an excellent reporter, lacked
the imagination of the novelist. His ability to re-create did not measure up to his ability to describe the observed. The shortcomings of *La
sombra del caudillo* do not keep it from being a very good novel; but
it lacks the encompassing power of Miguel Angel Asturias' *El señor
presidente*, a Guatemalan novel on a similar theme.

The chief value of *La sombra del caudillo* is in the implications of
the word "*sombra*" (shadow). The *caudillo* is never actually seen, but
his shadow is everywhere. He is the source of final decision, his authority exists in a way that transcends our normal idea of personal in-

fluence or persuasion. And although this novel is obviously an attack on the Calles regime, it is far more than that, because it is the shadow, rather than the man, that is important. The shadow exists as a kind of supernatural power, as if it were inevitably present. Subordinates acquiesce to the power. The physical agent of power may be challenged, even replaced, but the willingness to accept the shadow's domination is constant. The shadow and its acceptance constitute the major obstacle in the path of democracy, in Mexico and in the rest of Spanish America.

A confused awareness of the fact of the Revolution and its consequences became increasingly apparent in the novel. A little known novel of the Revolution, Agustín Vera's *La revancha*, was published in the same year as *La sombra del caudillo*. This book, published in San Luis Potosí, is an old-fashioned novel that resembles the combinations of Realism and Romanticism found in so much of the fiction of the last century. It is important because its author, although writing within a literary tradition that belonged to an age now past, sensed the importance of dealing with what had happened recently. The following year, Diego Arenas Guzmán published *El señor diputado*, another commentary on post-Revolutionary politics. And Jorge Gram (the pseudonym of a priest, David G. Ramírez) published *Héctor*, a defense of the *cristeros*.

Héctor is a one-sided account of the *cristero* movement. It is a poor novel, but an indicative one. The author was not really interested in writing a novel. He wanted only to defend the Church and its adherents while damning its opponents. We must wonder how he could possibly have ignored the atrocities committed by the *cristeros* themselves in the name of religion. However, his point of view and his artistic shortcomings are less important than the obvious need of the country to take account of itself.

In spite of the fact that two novels whose value rests purely on their artistic merit—Torres Bodet's *La educación sentimental* and José Martínez Sotomayor's *La rueca de aire*—were published in 1930, the trend was toward a novel committed to exterior reality. The writers of the *Contemporáneos* group were often justified in their fear that political propaganda might bury art, for that is exactly what happened in a number of books whose authors did not look deeply enough. The *avant-garde* novelists were, in a sense, one step ahead of the country's evolution. They were on the way to discovering the meaning of being Mexican, and of being man, before a prerequisite step had been taken. Before reality could be explored below the surface, Mexicans needed to know, in the deep sense of knowing, what had happened to them. And the first step was a review of events recently past. Around 1930 the Revolution began to acquire some unity in the minds of the novelists, and they had to write toward a clearer idea of this unity. They had to see the Revolution as a living entity, before the depths could be probed.

It would be proper to say that the intent of the novelists who were intensely aware of art was not refuted in the years following, but was held in abeyance until the proper moment. Happily, there were those who knew how to keep it alive.

 **10. The Mirror Image**
(1931–1946)

Almost overnight the novel became the novel of the Revolution. In 1931 there was not one novel of importance published that did not deal with the theme in one way or another. After the novels that were written concurrently, or almost concurrently, with the action they described, a decade passed before novelists paid any attention to the Revolution. Then late in the 1920's, Martín Luis Guzmán published *El águila y la serpiente*, Agustín Vera published *La revancha*—an isolated, provincial case—and two or three novels commented on political abuses and the *cristero* revolts. They mark a trend. But we are still surprised to see the coin completely turned in 1931: the Revolution is all pervasive.

The sudden turn to description of the Revolution suggests that the need was created by the nature of its political implementation—or to put it another way, by recognition of the nation's persistent problems and the shortcomings of the post-Revolutionary governments. This proposition, suggested by the intense cultivation of the "novel of the Revolution," is supported by specific protests and postures in the novels written during the next ten to fifteen years. There were two facets to the Revolution, even during its military phase: one was predominantly political and looked toward a genuinely democratic, capitalistic society; the other was social and anticipated fundamental changes in the economic structure. One was middle class, the other was proletarian. The first was the initial and predominant force. The second, whose principal exponent during the military phase was Emiliano Zapata, came later and was in the position of having to exert its influence on the middle-class, political revolt that had already started. The two facets are apparent in *Los de abajo*, one on each of the two planes which constitute the reality of the novel, and their co-existence is the basis of the apparent paradox in Azuela's attitude toward the Revolution. The same duality is present, though not as clearly, in *La fuga de la quimera, Fuertes y débiles,* and *El águila y la serpiente.*

The Constitution of 1917, although it is essentially a democratic-capitalist constitution like the Reform Constitution, shows the influence of the proletarian facet in some of its more radical provisions. However, the post-Revolutionary governments did not implement these provisions with any great enthusiasm, either because they were oriented toward the middle class or because the power struggle obscured the importance of social issues. The increase in leftist thinking during the 1920's aggravated the disenchantment of the more radical elements with the outcome of the Revolution. And President Calles' establishment of himself as the maker of presidents and source of power culminated an unsatisfactory political situation that displeased many who were interested primarily in political reform.

The Revolution had been a combination of heterogeneous forces. It was chaotic; and although sporadic moments of glory were apparent, the tragedy of civil war was even more so. The Revolution as an entity, as an achievement of men in search of freedom from a static society, could not possibly have been felt in the years immediately following, when the sense of tragedy prevailed. Because the interpretation of the Revolution was ambiguous, and its presence persistent, the need to discover its nature arose; and the first step was to look at what had happened.

The wave of novels of the Revolution in 1931 shows several different ways of telling the story, but with some characteristics that are common to most books on this theme: they are lineal accounts, episodic, with sketchily drawn characters. In general, everything—structure, style, characterization, even ideology—is subordinate to each author's need to tell what it was like. *Vámonos con Pancho Villa*, the first novel of Rafael Muñoz, is a fine example of a highly readable account which, on analysis, appears to be artistically defective in every conceivable way. It would be a waste of time to specify the book's faults, which it has in common with so many others. The essential question is why it is a good book if it has so many counts against it. One of the reasons is the author's narrative facility. Like many other novelists, he was a practicing journalist, and he carried over into his vignettes of Villa's men the easy, superficial description that characterizes a newspaper human-interest story. But there is something beyond this fact, perhaps a special kind of creativity: Muñoz has recreated his own eagerness to tell the story, and his reader is caught in the desire to know what the men were like. The answer is that they were fairly ordinary men with varying degrees of loyalty, persistence, heroism, who were united by an impulse—felt rather than understood —toward change. In *Vámonos con Pancho Villa*, the Revolution belongs to the people, not because it offers a proletarian economic argument, but because it sees the people as participating individuals in society. Political ideology is not important, the active role of the people is what matters.

Muñoz described from the outside. José Mancisidor, in *La asonada*, described the Revolution from the standpoint of a participant. His leftist ideology is apparent, as it is in all his novels, and it tends to inhibit his creative power. In *La asonada*, Mancisidor expresses fear that the Revolution will be betrayed by its leaders, and this means that the cause of the people will be lost. He does not declaim—his leftism was honest, profound, deliberate, and rational—but his ideas intrude too persistently. Unlike *Vámonos con Pancho Villa*, *La asonada* does not overcome its faults. Indeed, it is a very poor novel, but an important one because of its particular view.

The personal view of the Revolution had several variations. The novelist could write as a participant in his own story, or he could write the account of what others did, but from the standpoint of his having been a participant. He could also tell the story from the standpoint of the impact the action had on him. Nellie Campobello's *Cartucho* is a series of sketches that attempt to capture a child's view of the Revolution. The book naturally brings up all kinds of questions about child psychology, and I suspect the author's reflections are often lost among the readers' speculations. It seems to me that the

Revolution, in *Cartucho*, is exterior to the child's life, but the shock of its intrusion is felt less by the child than by the surrounding adults. Indeed, the child understands the noise and brutality of the Revolution to be the way things are, and in that sense she is very much the child of the Revolution. It is important that this book takes account of the fact that, in addition to participants and nonparticipants, there are people who grew up with the Revolution itself.

Cartucho is held together, if it can be said to have any unity at all, by the idea of the child's reaction. The view of the Revolution is, of course, limited by this device. However, the book apparently says what the author wanted to say about the Revolution, since she made no further contributions to the theme. This particular period in the history of the Mexican novel saw the publication of an extraordinarily large number of novels by authors who wrote only one or two books and who really did not belong to the main line of development of the genre. A casual count finds more than a score of such writers of limited production but with at least one book of some special interest. Not all of them deal directly with the Revolution. They range from General Urquizo's story of the common soldier in transition from the Díaz period to the Revolution (*Tropa vieja*, 1943) to Gustavo Ortiz Hernán's proletarian novel, *Chimeneas* (1937). In this group of apparently off-beat efforts are a traditionalist, *costumbrista* novel (Justino Sarmiento's *Las perras*, 1933), Leopoldo Zamora Plowes' very good historical novel of the period of Santa Ana (*Quince Uñas y Casanova, aventureros*, 1945), and Roque Estrada's two novels of the Revolution (*Liberación* in 1933 and *Idiota* in 1935) perhaps written after reading Dostoievsky and certainly unrelated to the literary trends of the time. The publication of more-or-less isolated works of this kind can be explained in part by the long-standing circumstance that few writers have been able to make a living by their creative efforts. Very often a man engaged in an entirely different profession has written a novel or two in order to satisfy a particular need for expression, without any intention of making fiction writing even a serious sideline. The concentration of such novels between 1930 and 1946 must mean that it was a period when a large number of people were impelled to make some specific statement that they considered relevant to their time. And from this general mood comes the feeling of urgency and incompleteness that characterizes the fiction of the period.

The best novel of 1931 was Gregorio López y Fuentes' *Campamento*, which is important not only for its intrinsic merit, but also for what it forecasts of a distinguished literary career. *Campamento* is less a story than an illumination of a revolutionary encampment. The author's view flashes across the entire scene and reproduces the reality of a night, a moment in the long struggle. The general effect is somewhat like the effect of one of the scenes from *Los de abajo*. The reactions of the revolutionaries are an intensification of ordinary human emotions. They are in a special situation which is becoming commonplace. They take advantage of the freedom that comes from the anonymity of belonging to the revolutionary band. The author accepts their state of anonymity as reality, and focusses his attention on the band rather than on individuals. Individuals do appear, but their real identity is with the group rather than as separate people. What matters in *Campamento* is what "the revolutionaries" do. López y Fuentes cultivated this device of the group protagonist in later novels, and also continued the same flashy style of obvious satire, easy irony, and broad antithesis. His prose is not beautiful, it is "catchy."

A year later, López y Fuentes published *Tierra*, a story of the whole course of the Revolution, with emphasis on the *zapatista* movement. Although this book is not a profound study, it is one of the clearest pictures of what happened from the end of the dictatorship to the end of the military phase of the Revolution. The lineal character of the narrative is emphasized by the use of dates as chapter titles. The real protagonist of the novel is the movement of the Revolution. Its effect on the *ranchería* (where the peons live on a large hacienda) is the central theme. It is mildly disconcerting that none of the characters, not even Zapata, is a protagonist; and it is possible to misread the novel if one tries to make it conform to a more conventional narrative method.

Tierra opens on a scene in which the peons are changing the boundaries of the hacienda. They know that the owner is able to do this because he has the power to influence the necessary authorities. But they are resigned to the facts of life. Several narrative sketches of the peons' life follow: payday, a death, a birth. The effect of these sketches is not surprising. They show the same picture of feudal society under the Díaz regime that is found in many different places, including the novels of José López Portillo y Rojas. López y Fuentes, however, makes a generalization of the condition, instead of allowing for individual differences as his predecessor did. He wins the reader's sympathy easily by quick character sketches that make you comprehend a man's social condition even though you don't know him very well. The peons on Don Bernardo's hacienda are not all stupid by any means. But the author makes it clear that they have absolutely no hope of freeing themselves from bondage. They vacillate between placid acceptance of Don Bernardo's patronizing despotism and unhappy recognition of the obvious inequality. They have no thought of rebellion. They are as static as the ruling class.

For reasons that are entirely unjust, Don Bernardo has Antonio Hernández, a young peon, sent away as an army recruit. When Antonio returns, well before he was expected, he informs the hacienda of the Madero revolt. The news does not impress the peons greatly. The action in the north is far removed from them. But Don Bernardo is frightened because his assumption that the revolt will not amount to much is shaken by the obvious feeling of freedom on the part of Antonio. It costs Antonio some effort to gather a small band, but he does so and wins a few skirmishes. When Madero is successful, Don Bernardo and other *porfiristas* take the lead politically, carefully including Antonio in their company but keeping him in his place. The peons' condition has not changed.

López y Fuentes introduces Zapata into the novel as an ideal and develops him into a legend. Antonio Hernández and his men join the *zapatista* forces. From this point on, the novel contains perhaps an overdose of Zapata's idealistic insistence on immediate redistribution of the land. More effective than Zapata's words is the author's description of the *zapatistas* as a farming army, taking time out from the Revolution to cultivate their crops on land that should belong to them. The Revolution does not give them what they need, and they continue the fight against the post-Revolutionary government until Zapata is killed treacherously. Antonio Hernández, the physical symbol of the Revolution, is killed in battle. Toward the end of the book, the author uses one of his literary tricks very effectively when he says that everyone knows Antonio is dead but no one knows where he is buried, everyone knows where Zapatá is buried but no one knows he is dead. Zapata has become a legend. The peons think they see him or hear him ride by, and their hope lives. Even if the Revolution physically ended in Antonio Hernández, its movement continues because the course that has been set cannot be reversed.

The year of *Tierra* produced three other important books: Mancisidor's *La ciudad roja*, Azuela's second best novel, *La luciérnaga*, and the first prose work of José Rubén Romero, *Apuntes de un lugareño*. Mancisidor's novel is the most clearly revolutionary of the group, but it does not say anything particularly surprising. It is a proletarian novel, set in Veracruz, and has the author's typically weak narration and strong ideological intrusion. Azuela's *La luciérnaga* is an entirely different case. Stylistically, it is the most radical of his works, and through skillful use of exterior and interior character development, he shows the unsettling effects of the Revolution's movement. The physical movement involved is from the province to the capital, where provincial values are jeopardized in the confusion caused by social displacement. Metropolis and provincial city are contrasted, and on this basic difference Azuela builds a series of contrasts that show the contradictory qualities of Mexican life: complacency and ambition, good will and egocentricity, desire for progress and stifling bureaucracy. The clearest characterization is a woman whose redemptive role recalls Heriberto Frías. I am not sure that Azuela is suggesting that people like her are the country's only hope, but there can be no doubt that her common-sense resistance to new customs illustrates the conservatism which became increasingly apparent in Azuela's later novels. His opinion of the new middle class is best seen in *Nueva burguesía* (1941).

Romero's *Apuntes de un lugareño* is a series of autobiographical sketches. They show an intense regionalism that is probably the outstanding characteristic of his works. Romero is undoubtedly one of the most read of Mexican novelists. He was a highly literate man who enjoyed posing as "just a plain, country boy." His humor is on the salty side. The combination of good writing, pose, and humor brought him a large audience. His ego was colossal, and all his novels are to a large extent autobiographical. One aspect of his egocentricity is the insecurity that tied him to his native state even though he travelled extensively. His pictures of provincial life are usually charming, even if the reader does sometimes tire of the author's presence. I suspect that in addition to Romero's personal need to remain spiritually within his native, provincial environment, his regionalism may be related to Azuela's approval of provincial values. The attitudes of both men seem to me to be a reaction against the movement of society that the Revolution started, a reaction against the uncertainty of society in a state of change.

In 1934, Romero published two novels, *Desbandada* and *El pueblo inocente*, that extol the virtues of the simple life. It is not a pastoral existence that he describes. Indeed, the simple life sometimes seems to be remarkably full of deceit. But Romero would have us believe that, for reasons which he never makes quite clear, human folly in a small town is less destructive than it is in a large city. Perhaps he believes hypocrisy can be seen more easily in the small town.

Desbandada is remotely related to the Revolution. It is the story of what happens when a group of revolutionaries sweeps through the town where Romero runs a store. Before their arrival, the author introduces a number of the town's personalities who come into the store. I suppose we should have some feeling for the town as a whole, but it never comes satisfactorily clear. We are aware only of the individuals' fear of the revolutionaries' brutality. The people of the town show some disgust with the Revolution, but one of them explains that these men do not represent the real Revolution. They are a perversion of it.

Romero's characterizations are good, though he tends strongly to caricature. Apparently he was so aware of individual differences that he was compelled to emphasize them. His somewhat picaresque view of humanity, including himself, is entertaining but not always convincing. *El pueblo inocente* is probably Romero's best gallery of provincial types, and the most successful characterization is Don Vicente, a fountain of practical wisdom who serves as a kind of tutor to a student who is home on vacation. In this book, better than anywhere else, we feel the author's ambivalence toward the province: an undying love for it mixed with a good deal of doubt about the honesty of human beings. One of the minor characters in *El pueblo inocente* is the town's philosophical bum, Pito Pérez, who became Romero's obsession and the outlet for his bitterness.

López y Fuentes published his last novel of the Revolution, strictly speaking, in 1934. *Mi general* is the story of a humble man who becomes a general during the Revolution and is unable to find a place for himself after the fighting is over. The book adds very little to what the author has already said about the Revolution. The general's career is rather similar to Demetrio Macías'. Having survived the fighting, he discovers that he has neither the education nor the influence to maintain himself in the circles of power, so he goes back to where he started.

Fernando Robles, a solid if not spectacular writer, published *La virgen de los cristeros* in the same year. It is, by extension, a novel of the Revolution because the *cristero* uprisings were a kind of postscript to the military phase of the Revolution.

In the midst of all this concern with the external, Jaime Torres Bodet found himself as a novelist, and kept alive the awareness of man's need to probe deeply into himself. *Primero de enero* (1934) looks a little strange among its immediate contemporaries, because its protagonist's concern is for the nature of his own being, rather than for the fact of the world outside. The first day of a new year is the occasion for him to do some thinking about what his life is like. He discovers that it doesn't make a lot of sense. It has come to be as it is because one circumstance has followed another in a building process accepted by the man, but not necessarily suited to his choice. He sees the possibility of making a life more to his taste, emerges from his house viewing the world in a new way, but discovers that he cannot become a different man, because his associates identify him as he is, in the world in which he lives. Or perhaps it would be better to say the world in which he dies, because there is nothing creative about his existence in a world where his identity is established by forces exterior to himself.

Primero de enero is obviously a much more revolutionary novel than any of the novels of the Revolution. Torres Bodet, always a good stylist, uses interior characterization in this novel with the excellent effect of stating a problem that does not ordinarily appear to be a problem. His book is a novel of protest of the most fundamental kind. The fact that *Primero de enero* was unique among its contemporaries emphasizes the anxiety that other novelists felt with regard to comprehending the external facts of what had gone on in Mexico, before discovering internal reality.

Although the Revolution continued to be the novelists' major preoccupation, the works published in 1935 and 1936 show two tendencies away from the account of revolutionary action: description of regional customs, and examination of the social problems that were apparent in post-Revolutionary Mexico.

José Rubén Romero's *Mi caballo, mi perro, y mi rifle* (1936) is an account of the author's participation in the Revolution, which was minimal. Far more interesting is the author's regionalistic viewpoint, which is present here as in all his novels. However, his regionalism is always a highly personal expression, and is different from that of his contemporaries.

In *Tierra caliente* (1935), a collection of three novelettes, Jorge Ferretis tries to capture the atmosphere of the tropical region of Mexico, but without great success, because his attempt to relate his characters to the region is too obvious, awkward, and incomplete. His apparent intent was to go beyond *costumbrismo* and relate the characteristics of the people to the natural characteristics of the area.[1] Such a procedure is, of course, much more complicated and profound than the regionalism of Romero. It is also a contrast to the general tendency of the period to view reality from the outside. The kind of regional *costumbrismo* used by Rosa de Castaño in *La gaviota verde* (1935) and *Rancho estradeño* (1936) is purely descriptive and seems to be the product of an impulse similar to the one that produces the lineal account of revolutionary action. The desire to tell what happened to the country is similar to the desire to describe the nation's way of life. And it may be a good idea to observe here that, aside from the Mexican Revolution, this kind of *costumbrismo* was common in the novel throughout Spanish America. It was a process of self-observation that amounted to a necessary step toward self-awareness.

---

[1] This relationship is referred to in Hispanic literary studies by use of the word *telúrico*.

Post-Revolutionary *costumbrismo* is different from the novels of the late nineteenth century, because the new *costumbrismo* shows no inclination to cling to tradition. Its intent is more in the nature of an examination than of nostalgic reflection. And, of course, such an examination is only a step away from social protest.

Normally, social protest came from writers whose political position tended toward the left. However, it is worth noting that one of the most violent protests of the 1930's came from the radical right. Jorge Gram's second novel, *Jahel* (1935), is a condemnation of any person or group that opposes the Church. The novel's bitterness is a measure of the intensity of the *cristero* reaction. The church-state issue was unique among social problems because both parties were endowed with considerable strength. Other problems involved some social element that was in a poor position to defend itself. Foremost among these problems was the question of the Indian and his position in the changing society.

López y Fuentes turned from the Revolution itself to the problem of the Indian (*El indio*, 1935) in what became one of Mexico's best known and most influential novels. Recognition of the Indian's separation from society was, of course, a part of the Revolution's awakening effect. In earlier literature, when the Indian appeared at all, it was in an idealized interpretation that exalted the virtues of primitivism and gave the Indian enough of the white man's standards to make him acceptable on the latter's terms. Such make-believe could not go on forever.

Mexico is one of several Spanish-American countries that have very large Indian populations. From the moment of contact of the two civilizations, the dominant European tried to ignore the Indian except when he wanted to take advantage of him. The Indian was not a functioning member of the social order, his life was tangential to it; and if he wanted to change this condition, he had to move from one culture to the other. In other words, although there had been from the beginning some intermarriage and some conjunction in the arts, the civil situation was one of confrontation and exclusion, rather than of conjunction. Toward the end of the nineteenth century, there began a slow-growing tendency in Spanish America to recognize the social injustice faced by the Indian, and later to take into account the ethnic characteristics that isolate Indian groups. The question is extremely complicated because it involves all kinds of considerations: ethnic, economic, social, political. And we must add to these difficulties the problem of plain human prejudice. The theme has become a major one in twentieth-century, Spanish-American literature, and López y Fuentes' novel set the stage in Mexico.

The people in *El indio* are not referred to by names, but by occupation, social function, or physical characteristics. This technique affects the reader in several different ways, and they are not all good. The anonymity produces a group characterization, and that, apparently, is what the author wanted to do. However, if López y Fuentes intended to spur his readers to active sympathy, he would have done better had he individualized his characters. Anonymity also emphasizes the primitive state of the people, perhaps more than the author intended. And it occasionally produces a "wise-old-chief-has-spoken" effect that is dangerously close to the noble savage foolishness of a century earlier.

A slender thread of story, concerning two lovers, connects episodes that the author chose to illustrate the Indian culture. The structure is typical of López y Fuentes. The episodes can be understood as an account of contemporary life, or as symbolic of the history of the confrontation of cultures. White men appear in the isolated Indian village. They look for gold and demand the Indians' help. They abuse the Indians' hospitality. The Indians retaliate and are in trouble. Later, a teacher comes. The Indians are obliged to work for both the Church and the State, to the detriment of their own interests. They observe the existence of two standards of justice, one for the white man and another for the Indian.

López y Fuentes' view of the Indian is the view of a social reformer, not an ethnologist. Basically, the trouble is a question of prejudice. The Indian is not a part of society because he is regarded as "other." The pictures of his life are shown in the *costumbrista* fashion; and although the author shows them with sympathy, he does not really enter into the Indian's being, as some later novelists have done. He sees what the Indian does, but he sees from his own point of view rather than from the Indian's. In general, this point of view does not greatly affect the novelist's intent, but it does have a tendency to make the book picturesque rather than profound.

Mauricio Magdaleno's *El resplandor* (1937) shows the nature of the Indian's "otherness" more clearly than *El indio* does. The author places his Indian characters in direct contact with white men and shows that the wall of separation is raised or lowered at the white man's convenience. The Indian is always different, though the wall may be lowered to allow the white man to approach if it is to his advantage.

Magdaleno's earlier works, though not very satisfactory, had already indicated a perceptive young novelist, willing to probe and to experiment. He is a much more resourceful novelist than López y Fuentes, and he had ways of giving his novel a perspective that is not present in *El indio*. He is keenly aware of the present as a spot on the continuum of history. After setting his scene, he flashes back to the past and we see the present as the natural result of its antecedents. In dealing with this particular group of Otomí Indians, the technique has the effect of giving them a quality of timelessness and endurance in the face of a terrible deprivation. Living on land that is too dry to produce anything, they look hungrily at the fertile lands that belong to the hacienda, "La Brisa." There is always a faint hope of something better, a hope that is always smashed by deceit. They are betrayed even by a mestizo child raised in their community. And it is clear that the circle of hope and betrayal will continue indefinitely. The mestizo boy does nothing to bring the two cultures together, but simply steps from one to the other, and from that point the people who had raised him were "other." His former friends remain, endure, looking at "La Brisa," with no real hope that life will ever be different.

While *El resplandor* sees the community as a whole, a number of characters are highly individualized and invite a wide variety of emotions on the reader's part. Lugarda, more than anyone else, communicates the feeling of endurance. Esparza, the storekeeper, has been close to the Indians long enough to break down the wall of separation, but self-preservation will not allow him to do it. Saturnino, the mestizo boy, may be simply an opportunist—or perhaps his betrayal of his people is based on the reactivation of historic "otherness." Magdaleno sees his characters from the outside, but also from within. He uses stream-of-consciousness passages in his attempt to enhance his re-creation of reality, and they work with the author's historical sensitivity to give the novel perspective. Many of Magdaleno's passages are highly poetic, both as to use of the language and power of suggestion. He is guilty of using some bothersome neologisms, but I think his general excellence is enough to earn him a pardon. *El resplandor* is the best Mexican novel of the 1930's.

El resplandor is, like *El indio*, an *indigenista* novel. But its scope is much wider. It is also a novel of the Revolution and a political novel. Perhaps even more important is the identification of the people with the land: the parched, stolid Otomies are human reproductions of the land they inhabit. Above all, it is a novel of social protest, against the failure of the Revolution to do something about the plight of the community, but even more against the lack of human concern for the oppressed.

By 1937 the novel's emphasis had clearly shifted from the account of revolutionary action to observation of the society that the Revolution produced. It is possible that this change may be related to the political change that brought Lázaro Cárdenas to the presidency in 1934. He gave Mexico the most revolutionary administration the country has had. His policies of radical social reorganization would naturally direct attention toward social problems.

In four novels published in four years, 1937 through 1940, Mariano Azuela expressed his bitter disapproval of the political implementation of the Revolution. *El camarada Pantoja* (1937) is a denunciation of the politics and politicians of the Calles regime. The author divides the latter into two classes, the vicious and the stupid. High and low are crushed by his wrathful satire. *San Gabriel de Valdivias* (1938) is the story of a community that is the victim first of the *hacendado*, then of an agrarian reformer who is just as greedy as the *hacendado*, and finally of a military man, sent to restore order and justice, who turns out to be as vicious as the others. Not even the Cárdenas administration escapes Azuela's needle. *Regina Landa* (1939) criticizes the stultifying effect of the bureaucracy which is capable of turning promising, well-intentioned men into mediocre tools of the administration. *Avanzada* (1940) attacks both agrarian reform and labor leadership. The peons are incapable of profiting from the lands they are apportioned. Labor leaders are a bunch of opportunists who have no real interest in the welfare of the people, but use their position strictly for their own advantage.

For the most part, Azuela's attack, in these four novels, is directed against the leaders. In later novels, he turned his attention to the people themselves and criticized their changing customs. As for the leaders, it is safe to say that his dissatisfaction was general and complete. We look in vain for an intelligent, humane, unselfish leader. This generalization of the attack defines Azuela's position as anti-Revolutionary, a tendency that is apparent even in *Los de abajo*, but which is much clearer and much more bitter in the novels dating from 1937. Azuela's extreme position was not typical, even of those who found fault with the Revolution. Most people recognized that some gains had been made, and worked for improvement within the existing circumstances. In his later years, Azuela was regarded as reactionary. However, since he is the only writer who has given us a series of novels covering the period of the Revolution from the years immediately preceding, through the military phase, the years of implementation, and what might be called the institutionalization, we need to be sure what his reaction means.

Azuela's view of Mexican reality must be understood on the basis of his early novels. However we may think of him as a participant in the Revolution, the fact is that he was a product of the Díaz period. The only real difference between his pre-Revolutionary novels and those of his contemporaries is that Azuela did not belong to the establishment. Since he did not, we sense in his novels the possibility of change rather than the need to cling to the past. The difference, therefore, is single but radical. The possibility of change that we find in his early novels is at the root of movement away from a static society—movement that was and is the very essence of the Revolution. But this movement acquired proportions that Azuela never anticipated. His novelist's vision discovered it in *Los de abajo*, and even there he viewed it with alarm. Azuela's views, like the views of many of the early leaders of the Revolution, were democratic, capitalistic, mildly nationalistic, humane, and intolerant of injustice and hypocrisy. The Revolution brought on such a ferment of ideas and actions that it produced its own injustice and hypocrisy, in an inevitably human way. This fact caused the disenchantment of Azuela. In some ways Azuela was more a man of the nineteenth century than of the twentieth. He thought less of changing institutions than of changing men. Indeed, he has written precisely that opinion. "With bitter sadness we consider that our great mistake was not in having been revolutionaries, but in believing that by changing institutions and not the quality of men, we would achieve a better social state."[2] I agree with Manuel Pedro González that it is not necessary in a book of this kind to say whether or not Azuela's opinions were justified by the facts.[3] It is important to know his position, and to know also that he was a conscientious citizen who, for reasons that are not always clear, was strongly inclined toward the contrary opinion.

Artistically, Azuela's novels from 1937 to 1940 are inferior to his earlier work. It is bad enough that he should have allowed moralization to become their dominant characteristic; it is even worse that moralization should be quarrelsome. Their great fault is in inadequate characterization. Azuela's characters had always been somewhat sketchy, but when they were related to a great theme, as in *Los de abajo*, they came alive because they did not stand alone. In the novels of political satire, the characters are like the drawings of a political cartoon, and the themes are not heroic enough to bring them into real existence. *San Gabriel de Valdivias* is something of an exception, because the life of the community supports the characterization. Within it, meaningful life still breathes. But in the pictures of political opportunism and bureaucracy, there is only the negation of meaningful life. Still, I would not want to give the impression that Azuela is not a competent novelist even in his lesser works. His is the professional touch; and even while writing under the anxiety of his dissatisfaction with society, his sense of what technique was appropriate to his purpose was exceptionally keen.

Azuela was not alone in his disapproval of politicians. Ferretis' *Cuando engorda el Quixote* (*When the Quixote Gets Fat*, 1937) is a rather poorly written novel of honest indignation, protesting the

[2] Mariano Azuela, *Cien años de novela mexicana*, p. 222.
[3] Manuel Pedro González, *Trayectoria de la novela mexicana*, p. 184.

change from idealism to opportunism. And of course, some political criticism is implicit in any novel of social protest. However, when a novel deals with the people rather than with the leaders, it seems to become more substantial, more communicative. Magdalena Mondragón's *Puede que l'otro año* (*Maybe Next Year*, 1937) for example, in spite of many faults often associated with a first novel, captures a feeling of endurance that is present only in *San Gabriel de Valdivias* among Azuela's novels of political satire. Perhaps it is wrong to feel that people are more enduring than bureaucracy or hypocrisy. Certainly Azuela feared that bureaucracy and hypocrisy were dominating people. But the majority of the novels that were contemporary with his do not take that position. Rather they anticipate reaction by the people. So it is in Ortiz Hernán's *Chimeneas* (1937), and in López y Fuentes' *Huasteca* (1939), a novel dealing with the exploitation of the oil workers.

Artistically, *Huasteca* is an example of the depths to which the novel can sink when it is inspired by propagandistic intent. Many pages of the novel are the exact equivalent of newspaper editorials. The author sets forth his case, but it is an explication of a problem, not a re-creation of life. In novels of protest, the artistic validity of the work depends on the author's ability to control his anxiety. It is not surprising, of course, that in post-Revolutionary Mexico it was hard for some writers to exercise the necessary control. The hard facts of social injustice and inequality, after a Revolution that offered the possibility of changing them, would hardly produce calm deliberation. The resulting novels show that the nation was still in the process of change.

Rosa de Castaño, in *Transición* (1939), tried to give a picture of the first stages of the change, from the last days of the Díaz period to the establishment of the post-Revolutionary government. It is her best novel, but suffers from the author's desire to do too much in one book. Obviously, what she is trying to do is make sense of the present in terms of the past—a present that was far from settled.

If nothing else had kept the country unsettled, the religious problem would have. José Guadalupe de Anda published, in 1937, the best novel about the *cristero* revolts, *Los cristeros*. Unlike Jorge Gram, Anda was more interested in the immediate social tragedy than in making propaganda. In many respects his techniques are similar to the ones Azuela used in *Los de abajo*. The effect is of the conflict between society in movement and society standing still. *Los cristeros* shows that the movement of the Revolution was partly realized, partly potential, and that it was not just the privileged, but often the humble people themselves, who refused to accept an extreme interpretation of the Revolution.

It is interesting, and mildly puzzling, to see that a slightly increased interest in a more universal kind of novel came with the shift from account of revolutionary action to social protest. It probably happened because social protest, at its best, tends to look deeply into human suffering. Several writers published works that are much more concerned with the inner nature of the human phenomenon than with the flaws of social organization. For the most part, they are minor works. Some are not novels. And they certainly did not constitute a new trend in Mexican fiction. But it is important that they kept alive a concern for the priority of art and for the less obvious human problems during a period when the dominant tendency was to examine the exterior.

Torres Bodet's *Sombras* (1937) is the best of these novels. It is one of his major works, worthy of comparison with *Primero de enero*. Through the suggestion of sounds, a woman recalls and examines her life. The author writes as well as in *Primero de enero*, but he does not make his reader feel as sharply the paradox of life that is not living. In the same year Eduardo Luquín and Rubén Salazar Mallén wrote books that intend to probe deeply, though in all fairness we must confess that Luquín's *Agua de sombra* did little more than scratch the surface. And in 1940 Agustín Yáñez published *Espejismo de Juchitán*, which is certainly not a novel, but which shows much of the deep sensitivity that is the author's outstanding characteristic.

In 1938 José Rubén Romero published a novel which appears to be entirely isolated from its contemporaries, unless its pessimistic view of man can be related to the dissatisfaction that most writers felt with regard to society. *La vida inútil de Pito Pérez* (*The Useless Life of Pito Pérez*) is a modern picaresque novel which is the author's statement of his personal obsession. Pito Pérez was a real person in Romero's home town. He was, in fact, the town bum. Presumably his antisocial habits were combined with some antisocial ideas that impressed Romero deeply. Pito's literary incarnation is probably a combination of the real man and the author himself. The book follows the general picaresque manner: Pito tells his story in his own language, he gets an inside view of the lives of different kinds of people, he trusts no one, and he thinks of himself as a victim of society. No literary form could have suited Romero better. He liked to think of himself—at least part of the time—as a *pícaro,* and Pito's book is a kind of "Walter Mitty" experience for the author.

La vida inútil de Pito Pérez is a very entertaining book. It may be a very serious book. We can never be quite sure about Romero. He was a clever writer, a literary prankster. We feel, on reading *Pito Pérez,* that it is the most natural narrative we've ever seen, and it is only on second thought that we realize none but a sure hand could juggle the language as Romero does. He is a natural humorist, though the "corn-fed" quality of his wit is a pretense. *La vida inútil de Pito Pérez* contains lots of dirty stories, and I am sure many people read the book for this reason alone. But in addition to the obvious humor, there is a much more subtle current that rides the line between tragedy and comedy in a wonderful fashion. The general tone of the book establishes the paradoxical union, and it is made more specific by various episodes like the re-enactment of the Crucifixion by a bunch of half-drunk jailbirds.

Pito's life is called useless, and indeed it is so from the standpoint of his contribution to society. His opinion of people is that they are just no good. Pito, however, gives people no more reason to trust him than he has to trust them. Still, this useless life may be regarded as the result of Pito's attempt to be himself. It may be that his life was useless because he wasn't permitted to live. His view of society raises questions about the honesty of a large variety of customs and institutions. From the point of view of society, Pito's values are perverted. From his own viewpoint, society makes little or no sense. He cannot change society, so he withdraws from its demands and becomes its victim. His life is active only when it is a negation of society, so the end result of his nonconformism is that his role is essentially passive. He cannot be what he would be, what his inner self would have him be. The novel, therefore, suggests a search for authenticity that is surprisingly similar to the problem in Torres Bodet's *Primero de enero*.

In 1941 Mariano Azuela published *Nueva burguesía (The New Middle Class)* in which he changed the point of his attack from the leaders to the people. These people are the humble who, after the Revolution, found themselves in economic circumstances that afforded them material things they had hardly dreamed of before. To a considerable extent *Nueva burguesía* deals with the disorientation of the provincial who comes to the big city. Azuela gives a panoramic view of this new social class, without developing a dominant story line. There is plenty of action which the author makes episodic and inconclusive in order to reproduce the feeling of displacement and lack of direction. Otherwise, his method of narration is objective statement in which he used none of the techniques he had mastered in recent novels.

Just as the movement of the Revolution had produced results in politics that displeased Azuela, so the changing values of the people brought down his wrath upon them. Sometimes he gives the impression that he wanted Revolution without change. We must continue to consider his basic views on the Revolution to understand why he was disturbed. There is no doubt at all that he wanted social justice for the humble. But he discovered in writing *Nueva burguesía* that the humble had not stood in their places to receive the blessings of a better life. They had become aware of the world's material joys, and had gone out seeking them. Azuela saw them living in a world of beauty parlors, movies, chewing gum, and second-hand automobiles. And interest in these material things altered relationships to the disadvantage of everyone. The author seems to feel a degree of sympathy for the people in their state of disorientation, but his expression of it shows impatience with them for their foolishness in not doing what was good for them. His advice is classically reactionary: they should go back, physically and psychologically, to their point of origin. His formula for man's happiness was to start the world turning in the opposite direction.

Nueva burguesía is a good novel because the people and the problem are real enough, and the author has reproduced them convincingly. The reader is put off only by Azuela's bitterness which is the result of anxiety. He could not see any more clearly than anyone else how the confusion of the present age may turn out. He might have done better to anticipate the recovery of the values he cherished by looking ahead from the present point, as he had done in his earlier works. Surely he must have known that the process of change cannot be inverted. Yet all his novels from 1941 until the posthumous *Esa sangre* are built on the reactionary advice to turn back. In the last novel, he seems to see that even going back would not remake the world as he wanted it.

The year of *Nueva burguesía* produced several books that, in their observation of society, tended to look inward, in search of man's inner nature. By far the most sensitive of these books was Agustín Yáñez's *Flor de juegos antiguos*, a volume of related stories that almost became a novel. Looking into the world of his childhood, Yáñez revealed both his profound Mexicanism and his sensitivity to the nature of man—a combination that has become his hallmark and his major contribution to literature. The fact that these stories deal with childhood does not in any way detract from their value as a study of the human phenomenon. No novelist is a better defender than Yáñez of the proposition that the child is father of the man.

But even the novels that were primarily concerned with exterior reality show deeper insight into the human condition than was common among the novels of the years immediately preceding and even immediately following. Rafael Muñoz published a novel of the Revolution, *Se llevaron el cañon para Bachimba*,[4] which is infinitely superior to his earlier one, and also radically different from it. Looking back upon the reality of the Revolution, Muñoz re-created rather than reflected what he saw. Taking the situation of a man who is facing defeat, he was able to re-create an episode that has the combined feeling of the Revolution as a limited, isolated operation, and also of the larger movement whose unity could be seen only from a distance.

In two novels of protest, José Revueltas and Mauricio Magdaleno went beneath the surface of the problem. Revueltas' *Los muros de agua* deals with a group of prisoners and their leftist views. It is a weak novel because very little happens and the ideas expressed are

---

[4] The title means "they took the cannon away to Bachimba." It is the title of a folk song.

terribly monotonous. However, as is always the case with Revueltas, his protest is firmly based on his desire to comprehend man's meaning. Magdaleno's *Sonata* is an even more searching novel. Unfortunately, *Sonata*'s panorama of life in Mexico City is both confused and confusing. Magdaleno was concerned with the different concepts of reality that make men act as they do, at different points on the broad spectrum of society that he describes. Perhaps he was hoping to find some common denominator. Sections of the book are excellent, but its total effect is confusion—in the novel and in the society—which is contrary to the apparent will of the characters and of the author.

Nayar, by Miguel Angel Menéndez, is a venture into the customs of the *cora* Indians that does a slightly better job than *El indio* of getting within the Indian culture. The customs are emphasized by having white men intrude into the *cora* world and by reference to the *cristero* revolts. Menéndez apparently thought that the use of enough detail would compensate for his basically non-Indian point of view. Although he moved slightly inward from the position of *El indio*, the world is still seen mainly from his standpoint, rather than from the Indians'.

From 1942 to 1946 the novel travelled largely along the same paths as in the preceding four or five years. Novels of protest outnumbered accounts of the Revolution. Regionalism is an important factor even in novels where it is not fundamental. Very gradually and subtly the novel probed more deeply into the meaning of the Mexican circumstance. A few books made understanding of the individual primary, and relegated the external social facts to a secondary position; but the common procedure was still to examine the new Mexico and to place people within the scene. The novel was hesitant: there was very little experimentation, yet the need to observe and describe was losing the intensity that characterized it ten years earlier. The nation itself was changing, also hesitantly. In the opposition of introversion and extroversion during the years since the Revolution, national introversion had been the stronger force. Mexico needed to be concerned for its internal problems, and the novels that examined the state of the country are a reflection of this need. However, they neglected the consideration of man's inner being.

The Second World War made it apparent that Mexico's destiny, whatever it might be, would be found in terms of its relationship to the world, rather than in isolation. The consequent turn to international extroversion revealed the universal community of man, decreased the amount of attention given to internal problems that were still unsolved, and emphasized the middle-class facet of the Revolution. Mexico was in a new stage of progress which could be highly beneficial, but which could be extremely dangerous if the nation lost its concern for the eventual incorporation of all social elements into the functioning structure of the country. The novelists were, for a few years, in a suspended state, faced with the nation's new outlook and still not certain that they had comprehended the old.

Revolutionary violence was still a preoccupation, partly heroic, partly tragic. José María Benítez, in *Ciudad* (1942), wrote descriptions of scenes in the capital during the years of violence. Benítez wrote from the point of view of a young boy, and did not try to generalize his observations. The scenes, which appear to be personal reminiscences, deal with the hardships faced by the boy and his family. A certain poetic strength comes from the author's imagery and his concentration on a single character; but this strength is not enough, because the people surrounding the boy are not clear enough to provide a background for his own troubles. The author's emphasis is on the tragedy of the situation rather than on heroic action, and the problems of a single person could not evoke an adequate reaction to the city's plight.

In 1945 José María Dávila published a book of reminiscences entitled, somewhat plaintively, *Yo también fui revolucionario* (*I Was a Revolutionary Too*). The book's motivation is more important than the result. I doubt that it adds anything to the understanding of the Revolution, but it shows the author's need, felt by so many of his countrymen, to identify himself with the movement and to tell what it meant to him. The date and the tone of the book make it a sort of postscript to a particular kind of writing. Of course, these accounts did not come to an abrupt end with Dávila's book; but it is safe to say that personal reminiscence has added nothing more to the comprehension of the Revolution's reality.

Although Francisco Urquizo's *Tropa vieja* (1943) is to a considerable extent personal reminiscence, it has more of the qualities of a novel because the author does not confine his attention to himself. *Tropa vieja* is a soldier's story of a soldier's transition from the Díaz period to the Revolution. Its authenticity is never in doubt. Urquizo certainly knew what he was talking about, and his humanization of the soldier is very competently done. The novel is a straight-forward account of what happened, in which the author used no particular techniques to communicate beyond what he had actually seen. However, Urquizo is so intensely human he inevitably saw the transition in terms of individual reaction. Life is what is important to the soldier of *Tropa vieja*. Ideologies and causes have their place, but they are just one of the factors that make up existence. The cause is no more important than sleeping with a *soldadera*. Without minimizing in the least the importance of the movement as a whole, Urquizo gave it the existential perspective of the participating soldier. This is not the perspective of the man who is drawn into the Revolution by the force of its movement, but of the man whose commitment is to soldiering and whose existence becomes a compromise between his interior self and the exterior forces that would direct him.

Francisco Rojas González's *La negra Angustias* (1944) was the first novel dealing with the Revolution written primarily for a reason other than to give an account of the action. The author's purpose is psychological. He analyzes, rather unconvincingly, a female revolutionary leader. It is possible that the protagonist, Angustias, may have an historical counterpart; but in general, the participation of women in the Revolution was not sufficient to indicate that Angustias was more than a special case. Woman's role in the Revolution was not often that of a soldier, and certainly not an officer. Her more characteristic role was that of the *soldadera*, who followed her husband or lover during the Revolution just as she had followed him earlier in Frías' *Tomochic*.

The *zapatista* movement provides the background for *La negra Angustias*, and some of the best moments of the novel come out of it. Rojas González combines innocence and brutality in several scenes that are at once amusing and frightening. But these scenes are intended to be nothing more than background. The author's purpose is to study the man-hating Angustias who is driven to cruelty by a distorted view of sex which was established during her childhood. I personally do not find the psychological justification convincing. And even less convincing is her reversion to womanhood when she falls in love with a puny young man who is literate and, therefore, possesses a kind of power that Angustias envies. Angustias loses the force of personality she possessed as *coronela* and assumes the self-abnegation of a *soldadera*. The young man is also transformed superficially. Although he remains as fundamentally weak as he ever was, he feeds on his domination of the strong woman. This kind of relationship is suggested by several Mexican novelists, most notably Heriberto Frías, but it seems that Rojas González has exaggerated its extremes.

It is possible that *La negra Angustias* might have been a more convincing novel if the author had not been a man of so few words. Often Rojas González etched a small amount of action on his background and leaves the reader wondering about details. This procedure is not the same as Azuela's elliptical narration, because Azuela always implies the necessary bridge.

Two novels dealing with the *cristero* revolts provided an addendum to the revolutionary theme: José Guadalupe de Anda's *Los bragados* (1942) and Jesús Goytortúa Santos' *Pensativa* (1944). The carefully planned narrative of *Pensativa* is its only real distinction. Its characterization is extremely weak, and Goytortúa's prose is far from elegant. But the construction of a real plot was a considerable contribution at a time when so many novels had been only lineal accounts. *Pensativa* is also important because it shows that the author is far enough away from the event to be able to re-create the circumstance rather than simply observe it.

In a different way, *Los bragados* also marks the *cristero* revolts as finished. Using the same staccato style he used in *Los cristeros*, the author deals with the residue of the *cristero* movement. Although an arrangement has been made with the government, the problem is not really solved. Cruelty and hate, when not active, are always waiting for the moment of failure in the tenuous communication between political system and human emotion. The official attack on the Church cannot be forgotten, nor can the violence of the reaction.

Social protest took several different forms. One of them is seen in *Los bragados*, which really doesn't take sides on the political issues, but is a protest against cruelty. Unlike many novelists who deal with society's ills, José Guadalupe de Anda takes a positive, constructive position. In *Juan del riel* (1943), which is his best novel, he tells the story of the struggle of Mexican railroad workers for suitable working conditions. On the face of it, this theme would promise dull reading. But the novel is more than an account of union activities. It deals with men who were exploited during the Díaz regime, played an extraordinary role during the Revolution, and finally achieved the status they sought. The author does not pay much attention to psychological development of his characters, but they do come alive within a limited range of reactions, and *Juan del riel* is a statement of how men can improve their situation. In a way, it is a case history, but the human qualities are not lost.

In the same year, 1943, Gregorio López y Fuentes published a satire on political opportunism, *Acomodaticio*. The theme was well worn by the time the novel was published, and it adds nothing to what had been said earlier, so far as politics is concerned. Whether or not the author intended to do so, *Acomodaticio* is likely to persuade the reader that opportunism is not the exclusive property of politicians, and that they are not the only people willing to sell themselves for immediate gain without regard for the principles involved.

The protest of *Acomodaticio* is like the protest of ten or fifteen years earlier. Younger writers turned from consideration of the structure of society and tried to communicate the actual conditions of the elements that were still not really incorporated into the social pattern of the nation. Magdalena Mondragón published *Yo como pobre* in 1944, the same year that Jesús R. Guerrero published *Los olvidados* (*The Forgotten*). These two novels belong to a group, by various authors, that show the most humble elements of Mexican society. They are written with a mixture of indignation and shame. Some people misread these novels because they expect to find individuals whose virtues make them worthy of help. But that is not the author's intent. What makes these miserable people worthy of help is the fact that they are human—or perhaps it would be better to say that they are supposed to be human and certain social factors have denied them the opportunity to be so. The novels are less a protest against the civic organization than against the fact that society shows a lamentable lack of concern for itself. The particular situations described are clearly Mexican, and the novelists may well feel their responsibility as Mexicans, but the problem is as universal as the arrangement of the planets.

Yo como pobre is Mondragón's first mature novel, and although she had not yet become as perceptive psychologically as she came to be in later novels, she made a brave attempt to put herself in the position of the people she was writing about. It is hardly surprising that she was not able to do so, because the condition of her subjects is really subhuman. Guerrero's people, however forgotten, are not quite as low on the social scale, and identification is easier. However, Guerrero did not have Mondragón's sensitivity, and his novel does not hit the human conscience quite as hard.

A year earlier, José Revueltas had published *El luto humano*, an attempt to see into the soul of poverty. This novel is the work that caused many people to expect a great deal of the author. Although he has never fulfilled his promise, and certainly *El luto humano* has many faults, the value of this early work cannot be overlooked. His insight into the lifeless living of his characters identifies him as a forerunner of the wider and deeper vision that characterizes the more recent Mexican novel.

The tendency to look more deeply is dimly apparent in a number of places: in *Yo como pobre*, in *La negra Angustias*, in *El luto humano*. Often obscured by regionalism, and even more frequently by the very apparent need to make a particular point, the combined study of the nature of man and the nature of Mexico became more insistent. It is apparent in a number of novelists in the mid-1940's: Raúl González Enríquez, Gustavo Rueda Medina, Federico Sodi. Their works, however, are not what should be regarded as the new novel. They are simply indications of deepening understanding.

In his second *indigenista* novel, *Los peregrinos inmóviles* (*The Immovable Pilgrims*)—published in 1944—López y Fuentes changed his position from outside to inside in such a way that the novel would not see the Indian as "other," but would see what "other" signified from the standpoint of the Indian. The people are uprooted, disputes arise, divisions take place, the white man imposes himself, the place to settle is found. The crossroads is the center of the world. The Indian stops—indeed, in a sense, he has never gone anywhere—and resists the insistent intrusion of the "other." He sits, defensively, and awaits the attack.

The author's new position anticipated the approach taken by more recent novelists, most notably Rosario Castellanos.[5] Unfortunately, López y Fuentes' efforts did not produce really satisfactory results, because his position is not consistent. The tendency to move inside is modified by the author's apparent desire to see the Indians' story as a gigantic symbol df the history of Mexico. He moves outside to get this view. And he fails because the story is partly related to time and partly removed from time. The reader is prompted to identify the symbolism historically, and then is deceived because symbol and history won't fit together. The result is that, after a first reading, he is likely to feel that he has missed something in a novel that is probably very good. But a second reading shows that he really didn't miss anything at all. The book tries to do two things that are not at all compatible, and the result is failure in both directions. What is left is an abortive attempt to see the world from the standpoint of the Indian, an unsatisfactory symbolism, and a wealth of external information about what the Indian is like. However, the movement toward the interior world of the Indian is sufficient to cast an entirely different light on the problem of his incorporation into society. *Los peregrinos inmóviles* emphasizes the egocentricity of the Indian point of view. *El indio* showed him living in a different world, but the later novel indicates that the separation of the two worlds is based on the assumption, held by both white men and Indians, that the world in which one lives is reality, and everything else is apart, unrelated, and naturally of little consequence.

A few writers forsook the mirror image of the nation and entered completely into a consideration of the inner reality of man: Agustín Yáñez in *Archipiélago de mujeres* (1943), Rubén Salazar Mallén in *Páramo* (1944), and Efrén Hernández in *Cerrazón sobre Nicomaco* (1946). Salazar Mallén's novel, in spite of its intense interiorization, is inferior to some of his other work because of a quality that I can

[5] Joseph Sommers describes the new approach in "Changing view of the Indian in Mexican Literature," *Hispania*, XLVII, 1 (March, 1964), 47–54.

describe only as melodramatic. In this novel, as in some other cases, the author was carried away with himself and allowed the value of his book to be jeopardized by his desire to shock his readers. *Cerrazón sobre Nicomaco* is an entirely different proposition. In highly poetic fashion, Hernández moved into the world of what we normally consider irreality in an attempt to extend understanding beyond the limits of the visible. Unfortunately, Hernández wrote very little more, but there is no doubt that he saw a possible road for the novel that very few other writers saw at that time. Among more recent novels, where prose fiction has often taken on the poetic role of venturing into an unseen reality, *Cerrazón sobre Nicomaco* is not nearly so rare a book as it was among its fellows of 1946.

Archipiélago de mujeres is an extremely important book because it completed the author's preparation for writing *Al filo del agua*. The novel is a kind of autobiography told in terms of famous women that belong to the western cultural tradition. Yáñez's style is neobaroque, and both style and theme make him a writer's writer. *Archipiélago de mujeres* marks the end of an autobiographical stage in Yáñez's work. Along with *Flor de juegos antiguos* and *Pasión y convalescencia,* and possibly some other early works, this book represents the author's basic study of himself as man. Having established this base and having proved himself aesthetically, Yáñez was ready to combine his understanding of himself, of man, of Mexico, with the mirror image, and write *Al filo del agua.*

The mirror image stands, sometimes shimmering brightly, sometimes shadowed by man's unwillingness to look at himself. Perhaps no nation can see itself completely, not even its external self. How can we be sure of what the mirror tells us? After all, we discover in it only what we think we see. And as we keep on looking, we discover that the appearance of the mirror image changes when we consider what is inside ourselves. The discovery of reality is not a question of choosing between interior and exterior, but of knowing the relationship between the two.

The years of hesitation in the novel were years spent on the brink of discovery. Introversion and extroversion would not quite coincide. And as long as they were separated, each suffered an inner conflict. The writers who were most inclined to turn inward nationally and

examine Mexico were the least inclined to examine themselves; those
who looked outward nationally—or internationally—were more inclined to look deeply into the nature of man, of self, of being Mexican. The combination of the two increased the dimensions of reality
understood. And if this immense and elusive reality sometimes appears to be beyond our powers of knowing, at least it offers a hope
not given to generations before our own.

Damián Limón, María, Gabriel, the town, the nation, mankind,
stood suspended—not only in 1910, but in 1947 as well—"al filo del
agua."

A CHRONOLOGICAL LIST OF NOVELS (1832–1963)

(This list is not a bibliography. Neither is it a complete list. It is an abridged version of the list on which the organization of this book was based.)

1832	*Don Catrín de la Fachenda.* José Joaquín Fernández de Lizardi.
—	*Netzula.* José María Lafragua.
1836	*El misterioso.* Mariano Meléndez y Muñoz.
—	*El criollo.* J. R. Pacheco.
—	*La hija del oidor.* Ignacio Rodríguez Galván.
1837	*Manolito Pisaverde.* Ignacio Rodríguez Galván.
n.d.	*Tras de un mal nos vienen ciento.* Ignacio Rodríguez Galván.
1841	*Un año en el hospital de San Lázaro.* Justo Sierra O'Reilly.
1845–1846	*El fistol del diablo.* Manuel Payno.
1848–1850	*La hija del judío.* Justo Sierra O'Reilly.
1849	*Amor y desgracia.* Florencio María del Castillo.
—	*La corona de azucenas.* Florencio María del Castillo.
1850	*La guerra de treinta años.* Fernando Orozco y Berra.
—	*Horas de tristeza.* Florencio María del Castillo.
n.d.	*Culpa.* Florencio María del Castillo.
n.d.	*Dos horas en el hospital de San Andrés.* Florencio María del Castillo.
1851	*Ironías de la vida.* Pantaleón Tovar.
—	*Los misterios de San Cosme.* José Rivera y Río.
1854	*Hermana de los ángeles.* Florencio María del Castillo.
—	*Amor de ángel.* Emilio Rey.
1857	*Impresiones y sentimientos.* Juan Díaz Covarrubias.
1858	*La clase media.* Juan Díaz Covarrubias.

1858   *El diablo en México.* Juan Díaz Covarrubias.

—   *Gil Gómez el insurgente o La hija del médico.* Juan Díaz Covarrubias.

1859   *La sensitiva.* Juan Díaz Covarrubias.

1861   *El monedero.* Nicolás Pizarro Suárez.

—   *La coqueta.* Nicolás Pizarro Suárez.

—   *Mártires y verdugos.* José Rivera y Río.

—   *El hombre de la situación.* Manuel Payno.

—   *Las tres aventureras.* José Rivera y Río.

—   *Fatalidad y providencia.* José Rivera y Río.

—   *Celeste.* José María Ramírez.

—   *Vulcano.* Hilarión Frías y Soto.

1862   *Ellas y nosotros.* José María Ramírez.

—   *Gabriela.* José María Ramírez.

—   *Historia de Welinna.* Crescencio Carrillo y Ancona.

1863   *La hora de Dios.* Pantaleón Tovar.

1864   *El oficial mayor.* Juan Pablo de los Ríos.

—   *El filibustero.* Eligio Ancona.

—   *Avelina.* José María Ramírez.

1865   *El ahorcado de 1848.* Gregorio Pérez.

—   *Astucia, el jefe de los Hermanos de la hoja, o los charros contrabandistas de la rama.* Luis Gonzaga Inclán.

1866   *La cruz y la espada.* Eligio Ancona.

—   *El santuario de la aldea.* Crescencio Carrillo y Ancona.

1867   *Las tres flores.* Ignacio Manuel Altamirano.

—   *Julia.* Ignacio Manuel Altamirano.

1868   *El cerro de las campanas.* Juan A. Mateos.

—   *Julia.* Manuel Martínez de Castro.

—   *Una rosa y un harapo.* José María Ramírez.

—   *El sol de mayo.* Juan A. Mateos.

—   *Monja y casada, virgen y mártir.* Vicente Riva Palacio.

—   *Martín Garatuza.* Vicente Riva Palacio.

—	*Calvario y tabor.* Vicente Riva Palacio.
—	*El tálamo y la horca.* Enrique de Olavarría y Ferrari.
1869	*Los dramas de Nueva York.* José Rivera y Río.
—	*Mauricio el ajusticiado o una persecución masónica.* Lorenzo Elizaga.
—	*El pecado del siglo.* José Tomás de Cuéllar.
—	*Sacerdote y caudillo.* Juan A. Mateos.
—	*Los insurgentes.* Juan A. Mateos.
—	*Las dos emparedadas.* Vicente Riva Palacio.
—	*Las piratas del golfo.* Vicente Riva Palacio.
—	*Venganza y remordimiento.* Enrique de Olavarría y Ferrari.
—	*El hambre y el oro.* José Rivera y Río.
—	*Clemencia.* Ignacio Manuel Altamirano.
1870	*La luz en las tinieblas.* Adolfo Isaac Alegría.
—	*La vuelta de los muertos.* Vicente Riva Palacio.
—	*Un hereje y un musulmán.* Pascual Almazán.
—	*Lágrimas y sonrisas.* Enrique de Olavarría y Ferrari.
—	*Los mártires de Anáhuac.* Eligio Ancona.
—	*Novelas.* José María Roa Bárcena.
—	*Esqueletos sociales.* José Rivera y Río.
1871	*La piedra del sacrificio.* Ireneo Paz.
—	*Isolina la ex-figurante.* José Tomás de Cuéllar.
—	*Las jamonas.* José Tomás de Cuéllar.
—	*La virgen del Niágara.* José Rivera y Río.
—	*Magdalena.* Francisco Sosa.
—	*Angélica.* Luis G. Ortiz.
—	*Ensalada de pollos.* José Tomás de Cuéllar.
—	*Historia de Chucho el ninfo.* José Tomás de Cuéllar.
1872	*Memorias de unos náufragos.* José Rivera y Río.
—	*Silveria de Epinay.* Vicente Morales.
—	*Gabriel el cerrajero o las hijas de mi papá.* José Tomás de Cuéllar.

1872   *Obras completas.* Florencio M. del Castillo.

—   *Las gentes que "son así."* José Tomás de Cuéllar.

—   *Antonia.* Ignacio Manuel Altamirano.

—   *Memorias de un impostor, Don Guillén de Lampart, Rey de México.* Vicente Riva Palacio.

1873   *Ernestina.* Vicente Morales.

—   *Gentes de historia.* Vicente Morales.

—   *El Doctor Cupido.* Francisco Sosa.

—   *El solitario del Teira.* José Francisco Sotomayor.

—   *Amor y suplicio.* Ireneo Paz.

—   *Beatriz.* Ignacio Manuel Altamirano.

1874   *Las ruinas del monasterio.* José Francisco Sotomayor.

—   *Amor de viejo.* Ireneo Paz.

—   *Angela.* Vicente Morales.

—   *Memorias de Paulina.* José Negrete.

—   *Gerardo.* Vicente Morales.

—   *Memorias de un muerto.* Manuel Balbontín.

—   *Caridad y recompensa.* Pedro Llanas.

1875   *Historias color de fuego.* José Negrete.

—   *Una hija i una madre.* Manuel Martínez de Castro.

—   *Sor Angélica.* Juan A. Mateos.

1876   *Pobres y ricos de México.* José Rivera y Río.

1877   *Doce leyendas de Francisco Sosa.* Francisco Sosa.

—   *Un santuario en el desierto.* José Francisco Sotomayor.

—   *Dos leyendas.* Victoriano Agüeros.

1878   *La mujer verdugo.* José Negrete.

—   *La niña mártir.* José Negrete.

—   *Lanchitas.* José María Roa Bárcena.

1879   *Leyenda de Navidad.* Victoriano Agüeros.

—   *El conde de Peñalva.* Eligio Ancona.

1880   *Atenea.* Ignacio Manuel Altamirano.

—   *El escéptico.* Vicente Morales.

— *Memorias de Merolico.* José Negrete.

1880–1887 *Episodios Nacionales Mexicanos.* Enrique de Olavarría y Ferrari.

1881 *Remordimiento.* Rafael de Zayas Enríquez.

— *Cuentos mineros. Un combate.* Pedro Castera.

1882 *Ensueños y armonías.* Pedro Castera.

— *Impresiones y recuerdos.* Pedro Castera.

— *Carmen.* Pedro Castera.

— *Los maduros.* Pedro Castera.

— *Satanás.* Adolfo Isaac Alegría.

— *Pocahontas.* Manuel Sánchez Mármol.

1883 *Doña Marina.* Ireneo Paz.

1885 *Eva. Memorias de dos huérfanos.* Manuel Martínez de Castro.

— *Perico.* Arcadio Zentella.

1886–1894 *Leyendas históricas de la independencia.* Ireneo Paz.

1886 *Baile y cochino.* José Tomás de Cuéllar.

1887 *Oceánida.* Rafael de Zayas Enríquez.

— *El grito de Dolores.* José Severino de la Sota.

— *La bola.* Emilio Rabasa.

— *La gran ciencia.* Emilio Rabasa.

— *Nieves.* José López Portillo y Rojas.

1888 *El cuarto poder.* Emilio Rabasa.

— *Moneda falsa.* Emilio Rabasa.

1889 *Elvira.* Manuel Martínez de Castro.

— *Staurófila.* María Nestora Téllez Rendón.

— *Del natural.* Federico Gamboa.

— *Entre el amor y la patria.* Demetrio Mejía.

1889–1891 *Los bandidos de Río Frío.* Manuel Payno.

1890 *Los fuereños y la nochebuena.* José Tomás de Cuéllar.

— *Los mariditos.* José Tomás de Cuéllar.

— *La Calandria.* Rafael Delgado.

— *La Rumba.* Angel de Campo.

1891   *La guerra de tres años.* Emilio Rabasa.
—   *Páginas de un primer amor.* José Rafael Guadalajara.
—   *Amalia.* José Rafael Guadalajara.
—   *La mestiza.* Eligio Ancona.
1892   *Inés.* Manuel Balbontín.
—   *El rayo del sol.* Crescencio Carrillo y Ancona.
—   *Juanita Sousa.* Manuel Sánchez Mármol.
—   *La estatua de Psiquis.* Atenógenes Segale.
—   *Apariencias.* Federico Gamboa.
—   *Pascual Aguilera.* Amado Nervo.
1893   *La línea curva.* Mariano Flores Villar.
—   *Angelina.* Rafael Delgado.
—   *Impresiones y recuerdos.* Federico Gamboa.
—   *Las cruces del santuario.* Joaquín Gómez Vergara.
1893–1895   *Tomochic.* Heriberto Frías.
1894   *La campana de la misión.* José María Esteva.
1895   *Naufragio.* Heriberto Frías.
—   *El bachiller.* Amado Nervo.
—   *Antonio Rojas.* Ireneo Paz.
—   *Reproducciones.* José Ferrel.
1896   *Suprema ley.* Federico Gamboa.
—   *Cuentos del general.* Vicente Riva Palacio.
—   *El último duelo.* Heriberto Frías.
1897   *Cuentos originales y traducidos.* José María Roa Bárcena.
—   *Del campo contrario.* Atenógenes Segale.
—   *Memorias de un guerrillero.* Juan A. Mateos.
1898   *La parcela.* José López Portillo y Rojas.
—   *Inri.* Juan N. Cordero.
1899   *Leyendas históricas mexicanas.* Heriberto Frías.
—   *Metamorfosis.* Federico Gamboa.
—   *El donador de almas.* Amado Nervo.
1900   *Adah, o el amor de un ángel.* Aurelio Luis Gallardo.
—   *Pacotillas.* Porfirio Parra.

1901   *El zarco, o episodios de la vida mexicana en 1861–63.* Ignacio Manuel Altamirano.

—   *El señor gobernador.* Manuel H. San Juan.

1902   *El teniente de los Gavilanes.* Rafael de Zayas Enríquez.

—   *Hermana de los ángeles* (new edition). Florencio María del Castillo.

1903   *Antón Pérez.* Manuel Sánchez Mármol.

—   *Santa.* Federico Gamboa.

1904   *Los parientes ricos.* Rafael Delgado.

—   *Memorias de un Alférez.* Eligio Ancona.

1905   *La siega.* Rafael Ceniceros y Villarreal.

1906   *Previvida.* Manuel Sánchez Mármol.

1907   *María Luisa.* Mariano Azuela.

1908   *Reconquista.* Federico Gamboa.

—   *El hombre nuevo.* Rafael Ceniceros y Villarreal.

—   *Pajarito.* Cayetano Rodríguez Beltrán.

—   *El amor de las sirenas.* Heriberto Frías.

—   *Los fracasados.* Mariano Azuela.

1909   *Los precursores.* José López Portillo y Rojas.

—   *Mala yerba.* Mariano Azuela.

1910   *Memorias de un juez de paz.* Salvador Cordero.

—   *Novelas cortas.* José María Roa Bárcena.

—   *La llaga.* Federico Gamboa.

1911   *La majestad caída.* Juan A. Mateos.

—   *El triunfo de Sancho Panza.* Heriberto Frías.

—   *Andrés Pérez, maderista.* Mariano Azuela.

1912   *La camada.* Salvador Quevedo y Zubieta.

1914   *Madero.* Ireneo Paz.

1915   *Los de abajo.* Mariano Azuela.

1916   *Las miserias de México.* Heriberto Frías.

1918   *Mirlitón.* María Enriqueta Camarillo de Pereyra.

—   *El secreto de la "Escala."* Francisco Monterde.

1918	*Las tribulaciones de una familia decente.* Mariano Azuela.
—	*El madrigal de Cetina.* Francisco Monterde.
1919	*Fuertes y débiles.* José López Portillo y Rojas.
—	*La fuga de la quimera.* Carlos González Peña.
—	*Jirón del mundo.* María Enriqueta Camarillo de Pereyra.
—	*Un ingenio.* Cayetano Rodríguez Beltrán.
—	*Ejemplo.* Artemio de Valle Arizpe.
1920	*Alas abiertas.* Alfonso Teja Zabre.
1922	*Doña Leonor de Cáceres.* Artemio de Valle Arizpe.
1923	*Sor Adoración del Divino Verbo.* Julio Jiménez Rueda.
—	*El corcovado.* Ermilo Abreu Gómez.
—	*La vida del venerable siervo de Dios, Gregorio López.* Ermilo Abreu Gómez.
—	*La malhora.* Mariano Azuela.
—	*Aguila o sol.* Heriberto Frías.
1924	*Moisén.* Julio Jiménez Rueda.
1925	*El desquite.* Mariano Azuela.
—	*La llama fria.* Gilberto Owen.
1926	*Pero Galín.* Genaro Estrada.
—	*El café de nadie.* Arqueles Vela.
1927	*Margarita de niebla.* Jaime Torres Bodet.
1928	*Dama de corazones.* Xavier Villaurrutia.
—	*El joven.* Salvador Novo.
—	*Novela como nube.* Gilberto Owen.
—	*El águila y la serpiente.* Martín Luis Guzmán.
—	*La hacienda.* Xavier Icaza.
—	*Panchito Chapopote.* Xavier Icaza.
1929	*La sombra del caudillo.* Martín Luis Guzmán.
—	*La revancha.* Agustín Vera.
1930	*La educación sentimental.* Jaime Torres Bodet.
—	*La rueca de aire.* José Martínez Sotomayor.
—	*El señor diputado.* Diego Arenas Guzmán.

—   *Héctor.* Jorge Gram.

1931   *Vámonos con Pancho Villa.* Rafael Muñoz.

—   *La asonada.* José Mancisidor.

—   *Cartucho.* Nellie Campobello.

—   *Campamento.* Gregorio López y Fuentes.

1932   *Apuntes de un lugareño.* José Rubén Romero.

—   *La luciérnaga.* Mariano Azuela.

—   *La ciudad roja.* José Mancisidor.

—   *Tierra.* Gregorio López y Fuentes.

1933   *Las perras.* Justino Sarmiento.

—   *Liberación.* Roque Estrada.

1934   *La virgen de los cristeros.* Fernando Robles.

—   *Mi general.* Gregorio López y Fuentes.

—   *El pueblo inocente.* José Rubén Romero.

—   *Primero de enero.* Jaime Torres Bodet.

—   *Desbandada.* José Rubén Romero.

1935   *La gaviota verde.* Rosa de Castaño.

—   *Patria perdida.* Teodoro Torres.

—   *La desventura del Conde Kadski.* Julio Jiménez Rueda.

—   *Idiota.* Roque Estrada.

—   *La consumación del crimen.* Diego Arenas Guzmán.

—   *Tierra caliente.* Jorge Ferretis.

—   *Jahel.* Jorge Gram.

—   *El indio.* Gregorio López y Fuentes.

—   *Campo Celis.* Mauricio Magdaleno.

1936   *Rancho estradeño.* Rosa de Castaño.

—   *Mi caballo, mi perro, y mi rifle.* José Rubén Romero.

—   *Concha Bretón.* Mauricio Magdaleno.

1937   *El camarada Pantoja.* Mariano Azuela.

—   *Cuando engorda el Quizote.* Jorge Ferretis.

—   *Los cristeros.* José Guadalupe de Anda.

—   *Arrieros.* Gregorio López y Fuentes.

1937	*El resplandor*. Mauricio Magdaleno.
—	*Chimeneas*. Gustavo Ortiz Hernán.
—	*Puede que l'otro año*. Magdalena Mondragón.
—	*Sombras*. Jaime Torres Bodet.
—	*Camino de perfección*. Rubén Salazar Mallén.
—	*Tumulto*. Eduardo Luquín.
—	*Agua de sombra*. Eduardo Luquín.
1938	*La vida inútil de Pito Pérez*. José Rubén Romero.
—	*San Gabriel de Valdivias*. Mariano Azuela.
—	*Claudio Martín, vida de un chiclero*. Luis Rosado Vega.
1939	*Transición*. Rosa de Castaño.
—	*Regina Landa*. Mariano Azuela.
—	*Huasteca*. Gregorio López y Fuentes.
—	*Manzana podrida*. José Meana.
1940	*Avanzada*. Mariano Azuela.
—	*Paludismo*. Bernardino Mena Brito.
—	*Sucedió ayer*. Fernando Robles.
—	*Espejismo de Juchitán*. Agustín Yáñez.
1941	*El canillitas*. Artemio de Valle Arizpe.
—	*Nueva burguesía*. Mariano Azuela.
—	*Se llevaron el cañon para Bachimba*. Rafael Muñoz.
—	*Sonata*. Mauricio Magdaleno.
—	*Nayar*. Miguel Angel Menéndez.
—	*La rosa de los vientos*. José Mancisidor.
—	*Los muros de agua*. José Revueltas.
—	*Flor de juegos antiguos*. Agustín Yáñez.
1942	*Ciudad*. José María Benítez.
—	*Los bragados*. José Guadalupe de Anda.
—	*San Antonio, S. A.*. Raúl González Enríquez.
1943	*Tropa vieja*. Francisco Urquizo.
—	*Juan del riel*. José Guadalupe de Anda.
—	*Acomodaticio*. Gregorio López y Fuentes.

—   *El luto humano.* José Revueltas.

—   *Los perros fantasmas.* Eduardo Luquín.

—   *Archipiélago de mujeres.* Agustín Yáñez.

1944   *Los olvidados.* Jesús R. Guerrero.

—   *La marchanta.* Mariano Azuela.

—   *La negra Angustias.* Francisco Rojas González.

—   *Pensativa.* Jesús Goytortúa Santos.

—   *Los peregrinos inmóviles.* Gregorio López y Fuentes.

—   *Yo como pobre.* Magdalena Mondragón.

—   *Norte Barbaro.* Magdalena Mondragón.

—   *Páramo.* Rubén Salazar Mallén.

1945   *Feliciano cumple medio siglo.* Federico Sodi.

—   *Quince Uñas y Casanova, aventureros.* Leopoldo Zamora Plowes.

—   *Yo también fui revolucionario.* José María Dávila.

—   *¿Quién tiene un sacacorchos?* Gustavo Rueda Medina.

—   *Los hermanos Gabriel.* Eduardo Luquín.

1946   *Rosenda.* José Rubén Romero.

—   *El santo que asesinó.* Fernando Robles.

—   *Las islas también son nuestras.* Gustavo Rueda Medina.

—   *Cerrazón sobre Nicomaco.* Efrén Hernández.

1947   *Donde crecen los tepozanes.* Miguel N. Lira.

—   *Lola Casanova.* Francisco Rojas González.

—   *El médico y el santero.* José María Dávila.

—   *Bajo el fuego.* María Luisa Ocampo.

—   *Lluvia roja.* Jesús Goytortúa Santos.

—   *Guelaguetza.* Rogelio Barriga Rivas.

—   *Más allá existe la tierra.* Magdalena Mondragón.

—   *Al filo del agua.* Agustín Yáñez.

1948   *Clase media.* Federico Sodi.

—   *La escondida.* Miguel N. Lira.

—   *Entresuelo.* Gregorio López y Fuentes.

1948	*Juan Pérez Jolote*. Ricardo Pozas A.
—	*El callado dolor de los tzotziles*. Ramón Rubín.
—	*La barriada*. Benigno Corona Rojas.
—	*El sol sale para todos*. Felipe García Arroyo.
—	*Murieron a mitad del río*. Luis Spota.
1949	*Sendas perdidas*. Mariano Azuela.
—	*La maestrita*. María Luisa Ocampo.
—	*Río humano*. Rogelio Barriga Rivas.
—	*Los días terrenales*. José Revueltas.
—	*El doble nueve*. Rodolfo Benavides.
—	*Ojo de agua*. Rubén Salazar Mallén.
—	*La paloma, el sótano, y la torre*. Efrén Hernández.
—	*Tierra grande*. Mauricio Magdaleno.
—	*Cabello de elote*. Mauricio Magdaleno.
1950	*Los pies descalzos*. Luis Enrique Erro.
—	*Huelga blanca*. Héctor Raúl Almanza.
—	*La estrella vacía*. Luis Spota.
1951	*Cuando el águila perdió sus alas*. Fernando Robles.
—	*La canoa perdida*. Ramón Rubín.
—	*Chicle*. Enrique Vásquez Islas.
—	*Más cornadas da el hambre*. Luis Spota.
1952	*El canto de la grilla*. Ramón Rubín.
—	*La mayordomía*. Rogelio Barriga Rivas.
—	*Candelaria de los patos*. Héctor Raúl Almanza.
—	*Ejercicios*. Rubén Salazar Mallén.
—	*Confabulario*. Juan José Arreola.
1953	*Frontera junto al mar*. José Mancisidor.
—	*El alba en las cimas*. José Mancisidor.
—	*Entre las patas de los caballos*. José Rivero del Val.
—	*El llano en llamas*. Juan Rulfo.
—	*Memoria de un espejo*. José Alvarado.
1954	*La bruma lo vuelve azul*. Ramón Rubín.

1960   *Las buenas conciencias.* Carlos Fuentes.

—   *Cuando el Táguaro agoniza.* Ramón Rubín.

1961   *Los extraordinarios.* Ana Mairena.

—   *El desierto mágico.* Concha Villareal.

—   *El picaflor.* Arqueles Vela.

—   *La voz adolorida.* Vicente Leñero.

1962   *Las tierras flacas.* Agustín Yáñez.

—   *La culebra tapó el rio.* María Lombardo de Caso.

—   *La muerte de Artemio Cruz.* Carlos Fuentes.

—   *Aura.* Carlos Fuentes.

—   *Oficio de tinieblas.* Rosario Castellanos.

—   *Detrás del espejo.* Héctor Raúl Almanza.

1963   *Bramadero.* Tomás Mojarro.

—   *Los antepasados.* Carlos Valdés.

—   *La feria.* Juan José Arreola.

—   *Los recuerdos del porvenir.* Elena Garro.

A SELECTED BIBLIOGRAPHY

The following list contains only books and essays that take a rather general and recent view of the Mexican novel. A more complete bibliography can be found in the *Breve historia de la novela mexicana,* which is cited below.

Alegría, Fernando. *Breve historia de la novela hispanoamericana.* Mexico City: Ediciones de Andrea, 1959.

Azuela, Mariano. *Cien años de novela mexicana.* Mexico City: Botas, 1947.

Brushwood, J. S. *The Romantic Novel in Mexico.* Columbia: University of Missouri Studies, 1954.

Brushwood, John S., and José Rojas Garcidueñas. *Breve historia de la novela mexicana.* Mexico City: Ediciones de Andrea, 1959.

Carter, Boyd G. "The Mexican novel at mid-century," *Prairie Schooner,* XXVIII, 2 (Summer, 1954), 143–156.

Castellanos, Rosario. "La novela mexicana contemporánea," *México en la Cultura,* no. 597, supplement to *Novedades* (21 agosto 1960), 1 & 5 & 10.

Fuentes, Carlos. "La nueva novela latinoamericana," *La Cultura en México,* no. 128, supplement to *Siempre* (29 julio 1964), 2–7, & 14–16.

González, Manuel Pedro. *Trayectoria de la novela mexicana.* Mexico City: Botas, 1951.

Morton, F. Rand. *Los novelistas de la Revolución mexicana.* Mexico City: n.p., 1949.

Ocampo de Gomez, Aurora Maura. *Literatura mexicana contemporánea: Biobibliografía crítica.* Mexico City: n.p., 1965.

Navarro, Joaquina. *La novela realista mexicana.* Mexico City: Compañía General de Ediciones, 1955.

Read, J. Lloyd. *The Mexican Historical Novel, 1826–1910.* New York: Instituto de las Españas, 1939.

Valadés, Edmundo, and Luis Leal. *La Revolución y las letras.* Mexico City: INBA, 1960.

Warner, Ralph E. *Historia de la novela mexicana en el siglo XIX.* Mexico City: Robredo, 1953.

Zum Felde, Alberto. *Indice crítico de la literatura hispanoamericana.* Vol. II, *La narrativa.* Mexico City: Guaranía, 1959.

INDEX

authoritarianism: in *Un hereje y un musulmán*, 100; in *Balbontín*, 111; in literature, 116
authority: in *Clemencia*, 102; in Cuéllar, 108; during Díaz regime, 137; in *La sombra del caudillo*, 202–203
autobiography: used by Orozio y Berra, 77; used by Frías, 166; used by Azuela, 183; used by Guzmán, 200–201; used by Romero, 200–201; used by Yáñez, 233
avant-garde, the: 188–189, 191–200, 204, SEE ALSO novel, *avant-garde*
Avanzada: 218–220
awareness. SEE reality, awareness of
Aztecs: and Conquest, 3, 56–59
Azuela, Mariano: 187, 229; and Frías, 166, 167 n., 168, 188; and Gamboa, 168; and Rabasa, 168; and Nervo, 169; and Zentella, 169; and López Portillo, 169, 178–179; and González Peña, 178–179; and *Contemporáneos*, 194; and Romero, 212; and Guzmán, 201; and Anda, 222
—, works of: 34, 50, 166–172, 173, 178–184, 206, 221; *La maldición*, 18; *Sendas perdidas*, 18; *Esa sangre*, 19, 224; *Los de abajo*, 46, 167, 171, 173, 178–181, 182, 194, 202, 209, 220, 222; *Andrés Pérez, maderista*, 170–172, 176; *María Luisa*, 167; *Los fracasados*, 167–169; *Mala yerba*, 169–170; *Las moscas*, 182, 200; *Las tribulaciones de una familia decente*, 183–184; *La malhora*, 188–189, 194; *El desquite*, 189; *La luciérnaga*, 189, 211; *El camarada Pantoja*, 218; *Avanzada*, 218–220; *San Gabriel de Valdivias*, 218–220; *Nueva burguesía*, 224–225

bachiller, El: 146–147, 148
background. SEE atmosphere; setting
Baile y cochino: 131
Bajo el fuego: 12
Balbontín, Manuel: 110, 111–112
Balbuena, Bernardo de: 60
Balúm Canán: 36, 42
Balzac, Honoré: influence of, 81, 90
Bandera de Provincias: 11
bandidos de Río Frío, Los: 116
bandits: defined, 178; liberals and conservatives as, 103; in *El Zarco*, 103; in Cuéllar, 108; in *Los bandidos de Río Frío*, 116; in López Portillo, 123; in

Nieves, 123; and Díaz regime, 137; and *hacendado* system, 176; in *Fuertes y débiles*, 178
baroque style: in Mexican literature, 60, 61
barriada, La: 22–24
Barriga Rivas, Rogelio: 12, 23, 24
battles: Chapultepec, 105; between Huerta and Madero, 176; Tacubaya, 83
Bazán, Jorge (fict. char.): 175
"beatniks": and *modernismo*, 149
beauty: in Aztec world, 58; in 18th-century literature, 63; and revolution, 63; in *Clemencia*, 102; in Sotomayor, 110; in *modernismo*, 143. SEE ALSO art; esthetics
beggars: of Díaz regime, 138. SEE ALSO poor, the; poverty
Benavides, Rodolfo: 22 n.
Benítez, José María: 227
Bermúdez, María Elvira: on the social novel, 16
Bernardo, Don (fict. char.): 210
Berta (fict. char.): 161
betrayal: in *La asonada*, 207; in *El resplandor*, 217. SEE ALSO traitor; treachery
Bible, the: in *Las tierras flacas*, 48; in *La vida portentosa de la muerte*, 63
"Biblioteca Breve" prize: for *Los albañiles*, 50
biography: in *Los infortunios de Alonso Ramírez*, 62; in *Astucia*, 93; in *El águila y la serpiente*, 200–201; in *Vámonos con Pancho Villa*, 206–207
birth: in *Ojerosa y pintado*, 46; in *Tierra*, 209
bitterness: of Azuela, 18, 218–220, 224; of Tovar, 78–79, 85; in *El monedero*, 86; in *Mala yerba*, 169; in *El pueblo inocente*, 213; in *Jahel*, 215. SEE ALSO anger; condemnation; cynicism; disillusionment; dissatisfaction; indignation
blindness: in *Santa*, 253–254
bola, the: defined, 122
bola, La: 122–124, 129
Bolaños, Joaquín: 63
Bolaños, Juan Nepomuceno (fict. char.): 176–178
bondage: in *Perico*, 118–119, 132–133; in *Niéves*, 120–121; in *Tierra*, 210; in *El resplandor*, 217. SEE ALSO prisoner

130; in De Campo, 134; in Gamboa, 134; in *La llaga*, 164; in *La fuga de la quimera*, 175. SEE ALSO poor, the
—, middle: in Azuela, 21, 211, 224; in *Entresuelo*, 22; and Mexico, 23; in *Justicia de enero*, 43–44; after Independence, 64; in Del Castillo, 77; in Díaz Covarrubias, 84, 124; in *Astucia*, 93; in *La linterna mágica*, 106; in Cuéllar, 106, 131; and novelists, 122; and Reform, 122; in Díaz regime, 122, 159; in Delgado, 124; in Rabasa, 126, 130; in *Suprema ley*, 151, 152; and the Revolution, 173, 184, 205–206; in *La fuga de la quimera*, 174; and the Ateneo, 185; in colonialist novels, 186; in post-Revolutionary governments, 206; in *Nueva burguesía*, 211, 224; during World War II, 227
Classicism: and romanticism, 116; and *modernismo*, 143–144. SEE ALSO Neo-Classicism
Claudio Oronoz: 148–149
Clemencia: 101–102, 103
clergy, the: in *Al filo del agua*, 10; in *El monedero*, 81, 87; in Mateos, 96; in *La navidad en las montañas*, 102, 103; in López Portillo, in *El bachiller*, 146. SEE ALSO Church, the; priests
clericalism: and Rivera y Río, 89
Clothilde (fict. char.): 151, 152
colonialism, post-Revolutionary: 185–187, 191
colonialista: 185–187
Colonial Period: 3; in literature, 55–68; in *El criollo*, 71; in 1820's, 69; in *El filibustero*, 91; in *El tálamo y la horca*, 97–98; *Venganza y remordimiento*, 97–98; and 19th-century liberal novelists, 186; and 20th-century *colonialistas*, 186. SEE ALSO *colonialista*; novel, colonialist.
Comala: 32
comedy. SEE humor; satire
commitment: of Revueltas, 26, 28; in Altamirano, 103–104; in *La navidad en las montañas*, 103; in Rabasa, 130; in *El donador de almas*, 148; in *Aguila o sol*, 188; in 1920's, 189, 195; in *Tropa vieja*, 228
common sense: in Romantic writers, 75; in post-Independence era, 81, 82; and the German, 86, 107; in "going-home"

theme, 108; and Reform, 108, 109, 112, 115; and nationalists, 166
— in work of particular writers: Payno, 73–74, 75, 77; Sierra O'Reilly, 75; Del Castillo, 77; José Ramírez, 89; Cuéllar, 100, 107, 108, 109; Altamirano, 104; López Portillo, 120; Gamboa, 151, 152, 154; Quevado y Zubieta, 166
— in particular works: *La voz adolorida*, 50; *Jicoténcal*, 70; *El fistol del diablo*, 73–74; *Amor de ángel*, 80; *El monedero*, 87; *Astucia*, 92; *El pecado del siglo*, 100; *Catequismo del moral*, 105 n.; *Suprema ley*, 151, 152; *La fuga de la quimera*, 174; *La luciérnaga*, 211
communal farm: in *La coqueta*, 88
communication: in *Caballo de elote*, 20; in Elena Garro, 53; in Cuéllar, 108; in Rabasa, 158; in *El café de nadie*, 193; in *La llama fría*, 196; in *Margarita de niebla*, 198; in *El águila y la serpiente*, 201; in *Los bragados*, 229. SEE ALSO human relationships; reader participation
Communist Party: and *Los días terrenales*, 27. SEE ALSO left, the; Marxism
community, the: in De Campo, 134; in *El resplandor*, 217; in *San Gabriel de Valdivias*, 218, 220; in Azuela, 218, 220
—, model: in *El monedero*, 86; the citizen in, 86, 87, 88; in Pizarro, 104; in Roa Bárcena, 104
compassion: in Bermúdez, 16; in modern Mexico, 16–17; and Azuela, 18, 180; in *Casi el paraíso*, 35; in *La región más transparente*, 38; of Romantic period, 117; in Gamboa, 151, 152; in *Suprema ley*, 152; in *María Luisa*, 167; in *Los de abajo*, 180; in *El resplandor*, 218; in *Los olvidados*, 230; in *Yo como pobre*, 230. SEE ALSO sympathy
complacency: in novel of Díaz period, 127; in *La Calandria*, 134; in *La luciérnaga*, 211
composer: in *La creación*, 45; in *Los precursores*, 161–162
compromise: in Independence movement, 64; in López Portillo, 119, 120, 121; in *Nieves*, 119, 120, 121; in Díaz period, 139, 158; in Rabasa, 158; in

Index

gueros de la Virgen, 61; *El monedero,*
85–86; *El Zarco,* 103–104; *Tomochic,*
155; *El indio,* 215–217; *El resplandor,*
217–218; *Nayar,* 226; *Los peregrinos
inmóviles,* 231–232
—, particular writers' treatment of:
Magdaleno, 21, 127–128; Rubín, 25–
26; Pozas, 25–26; Pizarro, 85–86, 103;
Altamirano, 103–104
indigenista theme: defined, 14 n.; discussed, 24–26; in *Donde crecen los
tepozanes,* 14, 25; in *Entresuelo,* 22;
in *La mayordomía,* 23; in *La canoa
perdida,* 26 n.; in Castellanos, 36; in
La región más transparente, 38; and
La muerte de Artemio Cruz, 40; in
Los hombres verdaderos, 45; in *El
resplandor,* 217–218; *El indio* as, 218;
in *Los peregrinos inmóviles,* 231. SEE
culture, indigenous; Indian; the
indignation, theme of: in *La barriada,*
22; in *Yo como pobre,* 22; in *Candelaria de los patos,* 23; in modern
works, 22–24; in Mondragón, 22–24;
in Zentella, 119; in La Rumba, 134;
and *Andrés Pérez, maderista,* 171; in
Los olvidados, 230; in *Yo como pobre,*
230. SEE ALSO anger; bitterness; condemnation; dissatisfaction
Indio, El: 215, 216–217, 218, 226, 232
individual, the: in *Más allá existe la tierra,* 13; in novel of 30's and 40's, 13,
226; in *Los recuerdos del porvenir,*
53; in Altamirano, 102; in *La Rumba,*
134; in *Tropa vieja,* 228
individuality: of López Portillo, 162–163;
of Azuela, 184; in *Contemporáneos,*
191; in novel of protest, 221
inertia: in *La muerte de Artemio Cruz,*
40; in *Los recuerdos del porvenir,* 53;
in *El libro vacío,* 42; in *Angelina,* 141;
in *Claudio Oronoz,* 149; after Revolution, 190; in *Sombres,* 222; in *La vida
inútil de Pito Pérez,* 223; in *El luto
humano,* 231
infidelity: in *Julia,* 99
influence: on Arreola, 28; in *Pedro Páramo,* 31; in *El cuarto poder,* 125; and
modernismo, 142; on Nervo, 148; in
Los fracasados, 167, 168. SEE ALSO inspiration; motivation
—, English: in 18th century, 62–63

—, French: in *Aura,* 39; in 18th cenury,
62–63, 64; in Independence movement,
64; in 19th century, 80, 81, 90; and
Inclán, 93; on Rabasa, 129, and *modernismo,* 142; in *Mala yerba,* 170; in
Mexican language, 187
—, hispanic: in colonialist novel, 187
infortunios de Alonso Ramírez, Los: 61–
62
inhumanity: in *La región más transparente,* 38; in Cortés, 70; of Díaz period, 126; in *Perico,* 133; in *Los de
abajo,* 180
injustice: in Almanza, 34; in *La hija
del judío,* 75; in *Nieves,* 120; in López Portillo, 120, 126; in *La siega,*
145; in *Tomochic,* 156; in *La llaga,*
165; in Azuela, 219; in Revolution,
220; in novel of protest, 221
innocence: in *Vulcano,* 90; in Cuéllar,
107, 108; in *Nieves,* 120; in *La Calandria,* 135; in *Los de abajo,* 180; in *La
negra Angustias,* 228. SEE ALSO purity
innovation. SEE discovery
Inquisition: in post-Independence fiction,
71; in *La hija del judío,* 75; in *Un
hereje y un musulmán,* 100; in 19th-
century novelists, 186
inspiration: in *La creación,* 45; in Altamirano, 95; of Luis Ortiz, 109; in *Reconquista,* 163; in *Los precursores,*
164; in *Aguila o sol,* 188. SEE ALSO
influence; motivation
intellectualism: and Independence, 63–
64; and *La vida portentosa de la
muerte,* 63; in *El donador de almas,*
148; in *Novela como nube,* 197
intellectuals: and Revolution, 63, 184–
185; in *Un hereje y un musulmán,*
100; and Reform, 82; González Peña
as, 184; and the Ateneo, 184–185; and
colonialist novel, 186
interiorization: in the novel, 8, 226, 233–
234; of Mexican character, 233
—in work of particular writers: Arreola,
51
—in particular works: *Al filo del agua,*
7–8, 10; *Pedro Páramo,* 32, 33; *La
muerte de Artemio Cruz,* 42; *La región más transparente,* 37; *La tierra
pródiga,* 47; *Las tierras flacas,* 48;
Clemencia, 102; *El café de nadie,* 193;
La luciérnaga, 211; *Primero de enero,*
213–214; *Tierra caliente,* 214; *El re-*

272

Mancisidor, José: works of, 21–22, 207, 211
manifesto, literary: and *Contemporáneos*, 191; and Revolutionary movement, 192
mankind: in *Ojerosa y pintada*, 46; in *Quevado y Zubieta*, 165–166; in Romero, 212; in Yáñez, 225, 233; in Revueltas, 225; in novel of 1940's, 231; in *Al filo del agua*, 233. SEE ALSO human condition; humanness
mannerism: in colonialist novel, 187. SEE ALSO artificiality
Manolito Pisaverde: 72
Marcela (fict. char.): 169
Margarita (fict. char.): 198
Margarita de niebla: 197–198
María (fict. char.): 10, 34, 45
María: 112
María Luisa: 167
Marina, Doña: and Conquest, 56, 58; in Cortés, 57; in Bernal Díaz, 57; in *Visión de Anáhuac*, 59
marines, Northamerican: in *Frontera junto al mar*, 21
marriage: in *La Quixotita y su prima*, 66–67; in *El diablo en México*, 85; in Cuéllar, 107; in *Suprema ley*, 151; in *Los precursores*, 161, 162; in *Margarita de niebla*, 198
Martínez de Castro, Manuel: 95, 116; works of, 99, 115
Martínez Sotomayor, José: 203
Mártires y verdugos: 89
martyr: in *La fuga de la quimera*, 176
Marxism: in Zentella, 118. SEE ALSO Communist Party; left, the
Mary, Virgin. SEE Virgin Mary
Más allá existe la tierra: 13
masculinity: in *Una mujer en soledad*, 16; in *La tierra pródiga*, 47; in *Jicoténcal*, 69; in *Aguila o sol*, 188; in 1920's literary dispute, 195
Mateos, Juan A.: 95, 107; works of, 96–97, 98–99, 139–140, 172, 173
materialism: in *Nueva burguesía*, 224. SEE ALSO greed
Maximilian: and French Intervention, 4, 91, 93; in *El cerro de las campanas*, 96
mayordomía, La: 23
Mazatlán, Mexico: 167 n.
médico y el santero, El: 12

Mexico in Its Novel

melancholy: in *La sensativa*, 83; in Altamirano, 102, 103, 104; in *Clemencia*, 102; in *La navidad en las montañas*, 102; in Sotomayor, 110; in *Angelina*, 142; in *modernismo*, 143–144, 149; in Realism-Naturalism, 144; in Claudio Oronoz, 149; in Azuela, 220
Meléndez y Muñoz, Mariano: 71
melodrama: in Rodríguez Galván, 72; in *Gil Gómez, el insurgente*, 84; in *El cerro de las campanas*, 96; in *Páramo*, 233
Memoria de un espejo: 34
Memorias de Merolico: 110
Memorias de un guerrillero: 97
Memorias de un muerto: 111–112
memory: in *La región más transparente*, 38; in *La feria*, 51; in *Los recuerdos del porvenir*, 53; in Rabasa, 130; in *Las tribulaciones*, 184. SEE ALSO reminiscence
Menéndez, Miguel Angel: 25, 226
Mercado, Miguel (fict. char.): 156, 166, 188
mestiza, La: 119
mestizos: in *Aguila o sol*, 188; in *El resplandor*, 217. SEE ALSO coras; Indian; peon; *tzotzil*
Metamorfosis: 152–153
Mexican, the: in *El médico y el santero*, 12; in *Los antepasados*, 52; in *El hombre de la situación*, 89
Mexicanism: of *Contemporaneos*, 11; and universality, 16, 234; and humanism, 41; in Realism-Naturalism, 135; and colonialist novel, 187; *avant-garde* on, 204. SEE ALSO Mexico; nationalism; nativism; reality, Mexican
— of particular writers: Rojas González, 13–14; Arreola, 30, 51; Velarde, 46; Altamirano, 94; Olavarría y Ferrari, 98; Rabasa, 129; Yáñez, 225
— in particular works: *La grandeza mexicana*, 60; *Astucia*, 92; *Cuentos del general*, 97, 140; *Fuertes y débiles*, 176; *Margarita de niebla*, 198; *Los olvidados*, 231; *Yo como pobre*, 231
Mexico: and Reform, 4, 81; after Revolution, 17, 190, 195; reality of, 17–18, 53–54, 159, 227, 233–234; and Juárez, 91; in Díaz regime, 140, 159; Christianity in, 164; and Obregón, 184. SEE

ALSO Mexicanism; nationalism; nativism; reality; Mexican
— in literature: and modern writers, 41, 162; in *criollista* poetry, 59; and *modernismo*, 143; and the Ateneo, 185; and *Contemporáneos*, 191; in novel of 1940's, 231
— in work of particular writers: Morales, 110; López Portillo, 162; Gamboa, 163; González Peña, 174
— in particular works: *La maladición*, 18; *Esa sangre*, 19; *Tierra Grande*, 19; *La muerte de Artemio Cruz*, 40; *El pecado del siglo*, 100; *Un hereje y un musulmán*, 100; *Santa*, 154, 163; *Los precursores*, 162; *Reconquista*, 163; *La llaga*, 165; *Al filo del agua*, 233
Mexico City: and the Conquest, 3; and Iturbide, 63; and French Intervention, 91; of "The Ten Tragic Days," 176; and Obregón, 182; and Carranza, 184; after the Revolution, 190
— in work of particular writers: Bernal Díaz, 57; Cortés, 57
— in particular works: *Casi el paraíso*, 28; *La región más transparente*, 36–37, 39; *Suave patria*, 46; *Ojerosa y pintada*, 46–47; *Los extraordinarios*, 50; *Los infortunios de Alonso Ramírez*, 62; *El Periquillo Sarniento*, 66; *El monedero*, 86; *Novelas mexicanas*, 125, 126; *Santa*, 153; *El amor de las sirenas*, 157; *Andrés Pérez, maderista*, 170; *La fuga de la quimera*, 174, 175; *La malhora*, 188; *Sonata*, 226; *Ciudad*, 227. SEE ALSO Tenochtitlán
Mi caballo, mi perro, y mi rifle: 214
middle age, theme of: 43
Middle Ages: of Europe, 71
Mientras la muerte llega: 15, 41
Mi general: 213
military, the: in Díaz regime, 137; in *Tomochic*, 155–157; in *Los de abajo*, 180–181; in *Mi general*, 213; in *San Gabriel de Valdivias*, 218. SEE ALSO soldiers; war
Mina, Javier de: 3
mirror image. SEE image, mirror
misfortune: in *Hermana de los ángeles*, 77; in Sue, 80; in *Nieves*, 121; in *La Calandria*, 124; in *Angelina*, 141; in *La Parientes ricos*, 146; in *Suprema*

ley, 151; in *La malhora*, 188. SEE ALSO tragedy
missionaries: Cortés as, 58; and the Indian, 58, 59
misterios de San Cosme, Los: 79–80
misterioso, El: 71
mistress: in *Santa*, 153; in *María Luisa*, 167
Moctezuma: and Conquest, 3, 56, 68; in Bernal Díaz, 57; and Cortés, 57
modernismo: discussed, 142–144, 146; and *Revista Azul*, 143; authors involved in, 149, 150, 157; and *Contemporáneos*, 191
modernity: of Díaz regime, 137; in *estridentismo*, 192; in *Panchito Chapopote*, 200
Moisén: 187
Mojarra, Tomás: 52
monarchists: in Independence movement, 68
Mondragón, Magdalena: works of, 13, 16, 221, 230–231
Moneda falsa: 122, 126
monedero, El: 85–88
money, theme of: in José Ramírez, 89; in *Vulcano*, 90; in *El ofical mayor*, 91; in Cuéllar, 107; in *Moneda falsa*, 126; in *La fuga de la quimera*, 174; in *Las tribulaciones*, 183, 184
monologue: in *La voz adolorida*, 49. SEE ALSO narration
Monterde, Francisco: 185
Montezuma. SEE Moctezuma
mood. SEE atmosphere
Moor: in *Un hereje y un musulmán*, 100
Morales, Vicente: 112; works of, 109–110
morality: in Romantic novels, 75, 126; in 19th-century writers, 86; in Porfirian novel, 160; in pre-Revolution writers, 160; of traditionalists, 165. SEE ALSO conduct; decency; ethics; honesty; virtue
— in work of particular writers: Orozco, 78; Pizarro, 87, 105, 105 n.; Mateos, 96, 97; Roa Bárcena, 104–105; Altamirano, 105; López Portillo, 121, 162, 174, 176–177; Delgado, 125, 135, 174; Rabasa, 126; Gamboa, 154, 163, 164; González Peña, 174
— in particular works: *La muerte de Artemio Cruz*, 41; *Jicoténcal*, 69; *El*

año, 221; in the novel, 221; in *Nueva burguesía,* 224
perception: of Pacheco, 71; of Cuéllar, 109; of Azuela, 171; of Mondragón, 231; in *El luto humano,* 231
peregrinos inmóviles, Los: 231–232
Pérez, Pito (fict. char.): 213, 222–224
Pérez Moreno, José: 36
Perico: 147; discussed, 118–119, 127–128, 132–133
Perico (fict. chars.): 65 n., 118, 119, 132–133
periodicals: after Hidalgo revolt, 64; *El Pensador Mexican* as, 65
Periquillo (fict. char.): 65 n., 66, 67
Periquillo Sarniento, El: 92, 104; discussed, 65–66, 67
Pero Galín: 191
perras, Las: 208–209
personaje, El: 34
personalism: of Díaz period, 126; in Rabasa, 129; in *La llaga,* 165. SEE ALSO ambition; greed; materialism
personification: in *Las tierras flacas,* 48; in *Los recuerdos del porvenir,* 53; in Cuéllar, 107; in *Los de abajo,* 179
perspective. SEE externalization; viewpoint
perversion: in *Mala yerba,* 169; in *Desbandada,* 212; in *La vida inútil de Pito Pérez,* 223. SEE ALSO corruption; evil
pessimism: of Rulfo, 35; of Fuentes, 35; of Castellanos, 35; of Yáñez, 35; of contemporary writers, 35; in *La guerra de treinta años,* 78; of Orozco y Berra, 78; of Payno, 78; of Tovar, 78, 79, 99; of *Romantics,* 78–79; of Díaz Covarrubias, 85; of Martínez de Castro, 99; of Altamirano, 102; of Rabasa, 131; of Gamboa, 134; during Díaz regime, 159; of Azuela, 182, 188; in *Mala yerba,* 182; in *Los de abajo,* 182; in *La malhora,* 188
Petra (fict. char.): 121
Peza, Juan de Dios: 110
Philadelphia, Pa.: and *Jicoténcal,* 69
Philippines: 61
Phillip II: 71
philosophy: in *La región más transparente,* 37; in *Ojerosa y pintada,* 46; in *Los sirgueros de la Virgen,* 60–61;

in *El donador de almas,* 148; in Nervo, 148; in *El pueblo inocente,* 213
pianist: in *Santa,* 153; in *Los precursores,* 161
picaresque, the: in *El médico y el santero,* 12; and Valle Arizpe, 22 n.; and Spanish literature, 62; in *Los infortunios de Alonso Ramírez,* 62; in *El Pensador Mexicano,* 65; in *El Perequillo Sarniento,* 65–66; in *Don Catrín de la Fachenda,* 67; after Independence, 70; in Payno, 77, 78; in *El fístol del diablo,* 74; in *Gil Gómez el insurgente,* 84; in *Astucia,* 92; in Cuéllar, 109; in *Memorias de Merolica,* 110; in Rabasa, 129; in Romero, 212, 222–224; in *La vida inútil de Pito Pérez,* 222–224
pícaro, the. SEE picaresque, the
picturesqueness: in *Las tierras flacas,* 48; in *Astucia,* 92; in *El indio,* 217
piedra del sacrificio, La: 98
pirates: and Alonso Ramírez, 61–62
Pitts, Zasu: in *avant-garde,* 196
pity. SEE sympathy
Pizarro Suárez, Nicolás: 97, 104, 105; and works discussed, 85–88, 90, 103, 105 n.
plot: in Rubín, 26; in *El siglo de oro en las selvas de Erífile,* 60; in Rodríguez Galván, 72; in *La hija del judío,* 75; in *Ironías de la vida,* 78, 79; in *Gil Gómez el insurgente,* 84; in *El monedero,* 87; in Riva Palacio, 97; in Sotomayor, 111; in López Portillo, 131; in Cuéllar, 131; in *Suprema ley,* 151; in *La camada,* 165; in *Los fracasados,* 168; in *Mala yerba,* 169; in *Andrés Pérez, maderista,* 170; in *La fuga de la quimera,* 175, 176; in *Fuertes y débiles,* 177; in *Los de abajo,* 179; in *Pensativa,* 229. SEE ALSO storytelling; structure
Pocahontas: 113
poetry: of Lira, 14; and *La región más transparente,* 40; in Galindo, 42; and Godoy, 49; of Mairena, 50; of Colonial Period, 55, 60, 61; of Axtecs, 58; of the *criollo,* 59; *La grandeza mexicana* as, 60; and Sor Juana Inés de la Cruz, 61; of the baroque, 61; *Profecía de Quatimoc* as, 72; in *Pizarro,* 87 n.; and *modernismo,* 143, 146, 149; of

Index